The Devil in My Friend

The Devil in My Friend

The Inside Story of a Malibu Murder

Ivor Davis with Sally Ogle Davis

ROWMAN & LITTLEFIELD
Lanham • Boulder • New York • London

Published by Rowman & Littlefield
An imprint of The Rowman & Littlefield Publishing Group, Inc.
4501 Forbes Boulevard, Suite 200, Lanham, Maryland 20706
www.rowman.com

86-90 Paul Street, London EC2A 4NE

British Library Cataloguing in Publication Information Available

Library of Congress Cataloging-in-Publication Data on File

ISBN 978-1-5381-8053-2 (cloth : alk. Paper)
ISBN 978-1-5381-8054-9 (electronic)

∞™ The paper used in this publication meets the minimum requirements of American National Standard for Information Sciences—Permanence of Paper for Printed Library Materials, ANSI/NISO Z39.48-1992.

For Sally Ogle Davis—

the loss of a wife is incalculable

Contents

Preface

For us it had all begun on January 3, 1981, a sunny Saturday. We were sitting in the breakfast room of our house overlooking the Santa Barbara Channel and its chain of islands when we read in our local paper that Verna Roehler and her son, Douglas, had drowned the day before in that same spectacular stretch of water we had been admiring. A front-page headline from the *Ventura Star* read: "Mother, Son Die, Effort to Save Dog Ends in Sea Tragedy."

There was a photo of the sole survivor, Fred Roehler, being transferred from the Coast Guard rescue helicopter into an ambulance.

We were stunned and saddened. We'd known Verna from 1970 to 1980, the ten years we'd lived in Malibu before moving north up the coast. She'd been a teacher's aide in our children's classes at Juan Cabrillo School. Our daughter and son, Rebecca and Gideon, were the same ages as her two children, Kimberly and Douglas Johnson.

We had known Fred since his storybook marriage to Verna, although we never knew his first wife, Jeanne. After they got married, we would often bump into Verna and Fred at school sports days and community celebrations, as well as at our children's birthday parties.

Fred came to me one day and gently asked if I would allow him to help coach the kids' soccer team, which Doug and my son Gideon were on. "I don't know a thing about soccer," he admitted, "but it's important for Doug and me to get to know each other and spend some father–son time together. I would be forever in your debt if you would allow me to help coach."

I was deeply moved. I knew that Doug had recently lost his birth father, who had died in a terrible accident in Los Angeles.

Fred showed up for midweek practices and all the weekend games. I was so impressed with his dedication to his son and the team that at the end of the season, after we'd won the regional American Youth Soccer Association (AYSO) championship, I presented Fred with a book about the rules of soccer at our pizza party celebration.

On April 4, 1981, three months after the drowning, another story assaulted us as we were once again reading the local paper over breakfast. Fred Roehler had been arrested for the murder of Verna and Doug. We did not tell our children. We didn't think they could handle it. We weren't sure we could either.

We talked about little else for weeks. The more we thought about it, the more we were convinced that jealousy and gossip had played a large part in what was happening to Fred. There had been rumors about Fred's unhappy first marriage, which ended when his first wife Jeanne Roehler had drowned in the backyard swimming pool. There were those who resented his new happiness and the good fortune that had resulted from combining his resources with those of his new wife.

We knew Fred was not someone who suffered fools gladly. He was not a man beloved by everyone, not one of those desperately social, partying types who had invaded Malibu. Or put another way, not one of the "beautiful people." We liked him as soon as we met precisely because he was so unlike those around him—quiet, speaking only when he had something to say; a man, we thought, of some substance and fortitude in the face of despair.

For some, losing two wives to drowning seemed too much of a coincidence, but we knew that life played peculiar tricks on people. We also knew that Fred Roehler was not someone who stayed home watching other people's adventures on television. We all respected the power of the sea. We'd lived by it most of our lives. We knew how dangerous and unpredictable it could be. Our son Gideon, like Doug Johnson, was a good swimmer, but the ocean was vastly different from a heated backyard pool.

When we were eventually able to visit Fred in jail in Santa Barbara, we were amazed at his reasonableness and calm demeanor. He was upset at not being able to get bail, but mainly because it separated him from his children. He worried about the psychological damage his incarceration would cause them. He was longing to hug them, he said. But he was coping surprisingly well. The prison personnel were fair men, he said, who were treating him decently.

Still, he looked awful. His tan had faded; his eyes were sunken. He looked depressed, as though he hadn't slept for a week.

Sally and I were also depressed. How scandalous: Our friend, an innocent man, had unjustly become a victim himself.

1

The Brady Bunch, Malibu Style

When Frederick George Roehler married Verna Jo Johnson on the beach in Malibu, California, on Christmas Eve, 1977, it was a fairy-tale ending to two sad stories. Verna, widowed two years before, had been left with two children, Kimberly, eight, and Douglas, five. Fred had been a widower for just over a year and was caring for his two children, Heidi, seven, and Kirsten, three. Verna had frequently been Fred's children's babysitter, and the four kids were friends from school and community sports.

From the day of the ceremony, the newly combined Johnson-Roehler tribe was greeted with warm smiles and universal affection wherever they appeared. People quickly began calling them "The Brady Bunch."

Verna was a sunny, all-American woman—tanned, athletic, always smiling. She was someone men gave a second glance at, even in Malibu, where aerobics-slim housewives did their shopping in thigh-high tennis dresses or abbreviated jogging shorts that left little to the imagination. She was in her early thirties, but her shoulder-length hair was prematurely gray, which, with her unlined face and youthful big, brown eyes, gave her just that touch of the unexpected. Verna was cute and sexy, and she knew it. She liked to flirt, but in a respectable, boundaries-set sort of way. She reminded me of a cross between the fragility of actress Natalie Wood and the outdoorsy beauty of Farrah Fawcett. Her tastes were simple. She bought her clothes at chain stores. Most of the time, she wore faded blue jeans, peasant blouses, and tennis shoes. And if she sometimes wore them just a mite too tight, she'd explain, "I may not be able to shop at Saks, but at least I can look like a real woman."

Before her first husband, Bill, died, they had lived in a simple wood-framed duplex close to the beach, surrounded by the much grander homes of people whose names were known the world over: Ali MacGraw, Steve McQueen, Jack Lemmon, Robert Redford, Dustin Hoffman, Rod Steiger, and scores more.

In the half-dozen years they'd lived there, they'd seen the one-mile-wide, twenty-six-mile-long stretch of coastline become a capital of world glamour. Malibu, like Monte Carlo or Beverly Hills, became synonymous with money, celebrity, and conspicuous consumption.

As Malibu changed around her, Verna worried that her intellect and education weren't on par with those of some of her high-powered neighbors. "Half the time, I don't know what the heck you guys are talking about," she'd sometimes complain to her friends. But then she'd laugh, adding, "I may not be all that bright, but I make up for it because I'm a warm and caring person."

In 1970, there was still a rural Malibu with a good population mix. Among the show business enclaves there were also small middle-class ranchers. They'd moved to Malibu in the 1940s and 1950s in search of cheap land and stayed to marvel at the real estate boom of the 1970s, which saw their two or three acres (picked up as scrubland on which to raise a few horses) grow to be worth more than they'd dreamed of making in a lifetime.

By the 1980s, single-acre, unimproved-view lots were selling for half a million dollars. The boom brought new neighbors. Palaces grew behind electric gates where once small wooden houses with chickens in the yard had held sway. Bob Dylan, the Sixties Pied Piper, built a Taj Mahal for himself complete with minarets and an onion dome and placed guards at the gates of his Point Dume estate to dissuade looky-loos. The real Archie Bunker, Carroll O'Connor, living far from his TV-series blue-collar Queens neighborhood, called a Moroccan-style mansion home. Barbra Streisand built a series of fantasy houses, each more extravagant than the last, at the end of a rustic canyon.

A pudgy, teenage Indian named Guru Maharaj Ji bought a white hilltop mansion and sent his young followers into the community to work as house cleaners and gardeners. It wasn't uncommon for disciples from around the world to knock on our front door and ask if they could use our bathroom before climbing the hill to visit "The Perfect Master of the Divine Light Mission." For his nineteenth birthday, his smitten followers bought him a helicopter, which became a familiar sight, whirring low over the rooftop of our house as the guru traveled to and from his regal residence.

Suddenly, Malibu people were hip. They shopped alongside Paul Newman and Walter Matthau at Trancas Market. Their kids went to school with Ali MacGraw's son Joshua; they ate pizza with Cary Grant's daughter Jennifer at the Malibu Pizza Palace. On the wide swathes of guard-gated trendy Malibu Colony Beach or several miles north to the very private wide sandy Broad Beach Road, you might bump into Carole King, Johnny Rotten, or Geraldo Rivera. At the Colony, Larry Hagman led a ragtag band of kids and worthy locals every Fourth of July as they marched along the sand, blowing whistles and banging drums. Jane Fonda and her husband, the French film director Roger Vadim, enjoyed cocktails with Rod Steiger and all the Mamas and the Papas. The Eagles set up a home and recording studio in the Point Dume Beach area. Liverpool-born restaurateur Richard Chesterfield opened his Monroe's café where, nearly every night, Johnny Carson walked from the Colony to his private corner table.

"Please don't bother Mr. Carson," Richard told other diners.

Once on Malibu's exclusive Broad Beach, local resident Steve McQueen angrily confronted a visiting rabbi friend of ours from Boston who was with his family, sitting on a deck chair enjoying the view. The actor pulled a gun on the rabbi and ordered him to leave, claiming he was trespassing on his private stretch of sand! The rabbi didn't argue and swiftly made his getaway.

Malibu was the most glamorous address in America, and its inhabitants proudly bought license plates for their cars declaring "Malibu: A Way of Life." For ordinary folks from ordinary towns, it was a heady experience, living on the edge of the fast track. The younger, more ambitious ones wanted in. But that took more than just an address. It required money and a high profile. I vividly recall going with a real estate broker to view a prime but tiny house on fashionable Broad Beach. We dallied for one day before making an offer. Next day the broker called.

"Sorry, the house sold last night," he said sheepishly. We were surprised. As it turned out, a sister of billionaire Norton Simon, who lived next door to the property, was so concerned about getting new neighbors that she'd bought the property with an all-cash offer—and then tore the house down to build a private tennis court!

For Verna Johnson, marrying Fred Roehler, an educated, handsome man, was a step up, her passport to a share in the glamour. It meant security for her two children and a new beginning for herself. In the sometimes flaky, often unreliable world of Malibu in the late seventies, Fred Roehler seemed solid, a man to lean on. A marine engineer and deep-sea diver by profession, he worked as a civilian consultant for the US Navy Pacific Missile Test Center at Point Mugu, some twenty miles north of Malibu on Pacific Coast Highway, just over the neighboring Ventura County line. Much of his working life was spent in the ocean depths all along the California coast and as far away as Hawaii, laying cables for navy war games and top-secret communications exercises. All of which were a long way from his roots.

Fred grew up in the small town of Centerville, Indiana (population 2,500), just a stone's throw from the Ohio border. His family was prosperous, prominent in the local Republican Party. He was dark and huskily handsome with a mass of curly hair, a heavy beard, and piercing pale blue eyes. His dry wit intimidated some but delighted those like-minded neighbors who found Malibu's "Have a nice day" platitudes grating. He was large and powerful, six-foot-two, 190 pounds, with huge hands, muscular shoulders, and strong legs. No one could ever remember seeing Fred in a suit and tie. It would have been like Plymouth Rock dressed by Brooks Brothers.

In the competitive, dizzyingly upwardly mobile world of Malibu, with its obsession with toys and status, Fred stood out. Display seemed of no consequence to him whatsoever. Dressed like a thrift-store reject in ancient jeans and work shirts, clogs worn invariably without socks, he drove around in a beat-up station wagon with the bumper missing and more dents and grazes than a demolition derby banger. There was always a quiet wall of reserve about him that added to the impression of substance. This was not a man you could know everything about in fifteen minutes.

He had been an exemplary father to his two daughters in the year after his wife died, taking them to school every morning—Heidi to Juan Cabrillo Elementary School, and Kirsten to Malibu Methodist Nursery School. He'd stay with Kirsten as long as it took to make sure she was comfortable, helping to tie the brightly colored ribbons in her thick, dark hair. Then he would stop to chat with the teachers about how his daughters were adjusting to the loss of their mother.

"Fred Roehler is a better mother than most of the real ones around here," Kirsten's teacher said. "He cares so much." And local women were heard to sigh, "I wish my husband were more like him."

More than a few Malibu ladies envied Verna, with her handsome new husband and her opportunity to start all over again.

The Johnson-Roehler children were picture-book pretty. Kimberly Johnson, now the eldest of an enlarged family, was the mirror image of her mother, Verna. She had the same lustrous, trusting brown eyes, full luxuriant hair, tiny well-formed features, and an even-toothed, wide smile. Heidi Roehler, one year younger, was tall and thin, coltish, a bit awkward, quiet and shy—not quite recovered from the loss of her mother, Jeanne.

Douglas Johnson, a little rapscallion of a boy, with brown hair and blue eyes, looked like his late father, Bill Johnson. He was mischievous, quick to learn, well-liked by his teachers and his squad of friends, loving the beach and the soccer field in about equal proportions.

Then there was Kirsten Roehler, always bringing up the rear of the family pack. The other kids at school called her "Raggedy Ann" because of her round cheeks, her hair tied in pigtails, and her perennial dimpled grin. She adored her new siblings and her new mother.

The Roehlers' new two-story, three-bedroom Sea Level Drive house sat close to the beach. It was a wreck when they bought it—a real fixer-upper—but they got it for a good price and immediately began working on it.

"You know Fred can do anything once he sets his mind to it," Verna told her mother, Camelia Zeitner. Cam was the resident grandma, even though Fred insisted all four kids frequently visit all four sets of grandparents. Verna's father, Zeke, had suffered from severe emphysema for years and was already fading at the time of their wedding. To Verna's delight, when she asked Fred if they could help her parents pay the rent to move into a retirement community, he had suggested instead that they move into a small studio apartment over the garage of the duplex where Verna had lived while married to Bill Johnson, allowing Zeke to spend his last months with his grandchildren. Sadly, two weeks after the Zeitners moved in, Zeke died. Cam stayed on to become a constant presence in their lives.

To all of us in the neighborhood, the Roehler-Johnson household seemed just about perfect. Nobody yelled, nobody was unreasonable. Tolerance and politeness were the prevailing order. Fred and Verna ruled with a firm but loving hand. On Sundays, the whole family trooped into the Methodist Church, well-scrubbed, smiling, staying behind after services to chat politely with friends and neighbors. It was no wonder that people sometimes wondered why their own families failed to measure up to the Roehlers, why their own kids seemed so much more contrary.

Malibu in the 1970s may have been nirvana for freewheeling adult seekers of "the good life," but it was a less-than-ideal place to raise kids. The easy lifestyle of sun and sea and plentiful possessions had its flip side: A fourteen-year-old who walked into the ocean wearing *de rigueur* swimwear and under the influence of Quaaludes didn't come out again. He was the son of the local sheriff's department's narcotics officer, who overdosed on a solution of pure strychnine that he thought was cocaine.

Fred Roehler had shunned community affairs during his first marriage, but now he lent himself to a myriad of sports and neighborhood projects. Besides volunteering to be my assistant coach for Douglas and my son Gideon's soccer team, the Malibu Lions, he and Verna also coached the softball team, holding regular practice sessions on the sand in front of their beach house. Fred was president of the Beach Residents'

Association and helped organize a program of enrichment classes at the elementary school. He volunteered to help run the church bazaars, organizing special family worship services. The local minister became a fond friend of the family. And always, the family was together, all six of them. One seldom saw Fred and Verna without the little ones in tow. This wasn't just a marriage of two people, they told friends; this was a marriage of families.

Shortly after her wedding to Fred, Verna discovered that she had inherited her family's tendency to have high blood pressure. Fred suggested she try to control it by running, and soon the entire family could be seen burning up the laps on the beach. It was fun to see them jogging past us as we picnicked on the sand, like the running-on-the-beach scene from *Chariots of Fire*.

It was the ocean, however, that was the true center of their lives. Fred, Verna, the girls, and Doug fished, surfed and swam, and rowed their little orange dory up and down in front of the house. Doug especially was a dedicated swimmer. He had taken swimming lessons every year since the age of three, and life-saving courses from the Red Cross. The Roehlers, parents and kids, were seldom out of their bathing suits during the summer.

Their Malibu neighbors felt the fairy tale was finally complete when they heard about the boat. The Brady Bunch was about to become the Swiss Family Robinson. They'd bought a yacht and planned to take the children out of school for six months to sail around the world together, shooting home movies and keeping journals of their adventures. Fred asked to join a local camera club set up by producer/director George Gage, who encouraged him to chronicle his seagoing adventures.

The *Perseverance* was a fifty-foot Flying Dutchman, a prototype number-one hull, all teak and brass with tall masts. The Roehlers first saw a photo of it at the Los Angeles Boat Show and immediately fell in love with it. Verna liked its domestic comforts. It had three heads, plus an extra shower, a beautiful master stateroom, a well-fitted galley, and even a fireplace.

The neighbors wondered how the Roehlers could afford such a luxury, but after much dickering over terms and maneuvering to make the deal, the *Perseverance* became theirs in April 1980. They spent most weekends on the yacht, with Fred teaching Verna and the children how to handle it until they felt comfortable in all possible situations and conditions.

They planned to leave on the first leg of their journey—a shakedown cruise around the coast of Mexico—at the end of the year. The start date was delayed when Fred's family from Indiana decided to pay them a Christmas visit. As soon as their visitors left, Fred and Verna assured the kids they would be Mexico-bound, "living the dream."

2

A Family Outing

He that will learn to pray, let him go to sea.

—BRASS PLAQUE HANGING IN THE MAIN CABIN OF THE *PERSEVERANCE*

THE DAY OUTING ON THE *PERSEVERANCE* ON JANUARY 2, 1981, WAS FRED'S mother's idea. The Malibu Roehlers were hosts to a large family group that Christmas. In addition to their four children and Fred's parents, Charlotte and Fritz, there was Fred's youngest brother, Scott, and his young wife Ginny, who'd also come in from Indiana. Fred's second brother, Ron, and his wife Elizabeth, known as Lib, were there with their three children. They were relaxing after the holiday rush at their Christmas tree farm in San Bernardino, some eighty miles east and inland of Malibu.

On Saturday, New Year's Eve, the family went on a picnic in a picturesque canyon near the house. From up there, the boats on the water looked like tiny Tinkertoys.

Charlotte seized the moment. "When are we going to get out and sail in your boat?" she asked.

Scott and Ginny, who were in their early twenties, were much more interested in Disneyland and Knott's Berry Farm than sailing. Fritz was also a reluctant sailor. "If I can hold on to the dock with one hand, I'll go," he told them. Ron and Lib said they had to be back in San Bernardino.

But Charlotte was not one to take no for an answer. Back at the house, she doggedly pursued the boat trip. "You know I'm crazy about sailing. Where do you think Fred got it from?"

That evening, the Roehler family's traditional New Year's Eve surf 'n' turf dinner had to be postponed when Verna announced she was coming down with a bug.

But that didn't deter Charlotte. The next day she began again.

"Wouldn't it be nice to start the year off with a day at sea," she pleaded to mostly deaf ears. "If I don't get to see that boat and sail on it," she told Verna, "I'm going to stow away with you to Mexico."

Finally, Verna gave in. "Okay. How about we go up tonight and sleep on board in the harbor? In the morning if nobody feels like sailing, we'll come home; otherwise, if the weather is good, we can take the boat out to Santa Cruz Island."

Charlotte quickly organized everyone to get their stuff together. The luggage was loaded into the station wagon and Scott and Ginny's van which they'd driven across the country. Fritz, Fred, and Scott tied the old dory on top of the wagon for the twenty-five-mile trip to Ventura Harbor. The battered dory had seen better days, but they used it as a backup safety boat to tow behind the yacht whenever they went sailing.

Verna suggested they bring Lady, the new beagle puppy they'd bought the kids for Christmas. "If she's coming to Mexico with us, it's time she started getting used to the boat," she said. "This will be good practice for her."

She was still holding the frisky pup under one arm when her mother, Cam, came down to kiss her good-bye. Cam had not been included in the invitation to sail and wasn't sorry. She found the senior Roehlers a somewhat intimidating prospect and was quite happy to stay behind. "Be careful out there," she whispered as she hugged her daughter.

Ventura Harbor, some sixty miles north of Los Angeles and thirty miles south of Santa Barbara, has long been a sailor's nightmare. Its narrow channel leads to the open sea past a breakwater, but over the years the channel has silted up so badly in low tide that the Army Corps of Engineers has dredged the bottom at regular intervals to prevent boats from being stuck in the shallows and stranded for hours until the next high tide releases them.

On the morning of January 2, 1981, Fred was taking no chances. He wanted to get out of there early, with the tide. Fritz Roehler, the reluctant sailor but early riser, had been the one who noisily roused everyone. He had abandoned any thought of avoiding the trip. Charlotte's mind was set on it, and after forty years of marriage, he knew it was useless to argue.

Fred, eager to please his mother, seemed equally determined to show off his magnificent acquisition, so, precisely at 8:00 a.m., the peak of high tide, Verna carefully backed the boat out of the slip and handed the wheel over to her husband to negotiate the tricky channel. In about half an hour, they were sailing as close to the wind as they could because it was a very light day. The fifty-foot *Perseverance*, a handsome ship by anyone's standards, silently cut through the steely gray waters with a grace and smoothness of handling that belied its size.

Out in the open sea, even with little wind, she soon hit a steady six knots for the three-hour trip to Santa Cruz Island. Charlotte's moment had come. When Fred offered her the wheel, she grabbed at it with gusto.

"I've seen Errol Flynn do this in the movies," she whooped, over-steering wildly.

Patiently, Fred showed her how to steer properly to keep the boat straight on the wind, and soon she was sailing as though she'd been at the helm all her life. She gloried in her pride in the boat and in the son who had miraculously acquired it.

Charlotte may have enjoyed every minute of the sail, but Scott's wife Ginny was violently seasick. Born and raised in the heart of the Midwest, she was a stranger to the ocean. She had refused the Dramamine Verna had offered her just before they'd set out. Now she was suffering horribly, shivering in the cockpit, leaning against her husband. Verna had also gone below. Having complained of a headache, she had taken a couple aspirin and was lying down.

By midday, the *Perseverance* was approaching Santa Cruz Island. Easily visible from the mainland, Santa Cruz is twenty and a half miles long and five and a half miles across at its widest point. The island is uninhabited except for a herd of sheep and cattle, and a privately owned campground where vacationers can enjoy California the way it used to be a hundred years ago.

With colorfully named harbors like Prisoners, Pelican Bay, Painted Cave, and Hungryman Gulch, the only communication with the mainland is by crank telephone and two-way radio, and access to the island is strictly controlled. Even hikers are required to get a permit from the Nature Conservancy before landing.

Little Scorpion anchorage, a popular harbor for weekend sailors, was almost deserted as the *Perseverance* sailed in closer. Located at the east end of the island, it's one of the easiest anchorages to find because it is protected on its western side by a looming landmark known as Bird Rock, a massive outcropping of brittle sandstone rising one hundred feet in front of the main island. On approach, it stands snow white against the green and gray of the main island.

"Oh, that's beautiful," Charlotte cooed as they sailed closer to the Rock.

Fred laughed. "You won't think it's so beautiful when we get closer and you get a whiff of the place."

It soon became obvious how Bird Rock got its name. What looks so attractive from afar is layer upon layer of encrusted bird droppings completely covering the Rock as if painted on by some malevolent artist with a bizarre sense of humor. Sailors give Bird Rock a wide berth when the winds are blowing across the bow. And the Rock does not welcome humans. Those unwise enough to set foot on it find birds dive-bombing inches from their heads, just as they did in Alfred Hitchcock's *The Birds*. The rocky ground is covered with a dense layer of bird skulls, carcasses, and shattered eggs.

The seas around the Santa Cruz Islands are cold in January—gray and chill and deep, unwelcoming, and unpredictable. But Fred Roehler knew these waters as well as he knew his own backyard. He had dived in them for lobster and abalone, trained with the navy around the island's kelp beds, sailed in and around the entire chain of islands, and knew every inch of Little Scorpion's coves and caves, its blowholes and shelves. He'd shot pictures under its deep dark waters, waters so treacherous that on summertime weekends scuba divers frequently drown, their bodies seldom recovered. He was as comfortable there as the sea lions perched on the island's rocky outcroppings or the seals playing in the chilly waters.

"Dad, get Verna up," Fred shouted to Fritz. "I need her to take the wheel while I anchor."

Verna was still fast asleep and Fritz had to shake her gently awake, but she quickly rubbed a wet towel over her face and went aloft.

As Fred began the routine of anchoring, Charlotte pulled off her lens cap to take the first pictures of her favorite son on the voyage she had so eagerly anticipated.

Moments later, she snapped a frame of Verna, silver hair fanning her face, her head obviously no longer throbbing as she posed with a smile at the wheel, while a cheeky Douglas mugged on the sidelines, trying to squeeze into the picture.

After everyone on board ate lunch, Ginny Roehler, who was still pallid and weak, pleaded to be taken to terra firma. Douglas, antsy and anxious to stretch his legs, jumped back into the forward storage cabin and heaved up the inflatable gray Avon dinghy that had come with the yacht. Immediately a clamor went up among the children to be allowed to go with Uncle Scott and Aunt Ginny. Scott, not as comfortable with the ocean as his older brother, and concerned about his gray-faced wife, said he would only take the two older girls. He didn't want to have to worry about the little ones.

It was not clear just who made the final decision that Douglas would not go with Scott and Ginny in the dinghy, but Scott clearly remembered Douglas begging to come with them. Charlotte also recalled that Doug complained bitterly to Verna when he was not allowed to climb into the rubber raft.

Fred, however, later insisted that from the moment the *Perseverance* had left Ventura Harbor, Douglas had been nagging instead about rowing the orange dory. "He didn't want to go out in the dinghy at all," he said. "It was his idea to wait for Verna and me to take the dory out."

Everyone agreed, though little Kirsten Roehler had had an unaccustomed fit of temperament. "If I can't go with Uncle Scott and Aunt Ginny, I'm not going anywhere," she pouted, and promptly went below.

Scott and Ginny, with Kimberly and Heidi aboard, set off rowing for dry land and Charlotte and Fritz went below for their usual afternoon nap. While Kirsten colored pictures in the cabin, they heard Fred and Verna loading the dory, preparing to leave the yacht.

Soon Kirsten, bored with her coloring, curled up on the bench seat by the dinette table and went to sleep too. Nothing stirred. The cove was quiet. There was no one on deck to enjoy the afternoon sun. Scott and Ginny's party were out of sight somewhere on Santa Cruz Island. Two other boats, who by this time had moored in the anchorage, were also silent. Little Scorpion seemed deserted.

Suddenly, six-year-old Kirsten awoke with a start. She had heard a scream. It sounded like her mother. What should she do? She couldn't disturb Grandpa; he got angry when you woke him from his nap. So, she waited. Soon all was quiet again.

Kirsten went back to sleep.

It had been a disappointing day's sail for the crew of the *Sound of Music*, a forty-four-foot cutter-rigged sloop out of Los Angeles. The wind had barely risen above five knots and the seas had stayed flat. They'd had to motor-sail all the way around Santa Cruz Island, ending up at Cavern Point at the westernmost end of Bird Rock.

Nevertheless, it was a pretty afternoon as they rounded the Point. The sun was shining, the temperature about 70 degrees, and Diane Wheatley, a striking, slim silver-blonde, relaxed at the helm as her sailing companions, Gerry Formiller and Carlyle "Mike" Davis, chatted together in the cockpit. The *Sound of Music* was Formiller's boat, but Davis was the more experienced seaman, having reached the rank of skipper in the sailing club to which they all belonged. He knew Santa Cruz well, having cruised there half a dozen times before. Formiller was using this trip to check out his new boat and to show it off to his date, Diane, an airline stewardess.

Formiller was the first to spot what looked like a red lobster pot floating in the water straight ahead. Around the Rock, the birds wheeled and dived noisily, filling the air with their shrill cries, but Mike Davis thought he heard a discordant note.

"What the hell is that?" he yelled to Formiller. He was sure it was a scream—a human cry for help.

"Look over there," Diane Wheatley said, pointing to the dark, dank face of Bird Rock. Amid the white surge of water rushing off the Rock and the looming overhang heavily shadowed by the cliffs, they saw a dark mass in the water, rising and falling with the surge. It was a human figure, perhaps a skin diver in his black rubber scuba gear.

The figure began to move heavily and awkwardly on his back toward them through the agitated water. As he got closer, emerging from the gloom like a sea creature from the deep, Davis gasped. "Oh, my God, there's more than one. They're in big trouble!"

The man, in ordinary sailing clothes, held two companions—a woman and a small child. Across some fifty yards of ocean, Diane heard him say to them in a voice compounded of both hope and despair, "We're going to make it. We're almost there."

"Hang on—we see you! We're coming!" Mike Davis shouted through cupped hands.

Formiller and Wheatley rushed to lower the mainsail as Davis swung the boat into a U-turn, motoring as close to the Rock as he dared. They had practiced overboard drills often at their club, but this was the first time they'd been confronted by the real thing. Wheatley, drilled in the artificial calm of an airline crew under emergency conditions, could feel her heart pounding against her chest as she watched the swimmer's painful struggle in the water.

At Davis's barked command, she got the boarding ladder ready and attached it to the starboard side of the boat. As they nosed closer to the Rock, Formiller on the bow prepared a heaving line with a weighted rubber ball on one end and hurled it toward the man in the water. He was nervous, overanxious about the danger to his boat from the razor-sharp rocks.

The line tangled and fell far short of its goal.

"Oh shit!"

Frantically, he pulled it back and aimed the ball again with all his force. This time there was no mistake. The line sailed true, just over the trio's heads, and somehow—Formiller didn't know how—the man in the water, with an almost superhuman feat of strength, moved the woman and child to one arm, and with a desperate lunge, grabbed the floating lifeline in the other.

Davis eased the throttle down and pushed the *Sound of Music* into reverse. Slowly they began to tow the three away from the rocks in the direction of the open sea.

By now a strange calm had overtaken Wheatley. She knew what she had to do. She and Formiller began pulling on the heavy towline, dragging the sodden figures now in, now out of the water, inch by inch, closer to the boat through the churning, punishing waves.

The man began to shout instructions. "You've got to help us here . . . we're going to need more help!" he yelled, sounding angry and panicked. He'd brought his companions into an almost vertical position alongside him, the woman, supported by what seemed to be his huge left hand, the child in his right, both with their faces turned toward the *Sound of Music.*

Formiller and Wheatley had pulled the three almost parallel to the boarding ladder. The waves were breaking over their heads, leaving them now submerged, now clear of the water, but whether under or not, the rescuers were appalled to see absolutely no reaction from the woman or the child. Not a blink. Not a twitch.

"Oh Jesus!" groaned Formiller. "I think they've had it."

For the first time, Wheatley found herself gazing straight into the face of the woman as the waves buffeted her in the water. She couldn't believe what she was seeing. This was not just a rescue at sea. This was the face of hopelessness and, dare she think it, of death.

She leaned over the lifeline alongside the boarding ladder and grabbed the child first, pulling the little body toward her into the boat. As she held the body and looked into the soft round face, for an instant she wasn't sure whether it was a boy or a girl. Then she cradled him in her arms like a baby. Gently coaxing, she spoke soothingly, as if her words alone could revive him.

"C'mon, little boy," she said. "We've got to get you breathing."

He was wearing an orange life vest fastened securely with straps and buckles. It wasn't ripped or waterlogged. It seemed in as good a shape as if it were brand-new. And yet the boy was ghostly pale, with the same bluish hue as the woman.

Mike Davis saw Wheatley's moment of hesitation. "Start CPR!" he barked.

She immediately began the routine she'd practiced in seagoing drills and as a stewardess. She continued mouth-to-mouth breathing, hoping against hope that her efforts might produce some sign of life.

Gerry Formiller had climbed down the boarding ladder as far as he could into the sea. In water up to his knees, he lifted the woman up to Davis, who carried her on board. Wheatley stopped working on the boy and began to undress the woman. It was weird, the things you notice at a time like this, she thought. The woman was wearing pantyhose under her jeans, with tennis shoes. How odd. You normally didn't see that among the boating crowd.

The two bodies, obviously mother and son, lay forward on the starboard deck, the boy's feet almost touching his mother's sodden head. The wintry California sun shone overhead, and the birds still wheeled and screamed, and the sea air, getting colder now as the sun lowered in the sky, made Wheatley shiver. It all seemed so incongruous, she thought. Nothing had changed, yet everything was different. Could death really be this ordinary—this peaceful?

Belowdecks, Mike Davis flicked the dial of his ship-to-shore radio to Channel 16.

"Mayday, Mayday, Mayday," he yelled breathlessly. He tried to stay calm. "This is the *Sound of Music . . . Sound of Music.* We're in Little Scorpion anchorage, Santa Cruz Island. We have a medical emergency."

Davis kept the Mayday channel open and went above again. The bearded survivor was still in the water, shouting now. "Get the Coast Guard! Get the Coast Guard for my wife and child!" His voice was commanding, strong, and deliberate. He tried climbing onto the ladder. It slipped, knocking him sideways. "No good," he said, apparently drained of strength. "I can't use my legs—they're useless." They tried leaning over to heave him on board. Dry, he was a big man; soaking wet, he was like a sack of concrete. They couldn't budge him and he fell back into the water.

"We're gonna need more help," Davis finally conceded, and sounded the ship's distress horn. Five short, sharp blasts echoed in the afternoon's still air, sending a flurry of seabirds shrieking into the sky.

Startled by the distress horn, James Squire ran up on the deck of his boat, the *Morning Star*, anchored in the harbor. He could see only the high mast of a yacht moving eastward behind Bird Rock. As it slowly nosed into the anchorage, Squire saw a man on deck jumping up and down, wielding an air horn. "We have an emergency. Come quickly!" he hollered.

Ten minutes later, standing up in his skiff to tie his bowline to the *Sound of Music*, Squire saw two bodies lying prone on the deck.

"What happened?" he started to say, but the crew on the *Sound of Music* motioned him sternly to keep quiet, gesturing toward the man still in the water.

From his sabot, Squire easily secured a line under the man's arms, first removing the camera that hung heavily from his neck. Boy, if I was drowning, he thought, I'd sure have dumped that damned camera.

Squire then concentrated all his efforts on guiding the man upright in the water to avoid bumping him, as Mike Davis attached the rescue line to the *Sound of Music*'s jib halyard, and slowly, with great difficulty, winched him aboard.

Squire, too, climbed on board and helped lay the sodden man forward of the mast and close to the woman and child. He was exhausted but alive, so Squire immediately turned his attention to the small boy. Diane Wheatley was still giving him mouth-to-mouth resuscitation.

Squire moved her aside and took over. He cocked the child's head back to clear an airway, plugged the nose, and breathed slowly and rhythmically into the boy's mouth. In between breaths, a steam of clear fluid oozed from the mouth, and Squire, taking it as a possible sign of life, would work on him feverishly, toiling for almost an hour.

Diane Wheatley moved over to the woman, trying to breathe life into her for what seemed like an eternity. She was also expelling a clear vomit, but eventually the acrid taste of the bile in her mouth changed. A more frightening odor came from deep within the body, a kind of stale air, which Wheatley felt in her own mouth and lungs, and in her every pore. Long after the Coast Guard cutter and the emergency evacuation helicopters were gone, when the *Sound of Music* crew was finally anchored for the night in Little Scorpion, Diane would still be trying in vain to get that taste out of her mouth. The taste of Verna Roehler. The taste of death.

Formiller and Davis were meanwhile undressing the man they'd pulled from the Pacific. Davis massaged his legs. He was surprised to find them un-cramped, the calf muscles loose. They wrapped him in blankets and Formiller laid his own bulky body on top of him to add extra warmth. The survivor was shivering with cold, but within ten minutes his breathing had returned to normal and his body temperature was warm; only his hands and feet remained chilled. Throughout the whole time they worked on him, they hadn't heard him utter a single word.

Edward Vernon had sailed to Little Scorpion to show off his boat to his son-in-law on his first ocean voyage. It had been a smooth sail; Vernon's wife, who got seasick at the first sight of a wave, hadn't even been slightly queasy.

Motoring into the anchorage at around 3:00 p.m., he'd just dropped his second anchor when he heard a quick, short alarm blast. A handsome sloop began circling Vernon's boat and the man on board shouted to him, "Call the Coast Guard! It's an emergency."

The crew on board the sloop was making frantic hand signals indicating to Vernon that they'd just pulled three people out of the water. After maydaying the Coast Guard, Vernon rowed over to the largest of the boats in the anchorage, the *Perseverance.* He pulled his dinghy alongside the sleek ship and hammered sharply on the hull. Receiving no answer, he tied up and climbed aboard.

Fritz Roehler roused himself reluctantly from his warm sleeping bag. He thought he heard footsteps on deck. When he climbed up, a stranger was standing there.

"There's been an accident. They've fished some people out of the water. Do you carry oxygen?"

Fritz called down to Charlotte below.

"Is there an oxygen tank anywhere down there?"

"Don't see one . . ."

"Do you know the Kiss of Life?" Vernon asked.

Fritz had never heard the expression and looked at Vernon as though he was one of the California weirdos he'd heard about.

"My son's out there somewhere. He's a diver with the navy—he's got all kinds of rescue experience and all that. Soon as he gets back, I'll send him over."

As Vernon left the *Perseverance*, he saw a gray dinghy with two adults and two little girls aboard slowly moving closer to the yacht from the island.

Scott and Ginny Roehler had had trouble getting the dinghy through the surf when leaving the shore. They were wet and bedraggled and glad to be back on board the *Perseverance*.

"We heard a boat horn," Scott told his parents. "And we saw something red floating out there."

"Yeah, there's been some sort of accident," said Fritz. "They pulled some folks out of the water."

The *Sound of Music* was anchored barely fifty yards from the *Perseverance*. Scott, standing on the deck, yelled over. "How many people you got over there?"

"Three," Mike Davis shouted.

"Is there a man with a beard?"

"Yes."

"Does the woman have white hair?"

"Yes."

Fritz Roehler let out an anguished bellow.

"Oh, God—it's Fred!"

Squinting in horror over at the *Sound of Music*, they saw a bundled figure, covered completely head to toe with a blanket, lying immobile by the mainsail.

Scott shuddered and crumpled slowly to the deck. "Oh my God! Fred's dead."

Minutes later, Vernon, now realizing where the victims had come from, rowed back to the *Perseverance*. "I'm going back over to the *Sound of Music*," he shouted up to the family on the deck. "Would any of you like to come with me?"

To his surprise, the woman answered quickly. "No."

The young man also shook his head, and the elderly gentleman, glancing sideways at his wife, never moved a muscle.

The children were screaming now, horrible cries coming from the three little girls huddled together in the main cabin. Charlotte Roehler had no time for that sort of carrying on.

"Your mother and dad don't need your tears," she told them. "They need your prayers. Now quit crying and sit down and pray. Pray just as hard as you can."

The little girls hugged each other as they waited and watched through the portholes as the Coast Guard cutter roared into the anchorage.

The first call to the Coast Guard had come in at approximately 2:30 p.m. at Channel Islands Harbor in Oxnard. Coxswain Virgil Estrada reckoned it took some forty-five minutes to speed to the *Sound of Music*. To the rescuers on board, it seemed much longer.

When Estrada jumped on deck, he saw a bearded man lying wrapped in blankets, shaking and apparently incoherent. The woman and the small boy seemed lifeless. Estrada immediately decided to move them to his cutter to wait for the medic's helicopter. He tied his launch to the *Sound of Music* and threw a gangplank from one deck to the other.

Mike Davis gently handed the boy's body to Estrada, and as he did so a strange involuntary rattling sound came from deep within the child. Davis reacted with a shudder. The Coast Guardsman paled and seemed even more shaken by it than Davis.

Estrada put Fred Roehler on a stretcher and carried him onto the cutter. Then they loaded Verna aboard and headed out of the anchorage into the open sea.

Some three miles out, the first of the helicopters hovered noisily overhead. Norman Branch, a young paramedic summoned from the Malibu Colony fire station, was lowered in a basket onto the deck of the cutter. He slapped electrocardiograph paddles first on the woman, then on the boy, holding them on their clammy skin for ten seconds. The line was flat on both.

"They're dead," he said.

Then he turned his attention to the man. He checked the pupils of his eyes; both responded equally to light. The hands and feet were cold, but the body seemed warm enough. There was no sign of an injury, but he appeared to be drifting in and out of consciousness. Branch did a response-to-pain test, digging his knuckles sharply and forcefully against the man's sternum. He winced visibly. He's not unconscious, Branch thought; he must be in some kind of shock. The man did not respond to any of Branch's questions and stared vacantly into space. But every so often he would look at the medic and silent tears rolled down his cheeks.

Quickly, they loaded him onto a stretcher and lifted him into the air and aboard the helicopter, which then roared off for the mainland. The navy would be by later to pick up the bodies of Verna and her child.

At 4:53 p.m., Brad Davis, the nurse on duty at St. John's Hospital in Oxnard, admitted Fred Roehler to the emergency room, wrapped in layers of blankets and lying in a Coast Guard litter. The patient's condition was strange, Davis thought, because although he was undoubtedly conscious, asking for the whereabouts of his wife and child, he apparently could not answer questions from Davis or the hospital's admissions clerk. He lay rigid as a marble effigy, his pale blue eyes wide open, staring fixedly at the ceiling as they asked gently, "Who are you? Do you know your name?"

His lungs were free of water, Davis recorded. His pulse was strong, his skin color good, yet for a long twenty minutes he seemed unable to speak. He seemed almost catatonic, yet there was nothing in his physical condition to explain his zombie-like demeanor. He seemed to have emerged from his ordeal relatively unscathed. A doctor, with the help of a resident priest, gently informed him that his wife and child were dead. He shuddered, his face contorted as if in agony. His chest rose and fell rapidly, and he rolled over on his side, sobbing bitterly, his whole body shaking. He asked that they contact his brother, his wife's mother, her pastor, and a friend of his, Dick Velthoen, who lived nearby and could come to drive him home.

Before leaving the hospital, Fred requested that his wife's eyes and those of her son be donated to the hospital's eye bank.

At first light, Fred Roehler, twice a widower in the space of five years, brought Heidi, Kimberly, and Kirsten into his bedroom and told them what they most feared to hear. These three little girls, who had been through so much in their short lives, sat on the edge of the big bed he'd shared with Verna. He put his arms around them and held them close for a few silent moments.

"I have something very sad to tell you," he began.

The girls started to cry. In their hearts, they knew what was coming.

"Mother and Douglas are dead."

Kimberly Johnson stared straight at him, a heartbreaking question in her eyes. "First my dad, then my mother and brother," she said. "I'm all alone now, aren't I?"

Heidi and Kirsten joined in, almost in unison. "Well, now we've lost two mothers."

He hugged them closer.

"But we're still a family," he said. "And Kim, you're every bit as much a daughter to me as Heidi and Kirsten."

They'd never seen Fred cry before. Somehow it seemed to make things worse.

Kirsten asked what had happened to their dog Lady. Her father explained that he'd put her up on a rock, and she would probably be okay. Then he explained in the simplest terms he could what had happened. All they could remember later was that it was something to do with the dog jumping out of the boat.

"I tried as hard as I could to help Mother and Douglas," he said. "I want you to believe that. But it just wasn't to be."

"Was it Lady's fault then?" Kirsten asked sadly.

"It wasn't anybody's fault. God must have been ready for Mother and Doug. They'll be in Heaven now with Bill and Jeanne."

"I wonder what it's like in Heaven," said Kirsten.

"I wonder if they'll like it there," murmured Kimberly.

Chapter 2

Santa Barbara, January 6, 1981

At 11:00 a.m. on Tuesday, January 6, 1981, Deputy Larry Gillespie, a stocky, thirty-six-year-old coroner's assistant with the Santa Barbara sheriff's department, sat in the crowded office he shared with a secretary and a plainclothes detective. He was trying to decide whether he had time to slip out to the County Hospital cafeteria next door and grab a hamburger and fries for an early lunch.

It had been a frantic morning. There were four unsolved homicides, but his stomach was growling, and finally, it won out. Halfway out the office door, his phone rang. Reluctantly he picked it up.

The woman on the line identified herself as Mrs. Candy Hinman of Malibu, a community some seventy-five miles to the south. She told him she was a neighbor of a man named Fred Roehler whose wife and stepson had drowned in the ocean at Santa Cruz Island off the coast of Santa Barbara a couple of days before. She had also been a close friend of Roehler's first wife, Jeanne.

Gillespie was used to strange calls; accusations, threats, and hysterical ramblings were all part of his daily routine. This one was different. The woman was businesslike and calm. She made her points clearly, logically, without excitement or nervousness. Gillespie realized she was no crank.

He cleared space in the middle of his cluttered desk, grabbed a notebook, and started writing. For ten minutes, he took copious notes, interrupting with a question here and there. As the caller finished her recitation, he put down his pen, pushed back his chair, and listened as Mrs. Hinman, her voice breaking for the first time, posed a dramatic question.

"This guy murdered his first wife," she emphatically declared. "Are you going to let him get away with this one, too?"

Gillespie put down the phone after talking to Candy Hinman and sat gazing at it for a moment. Then he picked up his notes and walked some twenty feet through the door into the detective division of the Santa Barbara sheriff's department.

3

Growing Up in Centerville

He was as solid as a rock—the kind of kid you'd want for your own son.

—Joel Rhodes, former Indiana legislator and editor/publisher of the *Centerville Crusader*

Charlotte Taylor Roehler's living room in her long stone ranch house in Centerville, Indiana, is like the mistress of the house herself: ample, elegant, and carefully appointed.

On one wall, a china cabinet lies open to display a collection of Hummel figurines. In the center of the room, a teal Early American–style pedestal dining table is permanently set for four, with peach-colored dishes on precisely matching placemats and coordinating napkins. Next to a soft pastel sofa is an armchair covered with the quilt Charlotte wraps herself in on chilly nights to watch television. A stack of *House Beautiful* magazines sits on an end table nearby.

The entire room, however, is dominated by the rear wall where portraits of the four Roehler sons hang in a descending diagonal line. The formal color photographs were taken on each boy's high school graduation, and in their dark suits and ties, they look strangely unanimated, giving little clue as to their character or temperament. On closer inspection, the reason becomes obvious: The pictures have been airbrushed. They are perfect, plastic, and utterly unreal. Nobody lives in those faces.

The picture of Fred Roehler, the eldest son, is the first and hangs highest in the tableau. In his case the airbrushing was superfluous. At age eight, at eighteen, and at twenty-eight, he was a startlingly handsome boy.

From the day the Roehlers and their two sons—Fred, six, and Ron, four—moved from the more sophisticated Pittsburgh to the flat and rather ugly town of Centerville, it was obvious that they did things just a little differently. They were big-city folks. They knew a thing or two. Charlotte, with her mane of dark hair, colorful tailored clothes, and skillfully applied makeup, would have been a standout in any middle-class neighborhood in America. On their street, Fenderville, she was a star. And Fritz, with his ramrod bearing and his air of confident *bonhomie*, would have been perfectly cast as a small-town bürgermeister.

Fritz had jumped at the opportunity when his older brother, Boots, offered him a degree of independence and a much-needed job selling for the aluminum awning factory Boots had bought in Hagerstown, Indiana, near Centerville.

The Centerville folks were impressed by the Roehlers despite themselves. Somehow the word got out that they'd both come from wealthy families in Pennsylvania and were a definite cut above the tombstone salesman or the Sears Roebuck plumber who lived down the street. They did things with just a little more flair, gave the place some excitement. It was good to have them around. They elevated the neighborhood just by being there.

Theirs was the first TV set on the street—a ten-inch black-and-white Motorola—the ultimate status symbol of the time. It was a long way to the nearest transmitter, but they rigged up a huge aerial themselves and put the TV set on the windowsill facing the garden, lining up chairs on the small lawn every afternoon so that the neighborhood kids could watch *Howdy Doody* after school without rampaging through the house.

All the other neighbors decorated their homes from the Sears catalog, but Charlotte bought decorator magazines and filled her modest house with scaled-down ideas from the grand homes of the Mainline and Grosse Pointe. She dressed her boys in preppy corduroys and oxford shirts until they begged to wear jeans and plaid flannel like the other country kids. Her own clothes had an elegance unseen in those parts before. Charlotte was the first woman in the neighborhood to wear slacks, a good ten years before anyone else did.

"You can always tell the worth of a woman by her shoes and her pocketbook," Charlotte liked to say. And hers were the finest for miles around.

Her neighbors often wondered how the Roehlers maintained such standards on what Fritz earned installing aluminum awnings and storm doors.

"They must be getting help from their families," they concluded, and left it at that. But there were no subsidies from home. The Roehler finances were the result of careful management, sleight of hand, and later, perhaps, something else. Their family history was never revealed.

No one knew that Charlotte's mother, after the birth of her last child, had had a severe mental health crisis and was in a deep catatonic state. She would be confined in a psychiatric hospital for the rest of her life. Coping with her mother's fate had given Charlotte practice in a skill she would later develop into a fine art. If something displeased her, she simply scripted a new version for herself. Hence, in the world according to Charlotte, children were handsome and well-mannered. Husbands were hardworking and attentive. Families were supportive and socially prominent. Poverty, teenage rebellion, sickness, and hard times appeared only in other people's families—a reflection of their inability to live up to the Roehlers' standards.

The Roehlers' firstborn, Fred, was a gorgeous child with dark curly hair, a cheeky dimpled grin, and twinkling clear blue eyes from which the mischief fairly shone. By sheer force of personality, it seemed, he soon had every kid in the neighborhood, younger or older, marching to his tune. Fred was the one who decided what games would be played and who would play them. New toys had to be first shown to Fred for his approval. It was to Fred's beat that they all marched.

When the family moved to Centerville, he had no trouble fitting in. At the elementary school, his teachers quickly warmed to the well-dressed, politely spoken youngster for whom nothing they wanted was too much trouble; he always seemed to go out of his way to please, and he was bright and curious about everything. His grades were good, and he had the makings of a great little athlete. He later became the scoutmaster's star pupil, making Eagle Scout quicker than anyone in town ever had before. He was eventually the senior patrol leader of his troop.

Two and a half years after they'd arrived in Centerville, Charlotte, Fritz, Fred, and Ron Roehler moved out of the house on Fenderville and into a brand-new ranch house they'd had built outside the town on the main state road to Richmond.

"You only saw the Roehlers at their best when they were prepared for you," one neighbor observed. "Going to their home was like being invited to a theater, waiting for the curtain to go up, to see what they'd staged for you."

Fritz gave his sons endless advice on saving money. He expected them all to bank half of everything they earned. He had mastered the art of living well on comparatively little, but money—the getting of it and the keeping of it—became increasingly important as the family grew.

"My children had a good German father," Charlotte would say proudly. "They all knew the value of a dollar."

Two years later, when the Roehlers had a third son, Scott, Charlotte resigned herself to being the mother of sons. Her husband called her "Queenie," and to her sons that was what she was—a queen to be protected, elevated, and served.

At Centerville High, Fred and Ron Roehler were the big men on campus. Fred was captain of the tennis team and star of the strength and endurance events in track and hurdles. But in Hoosier Country, only one sport—basketball—really matters. It's almost a state religion. Fritz instituted his own incentive bonus system, paying his sons twenty-five to fifty cents a basket. It may have increased their scoring average, but it did little for team spirit. Once the Bulldogs were out of the competition, Fritz's interest in basketball faded fast. "We support the Roehlers. Period," he explained. "All the rest is just a bunch of big Black fellas jumping on another bunch of big Black fellas."

There were two kinds of girls at Centerville High: those with the confidence to hope Fred Roehler would ask them for a date and weren't too shy to lobby buddies and brothers to intercede for them; and those who would have been scared to death by the very idea. "I was much too overawed by him to think about dating him," one of them said later. "I guess we put him on a pedestal. He was an Adonis. He seemed so far above us in high school. He was kind of the elusive butterfly. Everybody wanted him but nobody could catch him."

At age seventeen, Fred was six-foot-two, hard-muscled and broad-shouldered, with a pair of startlingly penetrating blue eyes, and sex appeal to burn. He was the star athlete, with the edge of arrogance that typically appeals to adolescents—always able to buck the system and get away with it. At the school costume party, he and a pal dressed as giant beer cans and danced all night with their dancing partners snugly tucked inside the beer cans with them, much to the chagrin of the edgy chaperones and the amusement of the other students.

"If he asked you to dance," recalled a classmate, "you were in heaven. A smile from him was enough to brighten any girl's day."

From the time he was sixteen to when he turned twenty-one, his brother Ron complained, "Fred wrecked every car my dad owned . . . every car he owned . . . and every car I owned."

The tales of crash woes grew. Fred tore a strip off his father's motor home the first time he borrowed it; he drove a convertible too wide around a corner and ended up stuck like a fish in a net between the telephone pole and its guidewire and had to be lifted out by a large tow truck.

The trouble with Fred, his friends reasoned, was that he got bored easily, so he took risks. He seemed to need to set challenges for himself.

Fritz Roehler carried insurance on Fred through his business and complained about the high rates his son's mishaps cost him, but never very strenuously. "That kid has the dumbest luck with cars," he griped.

And Charlotte agreed. "Yes, our Fred is accident-prone."

This continued to be the refrain when Fred's "bad luck" would be used to excuse more than the occasional fender bender.

4

The Midwestern Roehlers Discover Boating

THE ROEHLER FAMILY'S LOVE AFFAIR WITH WATER STARTED EARLY. A friend in Richmond, Indiana, invited Fritz, Fred, and Ron to go camping with his family on Big Bone Island on the Ohio River, twenty-eight miles south of Cincinnati, an experience the Roehler boys adored. A few weeks later Charlotte came along, too, although protesting all the way, "It's just not my thing."

Driving home two days later, however, she asked Fritz," How much do you think a boat would cost?"

Two weeks later, the Roehlers bought a twelve-foot Gibbs cruiser with a twenty-four-horsepower motor. The thrifty Fritz had wrestled long and hard with spending the money, but Charlotte said it was a healthy way to keep the family together, especially since Centerville in summer had little for the boys to do. It wasn't a fancy boat, but most weekends from then on were spent on the river.

The Gibbs soon made way for a twenty-six-foot cabin cruiser picked up for a bargain $5,500. Fritz souped up the engine so that it went fast enough for the older boys to water ski. When the cruiser hit top speed, all the boat's contents as well as the dishes in the galley spilled out and shattered.

"We need a real speedboat, Dad," Fred complained.

"And where do you think we'll get the money for that?" Fritz shot back.

In the spring of 1956, the Roehlers towed their cabin cruiser home and stored it in an unused warehouse at the local airport, across the street from their house. Not long after, a passerby spotted huge sheets of flames shooting from the warehouse roof. By the time the fire department had doused the flames, the Roehlers's cruiser had been badly damaged. The blaze was recorded as a "fire of unknown origin."

Luckily, the cabin cruiser was fully insured.

The next time the Roehlers appeared on the river, they were the proud owners of a $10,000, nineteen-foot Owens speedboat with a Chevrolet Corvette 225-horsepower engine, which they named *The Charlotte R.* It was the fastest boat on the river.

On a Saturday night late in the summer of 1956, the family was preparing to go to bed at a campground, where they were vacationing. As one of their boating neighbors was walking down to the river, he remembered Fritz Roehler calling to him, "You don't need to check my boat. I already did, and it's fine."

Around 1:00 a.m., the campground was jolted awake by shouts of "*Fire!*"

Racing outdoors, the campers saw a red glow light up the night sky. The Roehler boat was on fire, flames leaping hundreds of feet into the air, completely engulfing the hull. It was too far gone to even try to extinguish it. Even though the cause of the blaze was never determined, the insurance company paid the Roehlers in full for their loss.

It was not the last time fire was to visit the Roehlers. Some years later, after their two elder sons had moved to California, an old eyesore of a barn in their backyard burned down. This time, the claim was made on their next-door neighbor's insurance, as the fire had originally started on that property.

The fire came at a propitious moment, as their third son, Scott, was about to get married. With the insurance proceeds, the Roehlers built a two-story, picture-postcard barn with a white-trimmed apartment on top, complete with window boxes and frilled curtains. The barn looked particularly picturesque in the wedding pictures as Scott and his wife Ginny arrived in a fringed surrey to their new home.

Roehler's "bad luck" became a perpetual topic of conversation in Centerville.

"We should have disasters like old Fritz has disasters," noted one of Roehler's buddies at a coffee shop breakfast gathering.

5

Fred, the Ladies' Man

Not surprisingly, Fred—a handsome, popular teen jock—enjoyed the company of Centerville's young ladies.

There was the time that Ron, from his top bunk in their bedroom, looked down to find his mother's hairdresser snugly ensconced with his brother in the bottom bunk. Once when their parents were out of town with the two younger boys, Ron came home and followed a trail of ladies' garments to his parents' bedroom where Fred was entertaining a local lass.

This was a small, Midwestern town in the early 1960s, before the sexual revolution. There were good girls and bad girls, and everyone knew the difference. The boys in the Centervilles of America broke those rules at their peril, and no one was more conscious of the dangers lurking out there between rounds of the sexual mating dance than the Roehler boys.

Charlotte always made it clear to her sons: "If you ever get a girl pregnant, I want you to know that child will be my grandchild—a Roehler—and you'll marry that girl. I don't care who she is. And what's more, that marriage will last. There's never been a divorce in the Roehler family and we're not going to start now. Is that clear?" The two boys smirked at each other as Fred quipped, "Don't worry, Mom, we promise we won't get pregnant."

Girls who dated Fred for any length of time remember him fondly precisely because he was "such a gentleman." "He was so sensitive and romantic," recalls one. "He used to write me poetry about medieval knights and fair ladies. I knew his family well; they were all so close to each other, which I thought was great."

Chapter 5

When Fred graduated from Centerville High in June 1960, he received the Outstanding Senior Male Award. "There were people who were better than me academically but weren't any good at sports," he recalled. "And there were people who were better at sports, but duds academically. I got it because I was half good at both."

The award certainly helped him get into Purdue University, the number-one school for Hoosiers bent on engineering. Fritz and Charlotte had been pushing him hard to apply. His grades weren't the greatest, but with his Eagle Scout merits and glowing recommendations from his teachers, coaches, and other Centerville worthies, he was accepted.

First, there was a long summer to get through, and a job to look for. Fred applied as a lifeguard at nearby Liberty Lake in Richmond, which required him to pass a rigorous test of his ability in the water, competing against scores of other young men applying for the same job.

"Between us, we must have pulled sixty swimmers out that summer," a lifeguard recalled. "But Roehler was far and away the best of us. He was a whale in the water; no one else could touch him."

Handsome Fred enjoyed his status as a jock and ladies' man, and his sex appeal continued well into college.

Jane Anderson was a fellow engineering student at Purdue. She was tall with cool Scandinavian good looks, long legs, and a fresh complexion. She never forgot Fred, including the first time she set eyes on him.

"He was sitting in the sun on the edge of a campus swimming pool, with a spectacular tan, wearing a pair of tight shorts. He looked like one of those Hollywood pinups—Rock Hudson or Robert Wagner—gorgeous, everyone's dream man. I was pinned to someone else at the time, but the novelty wore off fast once I saw Fred. We got into the habit of having long, long late-night phone conversations. I would call him from my sorority house and pour my heart out to him. He seemed so much more sensible and caring than any of the other guys. I didn't think you could fall in love over the phone, but I did. I was absolutely mad about him."

Jane elaborated. "Here was this big guy with a black beard and longish hair, and he was so different from all the other fellows around there," she remembered. "I called him first and asked him out. From that first date, I stopped seeing anyone else. I gave up all my normal activities. I was his. Nobody else could measure up. I was twenty, he was twenty-three, and I was really in love. We couldn't get enough of each other. I tried to think up things to do outside of the trailer he lived in to get us out of there. Not that I didn't enjoy it, I just didn't want it to be the central thing in our relationship, and it was fast becoming that. I thought he was a marvelous lover, although it was usually over very fast."

What puzzled Jane most was his attitude toward family life. "Fred made it clear that the idea of ever settling down and having a family was completely repugnant to him. It was stronger than that, even—like the very thought of it made him sick or gave him physical pain—and yet he would talk constantly about his wonderfully close family and how terrific his mom and dad were. He made them sound like Ozzie and Harriet."

At times at Purdue, Jane said, he seemed to want to fantasize about their future together. "We were at a party at a local Unitarian minister's house. There was a big punch bowl, and standing around it, Fred took my hand and kind of went all mystical on me, gazing into my eyes. 'You know,' he said, 'I can see us on an occasion like this, years from now, and there's this big punch bowl like this, and we're celebrating something together.' It was the strangest thing, and so romantic. It was a real turn-on for me. He'd look at me with this kind of wonder in his eyes and tell me, 'I can't believe you're here. I can't believe I've found you.' To see someone who was as crazy about me as I was about him was just wonderful."

But then suddenly, he could go ice-cold on her. "It got so I never knew which Fred I was going to meet."

There was always quite a lot of tension in their relationship, sexual and otherwise.

She began to have dreams in which Fred was stalking her. In one such dream, he was stabbing her with a knife. "I told Fred about my dream. Immediately he got very excited. He took me into his room and set up his camera with the shutter on automatic so that he could take a picture of us together."

In the photograph he staged that day with Jane, Fred is holding a dagger, the tip pressed against her neck. His other hand is on his heart, as if in sorrow at losing his love. Jane is pointing a matching dagger at his chest.

"That wasn't part of my dream, but he suggested I do it," she recalled.

The photograph is chilling, a fantasy of murder. Jane Anderson is mugging for the camera, rolling her eyes back into her head in mock terror—a movie actress giving it her all.

Fred Roehler is in a different movie. His gaze is fixed, his concentration is total, and the expression on his face is one of deadly earnestness.

As time went on, she began to see another, more disturbing side of the man she loved. He dropped her off at her dorm one night after a date. An hour later, he called to say he'd been driving home and another driver had been following him too closely. Fred said he'd cut him off, jumped out of the car, and knocked the guy unconscious.

She asked if the man was all right.

"I don't know," he told her. "I just left him lying there."

He also told her he'd been to see a psychiatrist back home during his early years at Purdue. He never told her the reason. "It didn't help me, though," he said. "I ended up interviewing the shrink. Those guys are the biggest bunch of phonies around."

In June 1966, Fred graduated from Purdue and took his first full-time job that summer. He worked for the United States Navy at Lakehurst, New Jersey, as an electronics engineer—a lowly GS-7 civil servant at a salary of $7,511 a year. His first project was part of the escalating war in Vietnam, testing portable runways that let US aircraft land in difficult jungle terrain on aluminum matting dropped from helicopters. It was, Fred thought, the perfect way of avoiding the draft, a very real consideration for graduates of the class of '66.

The navy had paid the cost of towing Fred's trailer and possessions to Lakehurst, where, in the summer of 1966, he set himself up in a trailer park on Toms River, near the base. He was not impressed with the "jock officers," and called them "little tinpot gods striding around with their stripes. The only other thing around here are the surf bums who hang around the beach. What a bunch of losers."

His only salvation was the water and a tiny wooden boat with a single sail that he'd picked up cheaply. He spent all his off time out on the bay.

Later, he exchanged the boat for a Boston Whaler and ventured farther afield. At the end of August, Jane told him she was coming east with her parents on vacation before her final year at Purdue, and they would be staying near him at Ocean City. He immediately invited her to visit him.

The most extraordinary thing about her trip was that Fred Roehler suddenly started talking about marriage.

"He said I could always finish school later after we were married," Jane recalled. "He said he wanted to do things properly, to come back to Chicago and ask my parents' permission. It was a bit silly in retrospect, because they were staying just driving distance down the coast and he could have talked to them there and then. But he was saying all the right things, and though I didn't much like the idea of living in that awful trailer with him, this was Fred Roehler, and he was what I had always wanted."

In Chicago, she joyfully announced her marriage plans. "Everyone was so happy for me. I gave my notice at the country club where I was working that summer. I was on cloud nine."

Five days later, a letter arrived. It was simple and to the point. Fred wrote that he was sorry; he had made a mistake, and this was good-bye. It was nothing Jane had done. It was him. He wasn't ready for marriage. He wasn't sure if he'd ever be. He wasn't like other people; he'd always felt like a misfit. Marriage and family weren't for him. He was sorry, but good-bye.

She was devastated. She tried to call him. There was no reply. Then she remembered he'd told her he was going to a conference in Atlantic City.

"He knew when I got the letter, I wouldn't be able to contact him. I guess he thought that would give me a few days to calm down. When he got back, I called him two or three more times. He was almost brutal on the phone. It was kind of, 'I said all there is to say. Go away and don't bother me. It's over.' It was almost as if he were punishing me for something," she said, "but I had no idea what."

Jane went back to Purdue and tried to pick up the pieces of her life, but she never got over Fred. Years later, married and with a family, she was still painfully analyzing how he had been able to mesmerize her for so long.

"There was so little I knew about him. He was a repository for all my romantic fantasies. It had little to do with him, really. It's no wonder that for the rest of my life, no one could quite measure up to him. He was a creature of my imagination."

6

Fred

California, Here He Comes

The breath of the draft board was blowing uncomfortably close. The job in Lakehurst had provided a brief three-month deferment, but Fred's commanding officer, Captain James Lieber, refused to extend it. Fred sent a letter to the CO, signed by the chief engineer, stating that he was essential to the airstrip project and that he could not be drafted.

Lieber was not impressed. "What the hell kind of baloney is this?" he demanded of the chief. "This guy isn't even a senior man. Hell, he's only been with us a couple of months. You can't convince me he's essential to this mission. Deferment denied."

On the other side of the continent Tom Carr, chief engineer at California's Point Mugu Pacific Missile Test Center just north of Malibu, was delighted to receive Fred Roehler's call. Fred told Carr he was already working for the Navy, but wanted to do more ocean work and would move to California. Carr told him to come on out and that he'd arrange for a Navy transfer.

When Captain Lieber heard about the cozy arrangement, however, he blew his stack. He called his opposite number, the commander at Point Mugu, and told him how little he thought of Roehler. The job offer was abruptly withdrawn.

Tom Carr passed the message on. "Your captain out there isn't very fond of you, so we can't transfer you, but I really need engineers. So, if you show up here at the gate and we're still hiring, I'll take you on."

Roehler immediately submitted his resignation at Lakehurst.

"I wrote, 'To go to Point Mugu' on it in nice big letters and took off,' he recalled later, "but I had to pay them back the $900 they'd paid to move me from Purdue."

Years later, he couldn't resist boasting about his victory over the US Navy to a colleague at Point Mugu. "As soon as I hung up from the phone call with Carr, I jumped into my trusty Triumph and went streaking through the base at eighty-five miles an hour in a twenty-five-mile zone, burning rubber as I went. Then along comes one of the base police, and the guy writes me a ticket and chews me out. I drove out the gate, threw my security badge and the traffic ticket at the sentry, gave him a big salute, and took off. I knew I wasn't ever coming back there."

The Pacific Missile Test Center at Point Mugu is on the front line of global confrontation, testing projectiles to hurl across continents at some undesignated enemy, perfecting war games on and under the ocean for the benefit of the US Navy. The ugly base on 4,000-plus desolate acres houses rows of cement office blocks where civil servants and civilian engineers toil in lines of cubicles to invent new and better systems for war. It is a place for those comfortable with bureaucracy.

There has probably never been anyone less suited to Point Mugu than Fred Roehler. He moved into one of the cubicles in the Range Operations Division in October 1966. His immediate supervisor was Jack Burkhardt, a wiry, fair-haired, no-nonsense Westerner from Denver, Colorado. He'd been assigned four young men, all right out of school, to help operate his new geophysics division. Burkhardt was particularly impressed with the tall, rugged Roehler. He seemed bright, enthusiastic, and ready to tackle anything.

"He was a natural in the water," Burkhardt recalled. "He knew what he could get by with and what he couldn't. He was a terrifically strong swimmer and a pretty tough guy."

This was important, as much of the division's work involved installing weather buoys packed with electronic devices for measuring currents, surges, and wave actions, information vital to the smooth running of the Navy's military exercises. Burkhardt thought Roehler could be invaluable.

First, however, he would have to be Navy-certified by taking a thirty-day course at the Navy Diving School in San Diego. Roehler jumped at the idea because he was still worried about his draft status. "Mugu should fight a little harder for me," he wrote his parents, "having invested thirty days of schooling in me."

The naval port city of San Diego was no more to his liking than Toms River, and it didn't take him long to get on the wrong side of the chief instructor, a rough-and-ready, regular Navy type, a bosun's mate first class named Crooks who wasn't taking any guff from some wet-behind-the-ears civilian. Roehler seemed to delight in confronting the BM in class.

"Would you please not swear, sir?" he asked. "It offends me." His fellow students tried to keep their faces straight. The career Navy man looked at this bigmouth with the long hair (compared with the young naval recruits in the class) and dubbed him "the asshole college puke."

BM Crooks set up increasingly difficult ways to test the young divers' mettle, their courage, and their dedication to each other's safety. They would be left in pairs at the bottom of the swimming pool for twenty minutes during which, in quick succession, their air supply would be turned off, their masks yanked from their faces, their regulators pulled out, and everything possible done to encourage them to panic and rise to the surface. In a real diving situation that could cause the bends and an excruciating death. Panic could also endanger the lives of their comrades.

Crooks wasn't surprised when the "asshole college puke" panicked, failed to share his oxygen supply with his buddy, and surfaced to save himself.

"Roehler, you're out of here!" Crooks barked. He couldn't have been more delighted.

Back home in Centerville, Fred would have simply called his father, who would have taken care of it. But his father was a long way away, so he called Jack Burkhardt.

"Jack, you've got to help me," he pleaded. "Those dummies have flunked me. This Navy moron had it in for me."

Burkhardt made several calls to the diving school, but the Navy stood firm.

On March 8, Roehler drove back to Mugu alone, crestfallen and bitter. He commenced a process aided by his meticulous recordkeeping and his own perseverance, writing a lengthy report justifying his actions and reiterating his gripes. "I had kept dates, times, etc., for my travel reports," he explained. "Copies were sent to the Naval School's commanding officer, as well as everyone else concerned."

Jack Burkhardt was furious with him. He'd placed his faith in Roehler, and Roehler had let him down. "Listen, fella, we just lost one helluva investment here," Burkhardt said. "You had three weeks off from work and we still can't use you for diving. Why couldn't you keep your damned mouth shut?"

"But Jack, they wrapped the hose around my neck and tried to choke me," Roehler protested.

"Okay," said Burkhardt, "If I get you in again, you're going to show up with a Marine Corps haircut and you're going to sit in class and keep your trap shut until the end. Is that clear?"

Roehler went back that autumn with a short-back-and-sides haircut and graduated with a certificate on October 20, 1967.

With his diving credential, he was now spending at least half his working life in and around the Channel Islands off the coast, doctoring Navy buoys, being paid for doing what he enjoyed most: working in the water. In between jobs, he went fishing, using the Navy's best state-of-the-art equipment.

He wasn't happy with his transportation, however. He was learning that in California, you are what you drive. His battered TR4 had seen better days. Before he'd left Purdue, he'd rear-ended another car with it. The insurance company wanted to write it off, but he'd managed to salvage it. By now, it was in a sorry state. "I'm trying to come up with wheels," he wrote to his family. "A bike and a TR just won't hack it."

One afternoon in 1967, Fred Roehler sauntered up to Jack Burkhardt in the Point Mugu cafeteria line and asked an odd question. "Hey, Jack, is fire insurance good on your car if there's no collision?" Burkhardt told him to check with his insurance company.

Six weeks later, around midnight, Burkhardt's wife called him to the phone. "Fred's been in an accident," she said. "He's not hurt, but he's asking for you."

Burkhardt drove over to the beach just outside the Mugu property line. A couple of fire trucks had arrived first, and Fred Roehler stood among them in his warmups.

"Sorry to drag you out, Jack," Roehler said. "I came down to run on the beach, got in the car to head home, and some weirdo on a motorcycle came at me without lights. I had to swerve, lost control, and hit a tree stump." He had jumped out of the car, he said, just seconds before it burst into flames. By the time the fire department got there, the car had burned to its frame.

Several weeks later, Jack Burkhardt saw Roehler's insurance claim. It listed several hundred dollars' worth of diving equipment that Roehler said had been in the trunk of the car when it caught fire. As far as Burkhardt knew, the only equipment Fred kept in the car was dead diving bottles. Fred used the $1,600 insurance payoff to buy a spanking-new 1968 Volkswagen, the first new car he had ever owned.

His tales of traffic woes continued to the point where he was frantically seeking someone to save his driving license. A colleague at Mugu referred him to a judge in Oxnard who referred him in turn to a young local attorney he knew: Bill Fairfield, an energetic, attractive, and well-connected law partner of William Clark, who later became a key member of Ronald Reagan's cabinet. Fairfield was immediately charmed by the handsome, soft-spoken young man who sat rather sheepishly in front of him in his law office. He couldn't really have explained why. There was just something about the guy—a sincerity, he thought, a kind of goofy eccentricity that suggested he was his own man.

"Look," Fred said, "I've been an idiot. I've got three tickets in one weekend, and I know they're going to take my license away. Can you do anything?"

Fairfield bailed him out and saved his license. It was the beginning of a friendship between the two men that was to endure for the next thirteen years. Tall, fair-haired, athletic Fairfield, a ferociously competitive racquetball player, a driven A-type personality, but very attached to his own large family, became Roehler's lawyer, confidant, and friend. He was the man to whom Fred would turn when things went wrong, or when he needed to maneuver the bureaucracy—someone to pave the way for his ambitious plans.

In short order, Fairfield came to regard Fred as his best friend. He was sure that Fred felt the same way. Fairfield's wife, Donna, accepted Fred as a favored guest in their home and a fun companion on sailing trips, family picnics, barbecues, and swim parties. There was no one of whom her husband had a higher opinion. He would have trusted Fred Roehler with his life.

7

Jeanne

The First Mrs. Roehler

By the summer of 1969, Fred Roehler was traveling regularly to the US Navy's Pacific Missile Test Range at Kauai, Hawaii, setting up electronic surveillance equipment underwater, and directing recovery operations for target launchers in the ocean depths off the Islands.

In August, he and a Navy colleague were passing the time while they waited for United's red-eye from Honolulu to LA by liberally fueling themselves in the airport bar. By the time they boarded, the pair was feeling no pain. Fred Roehler was not so far gone, however, that he overlooked the tall brunette stewardess with the long legs who was serving drinks after takeoff. He later recalled that first meeting with Jeanne Schoonhoven in some detail.

"She had asked a tipsy tourist where he got the flower leis. She thought they were very pretty. The tipsy tourist gave her two, and she said, 'Thanks, I'll give them to my boyfriend.' And I thought, well, so much for her . . . she's occupied.

"Frenchy and I had both been drinking—he more than I. Jeanne was friendly and proceeded to get Frenchy to pass out—me, to become chatty. I went in the aft galley and BS'd for quite a while with she [*sic*] and her co-workers.

"I was waiting for a frozen bottle of champagne to thaw. Then a drunk passed out in the aisle and everyone said he'd had a heart attack. I said he was drunk, as I'd been in the same bar preparing for the flight in the same way. I asked if they wanted him out of the aisle; they said yes. I talked to him and helped him to the rear of the bus. They tried to give him oxygen, but it was turned off—then they wanted to give him coffee. I said, 'Do you want a wide-awake drunk for two more hours?'

"They put the coffee away and Jeanne locked up the frozen bottle, saying I'd had enough. I told her I was going to write her up and asked for her name and address. Later I wrote Jeanne to say hi and asked her to dinner."

Jeanne Schoonhoven and Fred Roehler had dinner for the first time together three weeks after they met, and they spent the following weekend at Fred's brother Ron's home some sixty miles from Los Angeles. Fred's dates were paraded down there just as regularly as they had once been trotted through the Roehlers' Centerville rec room.

Two weeks later, Fred invited Jeanne to visit him on his houseboat in the Oxnard harbor. He'd tired of trailer-park living and bought the thirty-six-foot boat for cash. It had all the right ingredients for a Roehler domicile. It was solitary, out of the mainstream, and cheap, and he liked the image it presented of a man unlike other men, not one of the herd—a man content with himself who didn't need to live surrounded by other people.

"Jeanne drove her '59 or '60 Ford up to my old boat," Fred remembered. "We had dinner and drove down to a beach hangout with some of the bachelor officers. I remember someone asking her how she liked flying and she said, 'Oh, it has its ups and downs.' I thought it was a pat line, but she was serious. We spent the night on the boat and made love for the first time. We did not discuss birth control, as we had two great Ernest and Julio Gallo Pink Chablis buzzes. . . . In the morning I went to the head and her padded bra was hanging on a towel rack. The dawn cometh."

When Carol Schoonhoven, a flight attendant with Pan American, visited her sister in Los Angeles soon after, Jeanne couldn't wait to tell her about Fred. "He's gorgeous, really neat, well educated, good job, and he lives in this cute little boat. So far there's only one problem. He's absolutely terrible in the sack, but I guess it'll get better—practice makes perfect, you know."

"Don't count on it, kid," Carol laughed. "Right now is as good as it gets."

A week or so after the night on the houseboat, Jeanne invited Fred to spend the weekend at the home of her friend Maureen Ross near Los Angeles Airport. Again, their lovemaking was a disaster.

"In foreplay, I ejaculated," Roehler recalled later, "much to Jeanne's surprise. I wasn't surprised and suggested that I get cleaned up and we start all over. Jeanne seemed preoccupied with the initial emission. I did not give it much thought at the time, but it seemed to give her a kind of guilt control over me."

"I don't know what the hell's wrong with the guy," Jeanne told Maureen. "He makes love like a fourteen-year-old."

Yet two weeks later, Jeanne told her astonished sister Carol that Fred Roehler was the man she felt she was going to marry. Fred obviously wasn't feeling the same way, for just two months after they met, he was ready for a change and jumped at the chance to go out with another woman. She was the daughter of a captain, a man of some influence at Mugu, and just the sort to impress the folks from Indiana who were coming to spend Thanksgiving with their son. Charlotte and Fritz dined with Fred, his new lady friend, and her father at the Officers' Club, and Charlotte was most impressed. Back in Centerville, she boasted about the delightful girl Fred was dating, the daughter of a "very prominent naval officer."

Just before Jeanne Schoonhoven left to spend the holidays on her family's ranch in Colorado, she received a letter from Fred saying he thought their relationship had become too serious; he was feeling pressured and wanted to end it. Besides, he added, he felt he was "maladjusted to society."

Carol Schoonhoven came down to breakfast the morning after Thanksgiving and found Jeanne bleary-eyed, her face stained with tears. "I'm not going to take this lying down," she said, "I'm going up there to have it out with him, once and for all."

Jeanne flew back to Los Angeles and drove straight to Oxnard. She and Fred went out to dinner and when they came back to the boat Jeanne began to cry. 'How could you do this to me," she sobbed, "especially now that I'm pregnant."

Charlotte Roehler had taught him well. This was one thing for which he was prepared. Fred proposed; Jeanne accepted. She had seriously considered having an abortion, but Fred wouldn't hear of it. He wasn't the least bit upset. On the contrary, he seemed elated.

"It was funny," Jeanne told her friend Maureen. "He thought my being pregnant was the neatest thing since cookies." It seemed to give him some sort of affirmation of his own masculinity. Whatever it was, she was just grateful that everything had worked out so well.

Five minutes after Jeanne accepted, they were on the phone to Indiana. Fred didn't tell his mother about the baby. In the letter he wrote following the phone call, he described a romantic proposal scene. "I suppose it's just the Christmas spirit or something, but I really felt all family-ish and good. So, I asked her—the big factor was that she said she would live with me on the boat. I may have it written into the marriage vows. I may tell you again I'm happy—very happy. I feel that Jeanne is the one and there will be no other, ever. I can already see a list of changes coming but that's just fine with me. Doing things with someone will be much, much nicer."

The wedding was set for the end of January, but first Jeanne took Fred to Evergreen, Colorado, to meet her mother and father. Jeanne's mother Marguerite was difficult to win over, but John Schoonhoven was immediately impressed. Fred was more than he could want in a son-in-law—a big man, a strong man, a good listener, and a charming talker. Fred Roehler was to become for John Schoonhoven the idealized son he'd never had. Whatever doubts Jeanne may have had were dispelled by her father's total approval.

Three weeks later, Jeanne nervously told her husband-to-be that her pregnancy had been a false alarm, but by then the date and place of the wedding had been set. The large, traditional, formal wedding was held on January 31, 1970, in Evergreen, Colorado. The snow lay even on the ground and the sun shone. Jeanne Schoonhoven was a picture-book bride in a Victorian gown of candlelight silk.

Charlotte Roehler, who wore apricot peach silk in the new shorter length, said of Jeanne, "I think that's the prettiest girl I've ever seen."

Fred and Jeanne Roehler's honeymoon night was a disaster. Before setting off for a week at the Schoonhovens's Maui condo, they spent the night in the old Brown Palace Hotel in Denver while Charlotte and Fritz Roehler checked into a motel nearby.

Jeanne had high hopes that once they were married their sexual difficulties would magically end. But that night, Fred climaxed prematurely yet again, and the tactless Jeanne burst into tears. "My sister was right!" she yelled. "This is never going to work."

Fred was furious that Jeanne had discussed his problem with her sister, and by the time the newlyweds stopped arguing, they were barely speaking. Two days later, on United Airlines notepaper, Fred wrote another of his long letters to his parents. It was an oddly detailed letter for a twenty-eight-year-old man to write on his honeymoon. Most honeymooners get by with a postcard, but Fred covered four pages, including a glowing testimonial, a kind of self-conscious reference to his parents' "wonderful" marriage. He signed it, "Your married bachelor."

The newlyweds returned to the Oxnard houseboat, a thirty-six-by-six-foot shoebox they called home. While it may have provided sufficient space for a casual bachelor, the cramped quarters aggravated their already fraught relationship. Jeanne was sociable and fun-loving with lots of close friends in the airlines, and she looked forward to showing off her handsome new husband. However, Fred quickly let her know he was not interested in that "brainless" crowd. He hated the airline gossip that Jeanne loved so much. She'd spend hours on the phone listening to her friends' troubles, consoling and advising them. It drove her husband up the wall.

Even though the pregnancy that had provoked Fred to propose had been a false alarm, Jeanne was pregnant again by the time they got married. She calculated the conception to be around Christmas 1969, when they had gone to Pennsylvania to Fred's cousin's wedding. She wanted to keep her job as long as she could and worried constantly about losing it. But that was settled when she blabbed about her condition to a fellow crew member who turned her in to the airline. United put her on suspension until six months after the baby was born.

With nothing to do all day, Jeanne was considerably frustrated. She and Fred argued constantly about the boat, which Jeanne felt was a lousy place to raise a child. They argued about money; Jeanne liked to spend, and Fred was extremely frugal. But underneath it all, most of their arguments were about sex. The constant tension was creating an atmosphere that made bickering inevitable.

Jeanne spent a boring and restless summer of 1970, attending Lamaze classes and practicing her natural childbirth exercises. Her complaints about the boat finally produced results, and they put a small deposit on a house, close to the beach in Oxnard. It was modest, but it was a home on dry land, and that was good enough for Jeanne. They bought the house, but by August Fred had found another houseboat, fifty feet, all electric, much more streamlined than their old clunker, and somehow he persuaded Jeanne that it would make fiscal sense to rent out the Oxnard house and live on the new boat.

They traded in the old one in part exchange, and in early August 1970, their friend Dick Velthoen drove them down to the Port of Long Beach to pick up the new vessel. Excited with their acquisition, they motored it back to Oxnard Harbor.

Soon after, the baby's arrival was upon them—a month early. The doctors worked hard to stop the labor, but finally, on August 24, 1970, with Fred at her side, Jeanne gave birth to a baby girl weighing four pounds, four ounces. She was frail and had breathing problems, but she was alive.

The prognosis for baby Heidi Roehler was still by no means certain, but not nearly as bad as her father apparently thought. The attending physician was astonished when Roehler approached him with a question that in all his years as an obstetrician, no father, no matter how perilous his baby's condition, had ever asked: "Do you think we could donate her body to UCLA or some other medical school to learn more about premature babies?"

"Mr. Roehler," responded the doctor, "we're nowhere near ready to consider something like that. Your daughter is going to be fine."

Heidi stayed in intensive care for another thirty days where her parents could visit her only through the nursery window, but the birth announcements were sent. "Having been slipped from her prime construction berth two months prematurely"—the "two months" was a sop to the tender sensitivities of the Schoonhovens and the Roehlers—"Heidi will be berthed at the Los Robles Hospital, Thousand Oaks, California, for additional ballasting prior to being officially piped aboard. Respectfully submitted, Fred and Jeanne Roehler." Even so, the Schoonhovens asked the couple to please not send birth announcements to their friends.

Jeanne liked the idea of moving to the Bay Area when Fred said he might be able to get into the University of California at Berkeley to pursue an engineering degree. She loved the area and could easily fly out of San Francisco for United.

Several friends from Los Angeles visited the Roehlers that summer. One afternoon, they had taken the houseboat out for a cruise around San Francisco Bay. Coming back into port, the water intake pipe became clogged and the engine overheated. "There's always a bunch of trash floating around in the Bay," Fred told his guests. "It must have been a bread wrapper or something that did it."

After two and a half years of marriage, Jeanne Roehler was not a happy woman. Matrimony had not given her the comfort and support she had hoped for, and Fred Roehler was not the man of her dreams. She was bored, depressed, and more important, still searching for a fulfilling relationship.

Then on one of her trips, she met someone who seemed to fill all her needs. She began an affair. Soon she was leading a double life with a man who, she confided to her friends, was everything Fred Roehler was not—sociable, fun-loving, playful, and attentive. The attraction was immediate. He was also married with a family, so the affair consisted mainly of brief sexual encounters in hotel rooms between long cooling-off periods. Her job enabled her to keep the liaison going, and although most of her friends knew she was playing around, Fred seemed unaware that Jeanne was straying.

That September, she searched for and found an apartment for the family near the University. "Heidi needs a more normal environment," she told Fred. It was also a good time to leave the Marina, which was trying to get rid of boat dwellers, and it seemed an opportune moment to move to dry land.

The move brought greater expenses, however. They were still paying off the mortgage on the boat. At $360 a month, with slip fees and sundry expenses on top of an apartment rental, the boat was a pain, and they were anxious to get rid of it. Selling it, however, was not easy. It was not in the best shape, and there was little demand for houseboats once the summer had passed.

One month after they had moved into the apartment, Fred suddenly switched his insurance on the boat to a new company, in the process upping his coverage to $35,000.

On December 22, three days before Christmas, the Roehlers's houseboat was destroyed by fire, burning right down to its bare steel hull.

It was not until January 2, 1973, that John Purmort of the Foremost Insurance Company in Walnut, California, came to see Roehler in his apartment in Berkeley, to take down his meticulous account of the fire. It was one of the most detailed accident reports Purmort had ever heard. Roehler handed him a full written account, spelling out every step of the catastrophe.

He'd planned, he said, to take some friends out on the boat for a picture-taking session to nearby Angel Island. He'd gone down to the marina early the evening before to warm up the engines and had left them idling for about ten minutes. Returning to the controls, he'd found that the starboard engine was overheating. This was caused, he discovered, by a plastic bag floating in the Bay that had been sucked into a valve designed to let in the cooling seawater.

"I got into the water and removed the bag," he explained. Then he said he took the boat over to the dock to fuel up for the next day's trip. It was by then a very pretty evening, so he decided to take the boat out in the Bay and take a few pictures himself. Motoring out toward the Golden Gate Bridge, however, he suddenly saw that the engine had once again started to overheat. He checked the seawater valve and again it was blocked, this time by a Wonder Bread wrapper. He made various attempts to cool everything down, he explained, but to no avail. In what seemed like an instant, the boat was on fire. He tried to control the blaze but quickly realized he couldn't, and dove over the side. He told the people on a passing sailboat who rescued him that he had been in the water for thirty-five minutes. When pulled out of the chilly water, he was wearing a full wetsuit. It was fortunate for him, he said, that he'd put it on earlier when he'd gone into the water to remove the bag from his intake. A few minutes more, he said, and wetsuit or not, he would have died of exposure. When picked up, he was carrying an expensive camera aloft, high above his head, out of reach of the waves.

Fred justified his $35,000 insurance claim by pointing out that his boat was of exceptional quality. It was a demo model and had never even been taken from the dock; the engines had clocked only two hours. He'd purchased the boat with a whole slew of accessories for $28,490, he said, and had added several expensive extras, including carpeting, drapes, and a fume detector system, which, he added, was not on board at the time of the accident.

He told the insurance investigator that he'd lived aboard the boat in Southern California and that he and his wife had the Wilmington Boat Movers of Wilmington, California, transport it to Berkeley. He also said they'd lived on the boat for only one month prior to moving into an apartment.

The insurance company balked at paying the full $35,000. They had no suspicions about the fire, which they said was logical, according to Roehler's account. However, they doubted the condition and worth of the boat, and offered a $28,000 settlement.

Fred sent a letter to his insurance carrier complaining of bad faith and threatening to sue if his claim was not paid in full. He also sent copies to the California Department of Insurance; to his district congressman, Barry Goldwater Jr.; to the man who had sold him the insurance policy; and even to the owner of the sailboat that had fished him out of the bay. On January 31, he filed a formal complaint with the Department of Insurance, but not before checking with Bill Fairfield, his lawyer, to see whether or not he should settle for the $28,000. In February, the Foremost Insurance Company paid Roehler $35,000, the highest claim of its type the company had ever paid.

Jack Burkhardt was surprised to receive in the mail a full report of Roehler's boat burning. He wondered what he was supposed to do with it, but noting his colleague's penchant for fires, when he next saw him, he kidded, "Is Jeanne wearing asbestos PJs yet?"

"Not yet, but she's thinking about it," Fred cracked back.

For Fred Roehler, it had been a profitable year. With his master's degree safely under his belt, he used the insurance proceeds on the boat to make an $18,000 down payment on a $68,000 house in one of the most prestigious residential areas in America. Roehler had arrived in Malibu.

The rustic house on Calpine Drive was a long way from the beach mansions. In a pleasant, country hillside area about a mile and a half back from the ocean, it had open-beamed ceilings and a backyard swimming pool, its privacy protected by tall, fragrant eucalyptus and pine trees on either side of the lot. The neighborhood was more down-home than manicured. Kids washed their horses in the middle of the street and some of the neighbors kept chickens and goats.

Jeanne celebrated the first real home they'd had by getting pregnant a month after they moved in. Kirsten Roehler was born in July 1974. It had been another difficult pregnancy, with Jeanne going into labor three times before actually delivering the baby, but Kirsten was a healthy, easygoing child, with none of Heidi's asthmatic problems. A friend of Jeanne's, who knew about her ongoing affair, told her own husband, "I hope to God the baby looks like Fred."

Some of her friends were beginning to be concerned about Jeanne's "other man."

"She told me Fred must never know," a friend later recalled, "but it was obvious to us it was becoming anything but casual. She would spend hours getting ready to meet him. She'd buy new outfits, get her legs waxed, make herself gorgeous. She was in love and, in her mind, there was no doubt about that."

After Berkeley, Fred Roehler was the only naval architect on the engineering team. He had brains, looks, and personality, and he quickly established himself as a star. He wasn't afraid to get his hands dirty, and his can-do attitude was infectious. It seemed there was no technical problem he couldn't solve if he put his mind to it, and the Navy provided him with the equipment he needed. Jack Burkhardt was impressed by Fred's skill in writing up requests for state-of-the-art expensive equipment for the department's projects; because of his meticulous documentation and paperwork, he almost always got it. He was rapidly becoming Mugu's blue-eyed boy, piling up patent awards for ideas he'd developed, and promotions were coming thick and fast.

8

A Diver's Death in the Channel Islands

On January 7, 1973, Fred Roehler led a crew of six Navy divers on a mission to San Nicholas Island, some eighteen miles south of Santa Cruz Island. They were going out to secure a weather buoy. Fred had invented a new device to help secure it underwater, and he was anxious to show it off.

Two previous attempts to do the job had failed because of bad weather. This time they had set out at 2:00 a.m., and it had taken them five and a half hours just to reach the buoy. At 12:32 p.m., after two failed attempts, Roehler ordered a third team of four divers to go down: Harry Kulu, a large, genial native of Hawaii; Don Weldon; Wayne Sullivan; and Robert Owen, a twenty-nine-year-old Navy photographer. It was Owen's first dive of the day, but the team had already made more dives than expected and there were not enough air bottles left to go around. Fred handed his bottle and regulator to Owen, telling him he had plenty of air left in his tank. Owen put them on and slipped under the waves to join his three colleagues.

Barely fifteen minutes later, Sullivan saw that Owen was in trouble, frantically switching his reserve valve up and down. He swam over to help, and Owen gave him the "out of air" signal. All three of his colleagues tried to assist him, but Owen, apparently panicked, dropped his mouthpiece and began to sink. For the next few minutes in the murky waters, seventy-five feet deep in the Pacific, a life-and-death struggle ensued.

Kulu watched in horror as Owen spiraled past him toward the ocean floor. He dived after him, caught up, and grabbed the cord on his life jacket, but was unable to inflate it. Finally, he gave up, inflated his own jacket, and, fast losing consciousness himself, rose to the surface.

Owen had vanished.

A Navy helicopter was summoned, but the body was never recovered.

All the participants were called to a naval inquiry, but Fred was the only one who could have seen the amount of air left in the bottle he'd passed to Owen. He insisted that there were 1,600 pounds of pressure left, according to the gauge—more than enough for a thirty-minute dive. Why, then, did Owen run out of air in just fifteen minutes? Why hadn't Owen tried to surface? Why didn't his jacket inflate? And where was his body?

Roehler suggested that perhaps Owen had somehow become entangled and was trapped, unable to free himself. Perhaps he'd been panicking all along and was breathing too fast, using up too much air.

Roehler later came up with a whole series of explanations for Owen's death: He'd had an automobile accident eight years earlier that left him with a fractured skull. He'd had a steel plate put in his head following the car crash, and often complained of dizzy spells. He shouldn't have been diving in the first place.

Owen's medical report, while acknowledging the accident and two episodes of light-headedness eight years before, made no mention of a steel plate and cleared him for underwater duty.

Roehler's explanations continued: Owen, he noted, had not kept up with his practice hours underwater; he was having marital problems; he may even have been drinking the night before. Later, he blamed Kulu for not dumping his or Owen's diving weights. "Even if it was just a lump you wanted to get to the surface, the first thing you do is get rid of the weights," Roehler declared.

What had probably happened, Roehler theorized, was that Owen had turned off his own air in confusion. Since the tank was never recovered, no one could disprove the theory.

The Navy reprimanded Owen's immediate superior officer who had not even been with them that day, and a letter of caution was placed in

Roehler's file that would be removed after a year, provided there were no further contraventions of regulations.

Roehler remained nervous about the incident, and called his personal lawyer, Bill Fairfield, just in case there was further trouble.

For months afterward, black humor circulated at Point Mugu. "Don't go out with Roehler," they quipped, "that guy's a killer." It was more in the order of taking Superman down a few pegs, however, than from any serious questions about Owen's death.

The diving death certainly did not appear to hurt Roehler's professional reputation. He had a new supervisor, Ed Mutz, who began calling him his High Roller, and wrote him up for a commendation. The word was out: When a task was difficult or impossible, send for Roehler.

His fellow engineers didn't share management's rosy opinion, however. They found him arrogant, incapable of listening to anyone else's point of view, and self-centered to the point where other people existed only to make his life easier.

"He felt so far above us," one of them recalled, "that he didn't even bother to hide it. He despised other people. They were simply pawns and tools to him."

Said another, "If anything went wrong it was always somebody else's fault. Fred never, ever made a mistake."

There was never any doubt that being under government regulations was not Roehler's idea of the best way to live, but he could handle it, he said. "The only way to get things done in the civil service," he once explained to a colleague, "is to bend the rules and to never give up. Just put up with all their shit, get through it a bit at a time, persevere—perseverance is the key—and, in the end, you'll get the brass ring."

Fred was having much less success on the personal front. There were moments when the Roehlers's relationship exploded into open hostility.

On one occasion, Jeanne and Fred invited Bill and Donna Fairfield and Dick and Linda Velthoen over for dinner. As on other evenings, the meal was followed by a session in the hot tub, a casual affair with the lights turned off, everyone mellow and in the nude, with lots of wine. It might not have played too well in the Midwest, but this was Malibu in the 1970s, and social mores were relaxed.

The party was getting raucous, leaping between the hot tub and the pool. At one point, Jeanne dove down into the depths of the hot tub and stayed for a few moments under the surface. Her husband suddenly erupted. Reaching down under the water, he dragged his wife out by her long hair. Jeanne thought it was vicious and cruel, and she told all of her friends about it. That hot tub story became an oft-told tale to friends in the Roehler circles.

In May 1975, Jeanne finally faced the fact that she was unhappy and went to see a psychologist. She told the therapist that her marriage had not worked from the beginning. She described her husband's sexual problems, and she wondered aloud why she had ever married him. Divorce was almost out of the question. She'd been brought up to think of it as an absolute taboo, and the idea of being a single parent terrified her. She confided about her affair, though she said her lover had recently called it off. He couldn't handle the guilt. She told the therapist that Fred had never known about the affair and would end their marriage if he ever found out. Still, he would not seek professional help himself. "He feels we should be able to solve it on our own," she said. "He's very, very rigid and he can't accept failure."

Would it make any difference, the therapist asked her, if her husband could get help for his sexual problems? "Doc," she said, "he could keep it up for a week now and it wouldn't matter a fart." As the weeks of counseling went on, she was becoming more and more convinced that she simply wanted out of the relationship.

Linda Schoonhoven, Jeanne's youngest sister, visited the family in Malibu that summer and was horrified at the state of her sister's marriage.

"When my parents came to see them, everything was lovely, but I was considered just a kid, so nobody ever bothered putting on an act for me. I couldn't believe Fred. He was just not of this world. He acted so superior to us all and so demeaning to Jeanne. He treated her as though she was a true moron. It was a 'pity the poor idiot' kind of thing. He played these endless mind games with her. It was real mental abuse. Somehow Jeanne tolerated it, but I guess she was trained to tolerate."

Carol Schoonhoven also visited the Roehlers around the same time. She had never had a particularly warm relationship with her brother-in-law, but this time he acted as though she were invisible. "He came into the house and although he hadn't seen me for months, he didn't even acknowledge my presence. He made not the slightest attempt at normal social intercourse. He was much worse than I'd ever seen him. It was as if he'd gone into himself completely—other people simply didn't exist."

By late 1975, Jeanne Roehler told her therapist she was ready to end her marriage.

Soon after, Fred Roehler came with her to a counseling session for the first time. He handed the psychologist a carefully written account of their marriage and a separate detailed account of their respective backgrounds. Roehler said that the psychologist needed to understand just who he was talking to. "We argued over money," Roehler had written. "She owed around $2,000 [Jeanne had changed the $2,000 to $400] . . . had a lot of clothes, a color TV, and a 1965 Ford. I had a 1968 VW, a boat, and $15,000 in savings."

At work, Roehler was propagating much the same attitude. Several colleagues in his department were getting divorced or were contemplating it. One of them remembered a conversation with Roehler on the subject. "He said he would never, ever consider a legal divorce. It simply cost you money and made attorneys rich. If things went badly in his marriage, he said, he would simply leave the house, Jeanne, and the kids, just take off to the Orient somewhere and disappear."

The marriage would continue to unravel over the next several months. At one point, Jeanne frantically called Fred's boss at Point Mugu and said that she was very worried. Fred had been on assignment in Hawaii for two weeks, and she hadn't heard a single word from him. When Roehler's boss ordered him to contact his wife, Roehler threw a tantrum.

"That damned woman wants to hear from me," he snapped, "all right, she will." He bundled up a roll of Navy communications/dispatches written in telegraphese and military jargon, without punctuation and totally incomprehensible to an outsider, shoved it into a large envelope, and mailed it to his wife without any other note.

They were both playing mind games. The angry Jeanne told her friend Maureen Ross that it was a relief to have her husband out of town: "At least I don't have to sleep with him."

Thus, their shaky marriage swung perilously between highs and lows. Fred conceded in his notes to the marriage counselor that they would settle into a routine only to find that things would soon start to come apart again. He gave the psychologist a treatise on their respective backgrounds, describing Jeanne's parents as religious fundamentalists, "very tight with money and very big on Christ."

During Jeanne's last visit to her therapist in the summer of 1976, she played a game of word association.

"Fred," said the therapist.

"Get him out," Jeanne responded.

"Divorce?"

"How to tell the family?"

"Divorce," the doctor repeated.

"How to start the lawn mower and fix the car."

For Jeanne, unhappy, confused, trying desperately to summon the courage to end her marriage, the counseling was of little help. After weeks of group sessions, she felt increasingly frustrated and even more convinced that she could never be happy if she was married to Fred, and she began to look for another answer.

Bill Fairfield was not at all surprised when Jeanne called him in the summer of 1976.

"I'm filing for divorce," she told him. "Can you recommend a good lawyer in Los Angeles?" Fairfield had known about the state of the marriage for some time, and told her, "I can't do that, Jeanne. I'm much too close to both of you. I don't want to even do a recommendation. If you really want to do this, you'll have to find one yourself."

During this period, Fred returned to Hawaii for almost three months, once again giving his wife the cold shoulder. While he was away, Jeanne took the opportunity to try something she'd been thinking about for a while. Her sister Carol had become an enthusiastic advocate of a movement called Lifespring. She had gone through its training, and her husband had, in fact, given up his job to work for the movement full-time. Lifespring was just the latest in a long stream of human potential movements from the early days of Esalen in Big Sur through Primal Therapy, Gestalt Therapy, Actuality Therapy, EST, and other related self-help movements that seemed to begin on the West Coast and spread rapidly throughout the country.

Carol Schoonhoven had told Jeanne how the movement—their motto, "A more fruitful individual . . . in a more harmonious world"—had opened possibilities in her life and helped her deal with some of the baggage she was carrying from childhood. "It's like she's found a new religion," Jeanne told Fred.

To Jeanne, a girl who had been raised in the old-time religion, this was like being born again.

In her application, she described herself as "attractive, five-foot-seven-and-a-half inches, down to 109 pounds" from her normal 120 pounds, adding, "Ali MacGraw appearance." The form also asked her what made her unhappy or tense. Her husband was first on her list, followed by the wife of her lover and then her children. When asked how things would be different if the course was successful, she wrote, "I will eventually be married to [her lover], have his present children, and will totally be happy. Of course, I plan on him attending Lifespring."

She wrote a letter to her therapist, terminating her counseling. "You should shut up shop," she told him, "and send everyone to Lifespring."

9

A Drowning . . . in the Backyard Pool

While Jeanne was undergoing the biggest psychological overhaul of her life, Fred was on Midway Island in the Pacific manning an underwater trenching machine, cutting deep channels in the ocean floor to house sophisticated communications cables. He had worked on a similar project in Kauai which had failed, and this mission too was doomed through a combination of bad weather and equipment failure. Fred's high hopes for another professional triumph were dashed. The project had fallen around his ears. His halo was tarnished, and he had been cut down to size.

His personal life was in equal disarray, yet there is no mention of that in a letter he wrote to his parents from Midway:

> It's tough being away from my California girls and I am so looking forward to getting back. This trip has been the hardest on Jeanne as she must run the entire house and work without my help. She does a good job of keeping the old homestead and the kids in good shape. I am usually happy to get her letters. She even sends me the *Los Angeles Times* comics, yet I feel distant and sad that I cannot be near them.

He was, however, in no doubt that Jeanne wanted a divorce. Along with his fears of the complete disruption of his lifestyle, the splitting of his assets, and the dreaded prospect of alimony and child support, he was certain that divorce was the one thing his parents would never accept.

On the first weekend in October 1976, Fred's Midway assignment ended abruptly. He had been away for almost three months. He had told his parents he couldn't wait to get home. Instead, he decided to take a week off and go sailing to the big island of Hawaii with his old friends, the Fairfields, who had been sailing in the islands close to Kauai that late summer. But just as they were preparing the boat to leave, Fred begged off.

"Sorry, folks," he told them. "Go without me. Jeanne's just called from Malibu. She wants me home for her birthday on October 5, and Heidi must go into the hospital to get her tonsils out. She's gonna need some help."

On October 5, Jeanne and her friend Rita Killeen, another flight attendant from United, arranged to meet at LAX so the two of them could have dinner together to celebrate Jeanne's birthday and catch up with each other's news. When the passengers boarded Rita's flight out of Honolulu, she was surprised to see Fred Roehler among them.

"What are you doing here?" she asked. "You're not supposed to be home. Jeanne and I have a dinner date tonight."

Meeting Rita's flight at Los Angeles Airport, Jeanne too was surprised to see her husband, whom she had obviously not been expecting.

"Sorry to spoil your evening, ladies," Fred blithely apologized, and headed home to Malibu with his wife.

On October 15, Jeanne had to go back to work. She woke before 4:00 a.m. and left for the airport at 5:30 to make United's turnaround flight to Chicago. After a two-hour layover in Chicago, the flight was back in Los Angeles by 6:00 p.m. the same night.

Heidi was in hospital. She had had a tonsillectomy that morning, and her father had been with her at Los Robles Hospital in Thousand Oaks, some thirty miles from Malibu. Fred reported that after leaving his older daughter, he picked up two-year-old Kirsten from Jeanne's friend Paddy Leitelt, who was babysitting her, and arrived home about thirty minutes before Jeanne pulled into their driveway at 8:00 p.m.

At around 9:00 p.m., Jeanne took a phone call from her friend and fellow stewardess Jeanne Sias. They chatted for nearly an hour. Jeanne had left the living room halfway through the conversation and picked up the call again on an extension in the bedroom. Fred said he then went out to the hot tub and waited for his wife to join him.

The night of October 15 was balmy and windless. Rudy Veland, an architect who lived next door to Fred and Jeanne Roehler, had just settled into a deep sleep when he was jerked into consciousness by an unexpected sound. He reckoned later it was between 10:30 and 10:45 p.m.

"Did you hear that?" he asked his wife, Barbara, as he forced himself awake, jumped out of bed, and stumbled to the deck outside his second-floor bedroom.

"Rudy, Rudy—help!" someone was calling. The cry was coming from next door. He switched on his outside lights but could see nothing through the trees.

"Fred?" he called into the darkness.

"Rudy, is that you?" a frantic-sounding Roehler shouted back. "Jeanne's hurt . . . get Dr. Morgenstern, fast."

Veland woke his son Eric and sent him racing to the home of Dr. Leon Morgenstern, a director of surgery at Cedars-Sinai Hospital in Los Angeles, who lived just across the street. Then Veland dressed, called the paramedics from the Malibu Fire Department, and hurried next door.

As his eyes strained to focus through the unrelieved blackness he could see Fred Roehler, naked, crouched by the swimming pool, administering mouth-to-mouth resuscitation to Jeanne who was also naked, soaking wet, and apparently lifeless.

Dr. Morgenstern arrived virtually at the same time. He moved the slender body of Jeanne Roehler backward and forward, turning her on her side, squeezing her furiously to force out as much water as possible. Then he began administering external cardiac massage while her husband continued mouth-to-mouth.

By the time the paramedics arrived, Morgenstern had gotten a very faint pulse started. Jeanne was quickly put into an ambulance and with Fred at her side, she was rushed to Westlake Hospital, thirty minutes away over a winding canyon road.

On arrival at the hospital, at 11:45 p.m., she was in complete cardiac arrest, her eyes fixed and dilated, her brain waves completely flat. A very faint, almost imperceptible pulse showed up on the ECG machine, however, so the physician on duty, Dr. Gunnar Larson, administered half a cc of adrenaline and one ampule of sodium bicarbonate to stimulate the heart. Automatically, the doctor checked Jeanne's breath and around her mouth for the aroma of alcohol and detected none. He put the patient on an artificial respirator and ordered more adrenaline and sodium bicarbonate, then vigorously tried resuscitation. Twenty-five minutes later Jeanne's heart began to beat spontaneously. Larson ordered a battery of blood tests and X-rays.

At 3:00 a.m. she was moved from the emergency room to the intensive care unit, where a nurse recorded her body temperature at 87.8 degrees.

That afternoon, the doctors examined the tests. The X-rays showed no injuries of any kind on her body. Her blood alcohol registered 0.10 millimeters—by this machine's calibration that represented a tenth of one milligram of alcohol per decimeter of blood, virtually none whatsoever—and so it was recorded. There was only enough alcohol in Jeanne Roehler's bloodstream on the night she drowned for her to have taken, at most, a couple of sips of wine.

When Carol Schoonhoven called Malibu the next morning, a neighbor who was looking after Kirsten told her what had happened. She flew immediately to California.

Her mother and sister Linda were waiting when she arrived at the hospital, both in their private hells, not even talking to one another. John Schoonhoven was en route from Iceland where United Airlines had tracked him down.

Carol slipped into the ICU. Jeanne was lying there, drained of color, her long dark hair hidden under a green surgical cap, her eyes covered by moist gauze, her thin body tied by a tangle of plastic arteries to a technological imitation of life.

She couldn't get Jeanne's letter out of her mind. It had been so bursting with life and hope . . . and now this.

Fred Roehler seemed in another world. He was apparently in deep shock, talking to no one. For the first twelve hours, he didn't seem able even to respond to Jeanne's doctor's questions. He seemed drugged, confused, his brother Ron calling him "a basket case." He lay rigid on a hospital bed near the ICU, staring at the ceiling for hours on end, eyes wide open, an expression of anguish on his face.

Ron Roehler summoned Charlotte and Fritz from Indiana. The attending neurologist, Dr. Seymour Herschfield, had given them little hope for Jeanne, but explained that he was mystified as to the cause of the drowning.

When a friend of Fred's from Point Mugu arrived the next morning to see him, Dr. Herschfield took him aside. "Were those two getting along all right?" he asked. "Do you know? Because this just doesn't make too much sense to me. There doesn't seem to be any reason for this to have happened."

The next day, Marguerite and John Schoonhoven were told that there was absolutely no sign of brain waves from Jeanne. They could keep her body maintained on machines indefinitely, but she would never regain consciousness. In the days to come, the Schoonhovens prayed for a miracle, and they had Baptists all over the country praying with them. Marguerite spent hours sitting by Jeanne's side, soothing her brow, holding her hand, quietly talking to her daughter.

The Roehlers were less inclined to resort to faith. Arriving from Centerville, Fritz declared that the whole thing was a futile exercise, doing no one any good except possibly the hospital's bank account.

But the Schoonhovens resolutely refused to allow the plug to be pulled on their daughter. God would decide when the time was right.

Fred had apparently recovered sufficiently to take in the news that there was no hope for his wife, even if she survived. She would remain a vegetable, they told him.

Her friends refused to give up. Verna Johnson was calling Fred regularly. "Please, please talk to Jeanne," she pleaded. "Even though she may appear to have no brain left. Talk to her. Tell her Paddy and I care about her and we're taking care of the kids."

Linda Schoonhoven called Jeanne's friend Maureen Ross to tell her the shocking news. For a moment, there was dead silence on the other end of the line. Then Maureen asked quietly, "Did Fred do it?"

Hospitals carefully train staff members in the delicate business of approaching the bereaved families of accident victims seeking donations of their loved one's organs so that someone else may have a chance at life through their tragedy.

The Westlake Hospital staff did not have to undertake this distasteful job in the case of Jeanne. Her husband approached them. On October 18, three days after she'd been fished out of the pool, he asked them to contact Stanford University. He wished to donate Jeanne's heart to their transplant program.

"She's young and in good shape and her heart is functioning well on its own," he told the doctors. "She and I both have those 'take any parts' stickers on our driver's licenses. She put hers on only a couple of weeks ago, but Jeanne would have wanted this."

He signed the papers to donate her liver, kidneys, heart, and eyes. Stanford Medical Center, however, had run out of the immune suppressant for organ transplants and could not accept the gift of Jeanne's heart, so her husband had to be content with donating her corneas to an eye bank.

But that would have to wait. The Schoonhovens still would not accept the fact that their daughter was dead. For five days, the two families waited, sleeping in nearby motels, the Roehlers watching over their firstborn as intently as the Schoonhovens labored to see any spark of life in theirs.

One afternoon, John and his daughter were leaving the hospital after visiting Jeanne when they bumped into Charlotte. "Doesn't Jeanne look lovely lying there?" John asked, trying to glean some meager comfort from a ghastly situation.

Charlotte stiffened. "Lovely? Listen, my Freddie can't take much more of this. How long is this going to go on? You've got to let him get on with his life."

At 9:00 a.m. on October 21, the attending physician at Westlake Hospital turned off the life support systems sustaining Jeanne Roehler's vital functions, waited for four minutes, turned them on again, and then declared her dead of pneumonia induced by drowning.

Because his lawyer pal Bill Fairfield was out of town, Bill's partner, Ron Harrington, arrived at the hospital and met with Fred.

"The reason to consult me," Ron recalled, "was to help Fred give the direction as next of kin to turn off the life support machinery. The doctor gave us the position and then left Fred and me together to consider what he'd told us. Within, I would say, thirty seconds, Fred said, 'Obviously there's no hope. We should turn it off.'

"Then he had me go over with him to the motel where Jeanne's parents were staying to explain to them that the decision had been made and to get their concurrence. I told them as next of kin the decision legally was Fred's, but that he would prefer it to be a decision of the entire family. They said they would do whatever Fred and the doctor thought was right."

An autopsy after almost a week on life support is difficult at the best of times, but the state of Jeanne's organs was completely consistent with a drowning death. There was no sign of injury to the brain or a cardiovascular episode. There was no doubt that she had neither suffered a heart attack nor a stroke. There were no external injuries to the head to indicate a fall, and no other external injuries. Virtually the only marks on her body were two symmetrical bruises on the front of her hips at the point where her husband had pulled her from the pool. There was nothing to indicate foul play.

Her death, the coroner stated, was entirely consistent with drowning, and the body's status was consistent with undergoing resuscitation and five days of hospital care in a coma.

A routine Los Angeles County Sheriff's Department investigation concurred. Police examined the autopsy report and the admissions tests and noted the 0.10 alcohol level. On the police intoxication scale, calibrated completely differently from the hospital scale, 0.10 indicates a blood alcohol level of 10, the level at which a driver is considered too intoxicated to drive. By misunderstanding the difference between the two scales, the police found it easy to conclude that Jeanne Roehler had probably fallen into her backyard pool while drunk.

But Fred had another explanation when he returned to work in November. He told his colleagues at Point Mugu that "a full coroner's inquest" had been held. Jeanne had suffered an aneurysm and died of a stroke. That was also the story Fritz Roehler relayed to the folks back in Centerville.

Soon after his wife's death, Roehler received a letter from the marriage counselor that he and Jeanne had been seeing. He wanted to know if Fred had considered the possibility that Jeanne could have committed suicide. She had told him about the "death exercise" at Lifespring and how she'd seen herself dying in the water. Her kind of personality was extremely suggestible, the doctor wrote, and it was just possible that in an exhausted state, she went for a late-night swim, flashed back to the Lifespring exercise, and just let herself sink under the water. If Fred wanted to explore the idea further, he said, he should get in touch.

He never heard from Fred Roehler.

The funeral Fred arranged for his wife was something no one who attended would ever forget. He would rent a boat, invite all their friends, and scatter Jeanne's ashes in the Pacific just outside Ventura Harbor.

The Schoonhovens cringed and outright refused to go at first. It would be a freak show, they said, a circus. They just couldn't take it. Their daughter Carol eventually persuaded them to attend for the sake of the family.

It was an elaborate ceremony—"A real Metro-Goldwyn-Mayer production," Carol later said bitterly. And certainly, no one at the funeral had ever seen anything quite like it. Fifty people boarded the chartered launch, and as the boat chugged out of the harbor, a short way into the open sea, Jeanne's favorite wine, Wente Brothers Grey Riesling, was poured. As the guests drank to her memory, the lyrics of the Rod McKuen song, "Jean, Jean, You're Young and Alive," came over the boat's PA system, filling the air.

Fred, walking slowly to the bow of the boat, emptied the contents of the small urn into the waves. Then each guest threw their wineglasses into the water followed by the long-stemmed red roses Fred had provided. Then he read a poem he'd composed about Jeanne, and his uncle, Charlotte's brother Carl Taylor, who'd played his trumpet at their

Colorado wedding seven years before, played "Taps" as Fred hung on the rail, sobbing.

There wasn't a dry eye on board except for Fritz Roehler, who, as he walked by John Schoonhoven and Fred, weeping on each other's shoulders, caustically observed, "Men don't cry."

Some of those present agreed that it was dramatic and wonderful and something Jeanne would have loved, while others recall that day with revulsion.

> "It was just too much," Carol Schoonhoven said. "My parents were dying through it. It was our mistake, Linda's, and mine. We should never have been there." Ever after, the Schoonhoven sisters referred to the funeral contemptuously as "The Harbor Cruise."

Jeanne's good Malibu friends and confidantes Verna Johnson and Paddy Leitelt were among the guests on board. They were both drained emotionally, comforting each other, in floods of tears, almost hysterical. After the ceremony, they adjourned to a nearby Mexican restaurant where, over a pitcher of margaritas, they proceeded to get drunk enough to ask each other the unthinkable. "Do you think he killed her?" Verna began. "How did he do it? Did he hold her down under the water? Did he hit her on the head? How did he get away with it?"

Two weeks after Jeanne's funeral, Fred returned to work at Point Mugu. He was a changed man. Gone was the hard-driving Mr. Fix-It. He was silent and gloomy, talking to no one, spending most of his time in his small office staring into space or talking on the telephone. His fellow engineers kept their distance. The only comment Roehler made in the weeks following was that Jeanne's life support machines had cost him "an arm and a leg."

As the weeks went on, Roehler showed little sign of snapping out of his grief and getting back to work. He would come and go pretty much at will, spending hours at his desk on the telephone dealing with personal business or doing the paperwork on Jeanne's insurance policies. The walls were paper-thin at Mugu, and his colleagues heard him tying up the loose ends to collect on the mortgage insurance on their house, some $49,000, which paid out on the death of either spouse, as well as a policy of $24,000 from United Airlines. He now owned their Calpine Drive house and their Oxnard rental property, free and clear.

At home in Malibu, Fred Roehler drove his adorable little girls to school every morning, producing pangs of sympathy among the women in the beach community. There was something so appealing about this big, sad-eyed guy with young girls to whom he was trying to be both mother and father. He was showered with invitations for dinner, brunches, and breakfasts, implored to, "bring the kids over to play" or to "leave the girls with me if you need some time to yourself." In the aftermath of his loss, he became something of a tragic hero.

At work, however, it wasn't long before the sympathy gave way to irritation, then resentment, then anger. Although he was the senior man earning more than the others, he was doing absolutely nothing.

While he sat on the phone tending to his investments, researching the price of land in the Santa Monica Mountains for a Christmas tree farm, or negotiating shares in a hotel/condo project in Costa Rica, they were carrying his workload.

"He'd sit there munching package after package of sunflower seeds, rubbing our noses in the fact that he wasn't doing a goddamn bit of work, and there wasn't a thing we could do about it," complained a colleague. What made matters worse was that their boss, Everett Bruer, seemed absolutely paralyzed, incapable of getting his underling to put in even a semblance of a day's work.

"Fred will come 'round," he said. "I'll talk to him . . . he's been through a lot."

The others burned: "He had a smirk on his face like he knows we know what's going on, but we can't do a thing about it."

Finally, Ed Mutz called Roehler into his office. At one time, Mutz had been one of Fred's greatest boosters, but now he was alarmed and puzzled at his eccentric behavior.

"It was just odd," Mutz recalled. "I told him I'd spoken to Personnel, and they said the government would pay for him to see a psychiatrist. Roehler listened impassively as if I'd suggested he take an extra hour for lunch. 'Fine,' he said. 'If you think I need help, I'll go.'"

But a couple of days later, Mutz called him, "Sorry, I goofed. We don't pay for that kind of treatment. You'll have to put it on your Blue Shield."

"Then forget it," said Roehler. "If the government won't pay, I'm not going."

Mutz issued a quiet edict to the department: Fred Roehler was showing all the signs of emotional disturbance following his wife's death, and he recommended that Roehler not be assigned any diving duties until fully recovered.

On April 1, 1977, the personnel department at Point Mugu received a letter from a Los Angeles doctor named Paul Remis. Roehler had apparently decided to consult a psychiatrist after all. Dr. Remis wrote that he had had four sessions with Roehler:

> In addition to job pressures, Mr. Roehler has revealed some personal difficulties which have occurred subsequent to the untimely and tragic death of his wife. It is my opinion that he should request a medical leave of absence in order to gain some time and sort out the major issues in his life. I have asked that he be absent from work for approximately three weeks to begin approximately on March 31st.

Roehler's emotional problems did not interfere with his romantic activities, however. By the time he had begun to see the psychiatrist, he was already involved with not one but two women.

His relationship with Verna Johnson had begun almost immediately after Jeanne's death. Two weeks after her funeral, John Leitelt had seen him coming out of the back door of Verna's apartment around 5:30 in the morning, as Leitelt was leaving for work. Soon after, Verna confided to Paddy that she was sleeping with Fred.

At first, it had simply been a matter of him dropping the kids off to her in the morning and picking them up in the evening, stopping for a glass of wine, and occasionally being invited to dinner. When they started sharing the same bed, they were discreet and careful. By November, they were openly dating without the children. They were both somewhat reluctant, they told friends. The kids had figured out how convenient it was for both families to again have a mother and a father, but the whole thing might be a bit *too* convenient. Verna kept telling Fred to date other people, and she told him she was going to continue seeing her old friends.

She was very concerned that the relationship be discreet; after all, Jeanne Roehler had been dead for only a few weeks. To Malibu, she was Fred Roehler's babysitter and nothing more. Only Paddy Leitelt knew differently.

Roehler's life began to settle into a comfortable routine. All of Malibu saw him caring for his kids, taking many hours off work to fill the void left by their mother. Soon, even those who had voiced suspicions about Jeanne's death were telling themselves they were being ridiculous.

Even Jeanne's friend Candy Hinman, who had had strong suspicions about Jeanne's death, caved. She invited Fred to dinner at her house to introduce him to a friend, Gloria Hunnicut, a sophisticated, stunning divorcee who was a fashion sales executive in Los Angeles.

The evening went well, as Fred recalled. "We had a lot of wine, a very nice dinner, warm fuzzies (coffee, Kahlua, chocolate), and then put the kids down to sleep. The music went on and the grass came out—the party got funnier fast. Candy went off to bed and Gloria and I played grab-bodies, and kissie faces. One thing led to another and to sex on the living room floor.

"I asked her if I could have her phone number. We dated in between my dates with Verna . . ."

The relationship with Gloria was hot and heavy for three months, but by late March of 1978, it was over. "I was getting pressure from her to see her more often," Roehler complained later. "It was not working too well. I made some rather creative reasons for not seeing her. One day I drove by her house, and before I could stop and get out, she came out and gave me back a book on Hawaii that I had loaned her.

"She said she was seeing someone else and wanted to part friends. I said okay. I never saw her after that time."

Gloria, too, remembered the day she said good-bye. "I didn't want him to come into my house. I wanted to end it amicably. I didn't want him mad at me."

By this time, Gloria was as wary around Fred as she would have been around nitroglycerin. The relationship that had begun so warmly in her friend's living room had quickly gone downhill. It had not taken her long to feel that something was wrong.

"He kept talking about the babysitter. He had to be home for the babysitter. Finally, I asked him if anything was going on between him and the babysitter, and he said, 'Oh no, no.' She was a friend of Jeanne's, and he would have dinner over there sometimes with his children. It was good for the kids, he said, and she was very kind to them."

"He told me she had two kids, a little girl who was very nice and a son who got on his nerves and was a 'real brat.'

"I kept asking myself why I just didn't kiss this guy off, but I would look at him and think, 'You should be so perfect, there's got to be something I can make of you.' I mean, he was good-looking and diligent with an interesting job and a nice life, so I hung on. I tried, but it was just useless."

10

The Widow Verna

SECURITY AND RESPECTABILITY WERE THE TWO MOST IMPORTANT things in Verna Jo Zeitner's life. She'd never had the first, but she'd hung on to the latter with a mixture of naiveté and obstinacy that together forged an iron will in a deceptively fragile-looking package.

As a child, home was a two-bedroom wooden house in a tiny court of identical bungalows in Eagle Rock, a working-class bedroom community just a few miles from downtown Los Angeles. The houses were small, and Verna's was often shared with an ever-changing cast of down-on-their-luck aunts, uncles, and cousins.

Verna's mother, Camelia Zeitner, was worthy of her exotic-sounding name. A tall, slim brunette, even her children wondered how on earth their parents had gotten together. Her father, Zeke, was a tiny, ferret-faced, unprepossessing immigrant from Romania, who compensated for his lack of presence by throwing his weight around at home. A compulsive gambler, he gave his wife $85 a month to run her household, and the rest of his check, as his wife often put it bitterly, was his own to "buy feed for lots of horses."

Cam worked as a waitress in local diners throughout her daughter's childhood, and during her husband's frequent bouts of unemployment, she was often the family's sole support. While her waitressing money supported the family, their clothes were often hand-me-downs from their more affluent friends. As Verna grew older, she became a skilled seamstress and could rework other people's castoffs until they looked like new.

For her sixteenth birthday, her parents bought Verna a sewing machine, and from then on she would save to buy the best fabric she could afford so her clothes looked every bit as good as those of the girls from the other side of the tracks in the tonier areas of Pasadena and San Marino.

After graduation, Verna enrolled in beauty school and became a hairdresser. She might have had higher ambitions, but in her own mind, she was not college material. She was cute and popular, but not even those who loved her would have described her as a great brain.

At twenty-one, she met and married Bill Johnson, an Eagle Rock boy with an engaging grin, a shock of light brown hair, and ambitions to become a race-car driver. Verna liked his ambition and his desire to get out of Eagle Rock, to be adventurous, to see the world.

Their first baby, Kimberly, was born in 1969. They decided the time had come to leave Eagle Rock. Bill had been working as an electrician since he'd left school. He'd made good money and he'd saved. Now he went looking for housing in a most unlikely place: Malibu—fifty miles away and a thousand cultural leaps from Eagle Rock.

He bought a small rickety duplex with a studio apartment above the garage, on two separate lots just yards from the ocean. He converted the two units into one house and rented out the garage apartment. It was a fine location with a million-dollar view, and before the seventies were over, their modest little home would be surrounded by houses selling upward of $400,000.

Verna's parents thought he'd gone mad. The $77,000 he paid for the house would have bought a mansion in Eagle Rock. Verna, too, was nervous. Malibu was a long way from home. She was uncomfortable at the beach alone all day. She had no friends there. But by the time their son Douglas was born in 1972, Kimberly was in nursery school and the gregarious Verna was making lots of new friends and was happier than she'd ever been. Bill was doing well in the California building boom of the 1970s, working on the huge steel-and-glass office towers that were rapidly altering the Los Angeles skyline. They lived modestly but well, and life for Verna was secure and relaxing for the first time ever.

For Bill, however, Malibu brought unexpected pressures. The old restlessness was still there. Verna wanted him to stay home on the weekends to work on the house, to bring it closer to the standards that the neighborhood was rapidly acquiring. Bill needed a more adventurous outlet for his energies. He'd once longed to race cars. Now he was hang-gliding off Malibu cliffs—another risky sport with an edge of danger to it. Verna was enamored with the upward mobility that Malibu offered her, but Bill was becoming increasingly withdrawn. As Malibu became more affluent toward the mid-1970s, and Verna seemed to bloom among new friends, he wondered aloud if he wasn't holding his family back, saying he felt like a millstone around their necks. His moods grew darker. His behavior was often irrational and his outlook constantly pessimistic. Through it all Verna was upbeat and smiling—the Mary Sunshine married to the Prophet of Doom. She had an image to protect. She and Bill had to be seen as the shining couple, in love and loving. On the weekends, she'd phone her friends, sounding like a parody of a song from the country-and-western albums she so loved. They became used to her regular request: "Can you take the kids this afternoon? My man and I need some good loving time."

"When Bill comes home from work," she told Paddy Leitelt, "we just tear our clothes off and jump on each other."

But from Bill, the Leitelts were hearing another story. They had become friends with the Johnsons when John and Bill had worked on a building together. They lived just north of Malibu, in Oxnard, and the two families took vacation trips together and often visited one another. One confessional evening Bill told Paddy that his now-frequent bouts of depression were making him impotent. John was getting an even more disturbing picture.

"He was in terrible shape. He told me he couldn't make the simplest decisions, like whether to get up and close the door. He was becoming paralyzed."

Finally, Bill was hospitalized. He wasn't sleeping, he couldn't eat. He was virtually unable to function. Verna found it hard to understand.

The complexities of mental illness were beyond her, and she was fast losing patience. "I'm fed up with this," she told him. "Either shit or get off the pot." Bill's depression, she reasoned, was a reflection on her as a mother and wife. How dare he shame her like this, and just when their lives were going so well?

On Halloween 1975, Paddy Leitelt stopped by to see Verna, who was out trick-or-treating with the children. Paddy was about to leave when Bill came out of the house. "He grabbed the top of my car window. His knuckles were white on the glass. He begged me to stay, and I saw he was crying."

At Thanksgiving, Cam and Zeke came down to visit, but Verna soon sent them home. "Bill's not very well," she explained. "You know how he gets. I think you'll have to go."

In the last week of November, Verna took the family dog Jadie to the pound. The mutt was one of the things that had been irritating Bill, so despite the children's protests, he was to be put down.

A friend of the family later noted, "I think Bill identified with that dog. It was a nuisance and they got rid of it. He thought he had better be gotten rid of, too."

That weekend he told Verna he thought he should start seeing his psychiatrist again. She blew up. "You promised you'd snap out of this before the holidays. It's not fair to the children. We just can't have another dreary Christmas."

Early the next morning, Bill, Verna, and the children took Douglas to a doctor's appointment in Los Angeles. Bill dropped them all off at the doctor's office, promising to pick them up in an hour. Three hours later, he still hadn't appeared. Finally, Verna called her sister-in-law to drive them back to Malibu.

Early that evening, a policeman showed up at the house. Bill Johnson had fallen from a building in Los Angeles. He'd parked his car on a nearby street, climbed over a parapet into a parking structure, and jumped off the seventh floor.

Verna refused to accept the fact that Bill had killed himself. His co-workers rallied around so that his life insurance wasn't threatened. But the coroner, following a psychological autopsy, ruled it a suicide.

In her first weeks of widowhood, Verna floundered. How would she manage the family alone? She had never lived by herself, not even for a week. She'd gone straight from her parents' home to Bill's. She came from a pre-liberation America where a woman's only obligation was to look pretty, raise well-behaved children, and have her husband's food on the table when he came home. She'd kept her part of the bargain. Bill had failed in his.

With the insurance payment, however, she began to realize that she would be secure financially. There was also a stipend from Bill's union pension and Social Security for herself and the children. An uncle helped convert her house back into a duplex so she could rent half of it for extra money.

The permissive 1960s had passed over Verna Johnson completely. She'd guarded her reputation religiously. She'd been a virgin when she married Bill; she'd spent the last year of his life with virtually no physical relationship with him, and she was about to make up for lost time.

"Part of it was just testing herself," a friend recalled. "Putting oneself out there on the meat market to see if she could still hack it." But this time the meat market was Malibu, where they play for higher stakes.

The first thing she did was to look up her old Eagle Rock boyfriend. Once she'd been the girl from the other side of the tracks; now she was a widow with means and her own home in Malibu. He'd married long ago, but Verna and he had a brief affair. Later, she told her sister, "Now I've got him out of my system."

She began to date wildly and not too wisely, she and Paddy frequenting the bars in the swinging singles jungle of Marina del Rey, an hour's drive from Malibu, where the newly divorced inhabited high-rise condominiums on the water. Verna would try and pick up a guitar player or a waiter, or the guy at the next table, just to see if she could do it, Paddy said.

The only other person besides Paddy who was aware of the extent of Verna's ventures was Jeanne Roehler. In their afternoon tête-à-têtes by the pool, Verna now had something to match Jeanne's tales. And Jeanne, who had trouble keeping her own secrets, let alone somebody else's, regularly passed on the titillating tales to her husband.

Even after Jeanne's death, when Verna had begun seeing Fred Roehler on a regular basis, her swinging lifestyle continued. On a ski trip to Aspen with the Leitelts, Verna told Paddy, "Now's my chance to sleep with a ski instructor. Everybody should sleep with a ski instructor once; otherwise, it's not a real ski trip."

Around the time that Gloria Hunnicut broke up with Fred, Verna was getting ready to take her children to Hawaii to visit friends who had moved there. Just before she left, she bumped into Candy Hinman at Malibu Methodist Nursery School.

"I've been meaning to call you, Verna," Candy said hesitantly. "I only just heard you've been dating Fred. If I'd known, I would never have introduced him to Gloria."

Verna was mortified, and when Fred called her in Hawaii, she refused to talk to him. Later she snapped, "I told you I was dating others, too. But you should have been honest with me. Now I don't think I can trust you again."

Roehler apologized profusely. "I meant to tell you, but it's over now."

"I think we should do some serious talking when you get back."

The Gloria Hunnicut episode seemed to change Verna's attitude toward her relationship with Fred Roehler.

"She decided she didn't want to lose him to anyone else," Paddy Leitelt recalled. "One minute she was going to Hawaii to see all the guys her friend had laid on for her, and the next she was back, and she and Fred couldn't live without each other."

When Verna returned from her vacation, the Fred–Verna relationship was in the open, and almost everyone was delighted.

That summer of 1977 they borrowed a motor home from a neighbor and took off across the country for Indiana to meet Fred's family and attend the wedding of Fred's youngest brother, Scott. It was Verna's first meeting with the Roehlers, and she found the prospect intimidating.

Charlotte had assigned Verna and Fred to separate bedrooms, but Fred set her straight from the beginning. "Mother, Verna and I sleep together. That's the way it is." Charlotte climbed down and from that moment accepted the inevitable.

Soon after they returned to Malibu from their cross-country trip, Verna and the children moved into Fred's Calpine house. "I don't love him," she confided to John Leitelt, "and he doesn't love me, but he's good for the kids. He presents a real good image."

The Leitelts were alarmed but not surprised. A good image, they knew, had always been important to Verna. Lately her own had been in danger of slipping.

11

Love and Re-Marriage

VERNA JOHNSON WAS NOT HAPPY IN THE HOUSE ON CALPINE DRIVE. Living publicly with Fred and her children while they were not married made her uncomfortable. She dreaded telling her mother of their decision to live together.

Verna was preparing for her new life with Fred in some almost comical ways. A friend remembered, "She felt she wasn't smart enough for him so she bought herself a set of encyclopedias to improve her mind so she could talk to him." But there were a lot of things that bothered her about him. He hadn't paid his taxes for years. "His thinking is a little different from ours," said the friend. "He didn't think you should have to conform to society."

She also didn't like living in Jeanne's house. She got rid of her things—the formal furniture Jeanne favored, her fine china and glass, the baby grand piano—but she couldn't rid herself of the swimming pool where Jeanne had drowned. Every time she looked out of the living room window, there it was. It gave her the creeps.

She tried fervently to exorcise the ghost of Jeanne in other ways. To those who might have been privy to Jeanne's confidences, she made a point of saying, "I want you to know this: Whatever problems Jeanne and Fred may have had, they are not our problems."

She told Paddy how wonderful her sex life with Fred was. He was a superb lover. She had never been happier. Then, taking her friend's hand in hers, she pleaded, "If you're my friend, if you've ever loved me, you'll forget everything Jeanne ever told us."

If Fred's secrets were an open book to Verna, so were hers to Fred. He had listened to endless stories from Jeanne about Verna's romantic exploits—"war stories," he called them. A balance of power of sorts was established; it ensured the status quo.

Verna was practical enough to know that her old duplex, as much as she missed it, wasn't big enough for the extended family, and they'd tried Fred's house. What they really needed, they decided, was "our house."

When Fred told her about a house on Sea Level Drive right below her old home, she was excited. Living on the beach was at the top of the Malibu totem pole. The house was a two-story, three-bedroom on a double lot, the front door just steps away from Broad Beach, one of the prettiest and quietest beaches in Malibu. Sea Level Drive was a secluded cul-de-sac, private and exclusive. However, the house itself was a disaster—the ugliest and most neglected thing on the street. The roof leaked and the ceilings looked as if they were ready to fall in. The two small bathrooms were mildewed and broken down, and the yard was a mess of broken bottles and discarded beach furniture. In Malibu parlance, it was a "fixer-upper," and it needed a small fortune to make it habitable.

"My God, they're asking $340,000 for this dump?" Verna exclaimed in disbelief. Anywhere else, the price would have been laughable, but in Malibu, it was considered a find.

"By the time we're finished with it, this place will be worth a million," Fred told her. "It's a great investment."

It did represent an enormous commitment, though, especially as Fred was earning just $30,000 a year from Point Mugu and Verna a mere $5,000 from the part-time job she'd taken as a teacher's aide at her kids' school. But there was $1,700 a month coming in from the children's Social Security, as well as Verna's Social Security and her small pension from Bill's union. What made it a real possibility, however, was Verna's legacy from Bill's life insurance. Even though they were not married, Fred convinced Verna that it would be ideal to invest the insurance money in the burgeoning Malibu real estate market.

To qualify for a loan, Fred refinanced his Calpine house, putting Verna's name on the deed to give him enough collateral. But he immediately had her sign a document relinquishing any claim on the property.

One of his neighbors met Fred on the street and was regaled by tales of high finance and hundreds and thousands of dollars. "Roehler was like a little boy," he recalled. "He just went on and on about how complicated the deal had been and how big-league it was. It was kind of 'Look what a clever boy I am.' He was virtually rubbing his hands in glee."

Moving in with Verna had given Fred Roehler the chance to jump from modest rural Malibu to the upper echelons. He was now an "on the sand" homeowner. Actress Ali MacGraw was their neighbor on Broad Beach Road and would drop by for a chat now and then. It was heady stuff.

They now also owned a valuable duplex property with an additional apartment, the Calpine house, and Fred's small rental house in Oxnard.

The only thing that still worried Verna when looking at the crumbling pile that was to be her new home was where on earth they would ever get the money to fix it up. They were already fully extended. There certainly wasn't anything left over for repairs.

On October 25, 1977, at 3:00 a.m., the Malibu Fire Department was summoned to 31685 Sea Level Drive. The call had come swiftly from an alert neighbor. A fire had broken out in a storage shed at the side of the still-unoccupied house. They quickly extinguished the flames, but in so doing, a six-inch water line supplying the closest fire hydrant burst, sending a shower of water, mud, and rocks cascading into the back of the house, undermining the foundation, and flattening a retaining wall. The fire department repaired the main with a sturdy clamp, but inexplicably, the next day, October 26, the line burst again, causing even more extensive damage to the back of the house.

The house was still in escrow and legally the possession of the seller, but immediately after the fire, Fred Roehler went to see him and suggested that he, as the new owner, take care of the negotiations with the insurance company and use the proceeds to repair the damage. The owner agreed, so it was Roehler who collected a total of almost $38,000. It was not achieved, however, without his by now customary battle with the insurance companies over the settlement.

The Malibu Fire Department's investigation of the blaze revealed that it had been deliberately set by someone making a pile of old paint rags in the center of the shed and torching it. "We think there was a vagrant sleeping there," Fred Roehler said later. "He must have set the fire."

The Los Angeles County Water Department, however, questioned how a pipe in good condition, with no evidence of deterioration, could have burst. It was most unusual, they noted also, for the type of clamp they'd used to repair the main to become undone. They denied liability for the break.

Roehler immediately organized his neighbors, part of whose properties had also slid, to file a lawsuit against the county for over $100,000.

Despite the mud, the broken foundation, and the now virtually nonexistent retaining wall, the Roehlers moved into their new home in November 1977. Their first night, despite the chaos, was a happy one. They hadn't moved any furniture in yet, but they lay in sleeping bags around a big log fire, on which the children roasted hot dogs and marshmallows. As they munched popcorn, Fred and Verna toasted their new life with wine.

The flames of the fire warmed the bare living room, making Verna feel cozy and safe. She had made the right decision. Fred would provide a solid home for Kimberly and Douglas. He was reliable, he was wonderful with the kids, and she knew she could give Heidi and Kirsten the hands-on mothering they'd seldom had. The relationship between herself and Fred, she had to admit, was scarcely a full-blown romance, but she felt sure it would grow into something deeper and more permanent. Into the small hours, they discussed their plans—Fred's for the house, and Verna's for bringing their families closer together. It was the last completely peaceful time she was to spend in that house. She remembered it often in the many nights to come as she lay awake, terrified that the steep hillside behind her house would come down to bury them all.

Soon after, Fred applied for a Small Business Administration loan to pay for retaining the back hillside, and with careful paperwork and his usual excellent documentation, he soon had a commitment for $55,800 of the SBA's money. With the $37,782 in insurance payments, he now had over $93,000 in working capital to begin his renovation.

Viewed from the outside, the house on Sea Level was a disaster; domestically, things were just as chaotic. For a family engaged in the difficult task of merging two sets of children, getting them used to a new parent, and making them comfortable with each other, it seemed sometimes as though Fred was determined to make settling in as difficult as possible. He pulled off most of the roof and began constructing a huge wooden deck on top of the house to take advantage of the spectacular ocean view. They lived surrounded by piles of rubble. They cooked in a kitchen torn apart as Fred installed new cabinets. They slept amid the debris of plaster, drywall, and wood shavings.

Some of Verna's friends thought she was looking older, more strained. She began to have severe headaches and was horrified to discover that she had high blood pressure. For the first time, she seemed aware of her own mortality.

"My children have lost one parent," she told her mother. "I can't afford to be careless with my health. They mustn't lose another."

As Christmas neared, Verna and Fred brought the children together and told them there would be a special Christmas present for them all that year. Verna and Fred were going to be married.

The wedding of Verna and Fred was the talk of Malibu for months afterward. It was a picture-book Christmas Eve ceremony. While most of the country shivered, the weather that day was in the balmy 70s, and no Hollywood director could have bettered the setting for mood and emotion.

They had painstakingly hauled Jeanne Roehler's old grand piano from the garage where it had been relegated. They parked it on the sand at Sea Level Drive, in front of Fred and Verna's new waterfront home, beside a huge scenic rock at the surf's edge, and decorated it with a silver candelabra, red candles, and seasonal bright red poinsettias.

The beach was pristine and quiet. John Hagar, the local Methodist minister, began to play from Bach's "The Well-Tempered Clavier" as Verna and the children slowly descended the steps to join Fred and their guests on the sand below. Much care had gone into choosing the dresses for the ceremony. Verna's was ivory-colored and floor-length. It was laced at the waist, peasant style, with a high neck and long chiffon sleeves, the tight bodice fastened up the front with tiny pearl buttons. It was the kind of dress a teenage bride might have worn, but no one remarked on this small vanity because Verna looked so happy. Her long silver hair was parted in the center and held back with sprays of baby's breath, and her big brown eyes sparkled.

The three little girls, lined up in descending order of age, wore identical long party dresses of red-dotted white voile, red petticoats peeking out from beneath their full skirts. They carried small nosegays of red rosebuds, baby's breath, and fern.

Douglas, looking uncomfortable in his finery, wore long white pants, a red, white, and blue open-necked shirt, and a navy blue knitted blazer adorned with a ship's wheel insignia. He sported a red carnation boutonniere matching those worn by Fred and Reverend Hagar.

Fred looked relaxed and handsome in tan slacks and a navy-blue blazer, welcoming the guests with a wide smile and charming ease.

The ceremony was timed perfectly to coincide with the sunset for maximum scenic impact. To some it might have seemed a trifle stagey—a too-perfect performance in a ridiculous, dreamlike setting—with Fred, Verna, and the children lined up some distance from the guests like actors putting on a play. But even the most cynical onlooker would have been caught up in the emotion of the moment. Everyone who should have been there was there. Fred hugged Bill Johnson's aging parents, Bill's sister and her children, and Verna's mother Cam and her husband Zeke, frail and sickly, shivering even though the day was mild.

Fred's parents were also in the wedding party. Fritz, ruddy-cheeked, barrel-chested, the perfect archetype of the successful Middle American, and Charlotte, handsome and beaming, wearing an eye-catching Christmas-red dress and white jacket trimmed with red braid to match the bridal party. She had quickly assumed the duties of hostess and was gleefully introducing herself around.

Only the absence of Jeanne's parents, John and Marguerite Schoonhoven, and Verna's closest friends, the Leitelts, were noted with some surprise. The Schoonhovens had decided the entire event would be too painful. It was, after all, only a year since Jeanne's death.

Reverend Hagar, at whose neighborhood church Fred and Verna's growing relationship had been nurtured, smilingly told the 150 guests, "A remarkably wonderful thing is happening here today where, in a way, two families are choosing each other." Throughout the late afternoon, the message was repeated again and again: This was the joining not only of two people, but of two families.

As they stood at the water's edge and the sun started to dip down below the horizon, Fred placed tiny rings on Douglas's and Kimberly's fingers. Kneeling to their eye level, holding their hands in his, he stared intently into their wide eyes and told them softly, "I'm your father, if you'll have me." Verna then repeated the process with Fred's daughters, placing rings on their fingers and smiling at them. "I will be your mother, if you'll have me." From this point on, they told the children, "We are one family."

Then Fred and Verna exchanged rings with each other, and the ceremony was over.

As the sun slipped finally into the waves, leaving the beach to children and straggling dogs, the guests returned to the house to toast the newlyweds with punch, beer, and wine, munching on hot hors d'oeuvres and a five-tier wedding cake. As they mingled happily in the beach house festooned with Christmas garlands of holly and pine branches, the chief topic of conversation was the fairy-tale quality of what they had just witnessed. They all agreed this idyllic coming together had restored their faith in "happily ever after." Two years after Verna had become a widow, and just over one year after Fred had lost his wife, the two of them had almost miraculously given their loved ones a Disney-style, bluebirds-and-sunset finale.

Verna's mother, Cam, was telling everyone, "You see, there *is* a God, and he looks out for us."

The elaborate ritual of the wedding ceremony on the beach, the idealized setting, the outfits and the music, all helped to obscure one fundamental fact: At no time during the ceremony did Verna Johnson and Fred Roehler take each other as husband and wife. They were not asked, nor did they respond to the traditional question that would have legally married them. And there was no marriage registered with the appropriate

Los Angeles County authorities. The wedding ceremony was, in fact, just that—a ceremony—an elaborately staged performance that legally signified absolutely nothing. Fred and Verna were as single after the ceremony as they had been before.

Fred had explained to his lawyer, Bill Fairfield, that if Verna married again, she would lose the $205 a month she received in pension benefits from Bill Johnson's union. It seemed a trifling amount, and Verna had great reservations about going through with what she couldn't help but see as a deception. But Fred said that he couldn't see the point of her voluntarily giving up the money.

Her minister, John Hagar, helped to reassure her. They would be married in the sight of God, after all, and they had constantly told their parents and friends that their coming together would be a merger of two families, not just two individuals. There was nothing deceptive about that.

Bill Fairfield assured them that there was nothing illegal in what they were doing, either; and if it made their families more comfortable, what was the harm?

The beauty of the ceremony seemed to settle Verna's mind. As far as she was concerned, from that moment on, she and Fred were married, just as surely as if all the i's had been dotted and the t's crossed.

12

Raising the Kids

Bill and Verna had run a loose, relaxed household up until the time of Bill's illness, deciding they didn't need rigid discipline. Fred was cut from a very different cloth. In his world, a family was supposed to run perfectly—to look good and sound good and present a shining example to the rest of the community. For him, parenting was no different from any other difficult project. There was a right way to bring up children. He immediately began instituting a system of rules and orders, rewards and punishments, as rigid at times as those in a military academy.

He introduced a token system. Each child had their own jar with their own color-coded tokens. Every night, they had to come up with a nice or helpful thing they had done that day, and for each one, they got a token. Tokens could be spent for extra television time or to have their mother or father spend extra time with them individually.

Later there was another system, from *T.A. for Tots*, a manual produced by the Transactional Analysis Group: Positive things were rewarded with "warm fuzzies," and negative things by a "cold prickly."

Fred made a cold prickly out of a brown-paper-covered brick. When one of the children did something wrong, they had to take the cold prickly with them wherever they went. Later, they bought a kitchen timer, and an errant child would have to sit out by themselves until the timer went off. This worked until Douglas, who was generally the one sidelined, put an end to the system by removing the timer's inner works.

It was the running, however, that Fred decided worked best. Every misdemeanor, every prank the children came up with, drew a set number of laps on the beach, up and down, until the punishment was run out. Even three-year-old Kirsten, a little dumpling of a child, had to join in. The beach dwellers became used to the sight of the little Roehlers and Johnsons burning up the miles on the sand. "Wonder what they've done now," they'd ask each other.

Running was also part of Verna's health regimen. Eventually, she could run for forty-five minutes, and when she ran, the Johnsons and Roehlers followed, though often Fred paced her on his bike. To friends and family in Malibu, Fred would expound on his wife's progress. He was proud of their success in the Malibu Marathon, where Verna and Doug had earned second place in their categories.

In his other world at Point Mugu, however, he complained to a fellow engineer. "We have to eat this damned health muck at home all the time because of her high blood pressure, but if Doug complains, she'll make him special food. That kid can wind his mother 'round his little finger. He's a spoiled brat."

Verna was having difficulty coping with Heidi, Fred's older daughter. Despite her best efforts, she felt she wasn't getting through to the child, and it was a worry to her. It gave her something on which to focus her growing sense of unease.

Paddy Leitelt, living in Verna's duplex, sensed her friend's distress, though she never expected to hear about it from her. Verna had gone through too much to make this new marriage with her Prince Charming work, Paddy thought. "There's absolutely no way she's going to admit she made a mistake," she told her husband John, "not after Bill, not after the fairy story with the happy ending. She's in it for life."

Fred's disciplining methods with her children, however, were beginning to bother Verna. "It's the biggest source of conflict we have," she told a friend. "Those kids of mine have been through a lot, and if they need disciplining, I'll do it."

She resented what she saw as Fred's singling out of Douglas for extra discipline. The boy obviously challenged his new father more than the girls because he wouldn't buckle under. He was all boy, and Fred, who'd only had experience with girls, didn't like the challenge. It was particularly bad, Verna said, when his parents visited. Her kids had difficulty getting a look in.

At Juan Cabrillo Elementary School, Douglas was a little star at everything he did, genuinely enthusiastic and talented, but the more he shone, the more irritated his new father seemed to become.

Playing tennis with John Leitelt one day shortly after the "wedding," he confided that he thought boys were a lot more trouble than girls. "Girls you can just make nice with; boys, you've got to do things with, like show up at their sports and coach them and stuff. They take up a lot more of your time. They're a pain."

Some of Verna's friends were telling her the outgoing little boy seemed quieter, more reserved, and it bothered her. She didn't want Fred's strength to break Douglas's spirit. Fred, however, continued to insist that all would be well if they would just stick to his system.

To the outside world, the Johnson–Roehler household seemed about as perfect as it was possible to be. They were well turned out, always shining and clean. In fact, like the families in Centerville years before, when faced with the Roehlers, the Malibu folks also began to wonder why their own families couldn't measure up.

Chuck Menville and his wife Dottie had been neighbors and frequent visitors of Verna and her family when she was married to Bill, and their friendship with the combined family continued. They had two young sons of their own who were quite a handful; their house was noisy, chaotic, and scruffy most of the time. "Then I'd go over to the Roehlers,'" Chuck remembered, "and everything would be smooth as silk. The kids, sitting down to dinner and everything, 'May I?' and 'Thank you' and 'Please pass the . . . ,' all dressed smart and clean, not a hair out of place, napkins folded on their knees. I mean, it was incredible. It gave me a complete inferiority complex. I used to think, 'Why can't I be more like Fred? This guy has really got it together.'"

Not everyone was convinced, including Dottie Menville, for one.

"Bill and Verna had been very down-home," she remembered, "relaxed and unpretentious. A lot of friends came to Verna's house as a place of fun and uplift and nurturing. She was very warm and caring for her friends. That sort of stopped after Fred. Show was more important in this marriage. Verna had made a big social leap in marrying Fred. He appeared to have more money and more education than Bill, and they were now a very visible couple in the community. There wasn't as much time for spontaneity. You couldn't just drop in anymore. Appearance was very, very important to both of them."

Verna began to spend. No longer happy with her bright sassy, inexpensive clothes, she slimmed down to a svelte hundred pounds and started wearing designer jeans and putting the kids in the latest fashions. Shopping became one of her favorite activities. The Menvilles watched her transformation with amusement. "She got skinny and tanned and sleek and began to look like the typical Malibu housewife," said Chuck. "I expected to see her driving a Mercedes any day."

Even her mother became concerned, and on one of her shopping trips, as Verna's bill climbed, she protested, "Haven't you spent enough?"

Verna whirled on her angrily. "Mother, if Fred doesn't mind, why should you? Stop nagging, or I'll never take you shopping with me again."

Fred apparently did little to discourage her, at least outwardly. "If we have a spat and she squawks at me," he told Chuck Menville, "I just hand her a credit card and say, 'Go buy yourself some clothes.' It works every time."

His actions, however, belied his words. He got rid of the weekly maid and paid off the gardener. "We've got four kids," he told Verna. "Anything needs to be done around here, they can do it." And he took over the grocery shopping himself, searching long and hard for the cheapest cuts of meat, marinating them for days in the refrigerator to make them palatable.

The Leitelts, with whom Verna had been so close, stopped coming around to visit. They felt Fred had made it clear they were not welcome, and they were becoming increasingly worried about something more serious. Verna had had several conversations with Paddy about protecting her estate for her children.

"Fred and I are looking into a family trust," she told Paddy. "Our estates are about equal, so we can put them together and then divide them equally among the four children if anything happens to either of us."

"But your Broad Beach house is beach property, Verna," protested Paddy. "It's worth much more than Fred's place on Calpine and that tiny place he has in Oxnard. You're not getting a fair shake here." Paddy said that Verna, in her naiveté, went straight to Fred, in front of her, and blurted out, "Paddy thinks you're trying to rip me off." Fred gave Paddy a look that went right through her. "After that, needless to say, we weren't exactly welcomed with open arms," Paddy recalled.

In October 1978, less than a year after the idyllic beach wedding, Malibu was hit with one of the worst fires in its history. The blaze, fanned by hot winds from the desert, swept through the canyons to Malibu and burned thousands of acres right down to the ocean.

Fred Roehler sat on the roof of his Sea Level Drive house and hosed it down, as well as those of his immediate neighbors. After the flames were quenched, he was a hero; Verna, however, had lost one-half of her duplex. While Fred had saved the house on the sand, just yards away, part of Verna's old home was damaged beyond occupancy.

As a result of the fires, John and Paddy Leitelt lost their home. They moved to a townhouse farther north on the Malibu–Ventura County line.

Fred decided to leave the duplex as it was, with one half burned out. Verna's disappointment at losing the Leitelts as neighbors soon faded when, at Fred's suggestion, her mother and her terminally ill father, Zeke, moved into the remaining half.

When Zeke died, just two weeks after the move, Cam moved to the small studio apartment over the garage, enabling Verna and Fred to rent out the larger unit. Verna's duplex had been insured to the tune of $69,630. Once again Fred conducted more battles with the insurance company over the amount of the payout, threatening lawsuits and writing yet again to the State Department of Insurance.

In November 1978, a month after the Malibu fire, Roehler went to his boss, Everett Bruer, and asked for a year's leave of absence so he could work on his house. Bruer was apologetic but firm: Roehler was needed at work. There could be no time off.

A month later, Roehler was carrying a videotape machine out of a trailer near his office when he tripped. Stumbling to his desk, his face contorted, he seemed in dire pain as he yelled to a colleague: "I've done something to my neck and shoulder."

He took forty-five days off on paid leave before going on a leave of absence and applying for workers' compensation. His back injury made it impossible for him to sit at a desk, he explained.

The "bad back" was the culmination of a year of open warfare between Fred Roehler and his superiors at Mugu. "Roehler's games," as they came to be called, had begun with the psychiatrist's letter in April 1977, getting him off work for three weeks. Then it was extended to six. Toward the end of April, Ed Mutz sent a confidential memo to Bruer and his other engineers, laying down the new guidelines for the handling of his recalcitrant employee: "It seems that we must carefully document all of Mr. Roehler's assignments in the future and give him completion dates for every action requested . . . a weekly review of his accomplishments should be noted and discussed with him."

By the end of 1977, Roehler's performance evaluation told the story. He was described as "uncooperative and disorderly . . . hampered by fixed ideas, resistant to change."

After the Malibu fire of October 1978 and his back injury in December, Fred Roehler was off work continuously for the whole of 1979, and, as it would turn out, for most of 1980 as well.

When he eventually came back in March of 1980, his boss's patience had been exhausted. He took steps to fire him. He was moved to a tiny office by himself to wait out the thirty days it took for the action to become effective. He immediately filed an appeal.

While the US Navy tried throughout 1979 and the spring of 1980 to resolve the Fred Roehler problems, the source of their frustration—supposedly so badly incapacitated that he couldn't even sit at a desk—was literally moving mountains in Malibu.

It was the most ambitious engineering project of Fred's life. He was building an intricate wall in his backyard to hold back the crumbling cliff, using an expensive and difficult technique for retaining riverbanks in flood areas which involved encasing hundreds of tons of small rocks in a series of linking wire baskets. He rallied the neighbors, telling them he would tackle the immense project himself, charging them $45 an hour for his services (nearly $170 per hour in 2023 dollars). No sooner had he begun than one of his neighbors threatened to sue if Roehler proceeded, claiming the whole project was excessively expensive.

Horace Bresee, a retired high school teacher in his mid-seventies, living on a tight budget, said he was worried about the Roehler wall turning into an overpriced boondoggle, and wanted out. "That old idiot is holding up the entire project," fumed Roehler. Bresee soon became his public enemy number one.

On January 15, 1980, a fire of unknown origin broke out in the back bedroom of the Bresees' beach house. His neighbor Fred Roehler had discovered it. He had broken a window, reached into the house with a hose, and extinguished the flames, but not before the building had sustained substantial damage.

Arson investigators said the fire had been deliberately set. Someone had neatly piled used paint rags in a closet of the bedroom and set it alight. The Bresees blamed the fire on a former tenant, but shortly afterward they were surprised to receive a letter from Fred Roehler, offering to take the fire-damaged house off their hands for $87,000. They turned him down, explaining they intended to fix it up themselves. They later found out that the fair value of the house was closer to $200,000.

In between his herculean labors in his backyard, Roehler, who had been virtually invisible in his former life in Malibu, was coaching eight-year-old Doug's soccer team, along with the local softball and baseball teams. He was arranging photography and extra education classes at Juan Cabrillo Elementary School and revitalizing the local Methodist church, doing just about everything except baking cakes for their annual bazaar. He was, in fact, becoming Mr. Malibu, piling up brownie points for himself. While all the other fathers were at work, he was at home all day—a more and more visible presence in the neighborhood.

"I had to admire the guy," said neighbor Chuck Menville. "He knew how to make the system work for him. He was getting workers' compensation; he was suing the County for $100,000; he was engineering a hill and rebuilding his house. He liked to boast to me when he'd pulled off something clever. At first, it didn't bother me, but when a couple of years went by and he was still so manipulative, it got under my skin. There I was, working my tail off, and he's home all day, jogging with his kids and getting paid for it. He had a smugness about it that I couldn't take."

Fred's sailing buddy Dick Velthoen, manager of the nearby city of Port Hueneme, was also turned off by Roehler's attitude, but even he was stunned when Fred turned to him one day and said, "Dick, I have absolutely no intention of ever working again." On August 15, 1980, three months after Roehler had been fired, a US Navy board at Point Mugu met to hear his wrongful dismissal appeal. He was represented by two civilian attorneys, both specialists in civil service disputes. The navy's representative was the head of Mugu's civilian personnel office, not a lawyer.

Roehler had kept meticulous records of every communication he had received from the navy during his absence—every visit, phone call, and note to his doctor. The navy's records were sloppy, begun only when they'd finally decided that Roehler had rubbed their nose in it once too often. They could not produce one iota of solid evidence against Roehler, and seemed more concerned about passing the buck on who had made the decision to fire him in the first place.

Roehler's family doctor, Jeff Harris, confirmed that indeed his patient was totally incapacitated by his back injury, and that he had complied with every form sent to him by the navy. The navy's counsel did not ask Dr. Harris a single question, nor did he make a closing statement. It was almost as if he were embarrassed by his role and wanted out of his predicament.

Roehler's attorney, on the other hand, burned with righteous indignation. "This whole thing is a tragedy," he snorted. "I have never seen such an arbitrary decision without a scintilla of evidence to back it up."

In December 1980, the Board handed down its decision: Roehler was to be reinstated with full back pay for three-quarters of the year, amounting to $21,600. All documents referring to the attempt to remove him were to be withdrawn from his personnel file, and he wasn't obliged to return to work until January 16, 1981—the date the decision of the board became final.

His triumph was complete: The US Navy had been humiliated, and he'd virtually been given carte blanche for his future dealings with Mugu. Any further attempt on their part to get rid of him could be construed as a vendetta. From now on, as far as the navy was concerned, Fred Roehler was untouchable.

What had made the whole thing even more galling to his bosses at Point Mugu was that on September 12, 1980, the *Los Angeles Times* had carried an article titled "The Art of Living with the LA Brush Fire Season." The story featured burned-out residents of Malibu rebuilding their lives after the ravages of the 1978 fire. It was illustrated by several pictures, one of which showed an earnest, hale and hearty Roehler working on his Malibu duplex.

There was never the slightest doubt in Roehler's mind that he would win his case, a fact that had led him, on March 31, 1980—having just been informed that the navy had instituted proceedings to fire him—to sign papers to buy a 50-foot yacht valued at $150,000. It might have seemed an inopportune moment to take on such a heavy commitment. He was about to lose his job, he had house payments on four properties, plus tens of thousands of dollars of work still to do on the Sea Level Drive house. But it didn't seem to concern him.

He told Verna, after the sail to Mexico in the *Perseverance*, they might just keep going and do a complete 'round-the-world sail, keeping a journal and film record of the trip. He talked to some of his Malibu neighbors in the movie business about helping him market their seagoing adventures for film or TV when they returned.

Chuck Menville, a film writer, remembered one such conversation. "If anyone else had told me he was going to do this with a completely inexperienced family and no other crew on board a boat that size, I'd have said he was crazy. But this was Fred. I mean, the guy had built a mountain of stone behind his house, which everyone else had thought was impossible. He needed a bulldozer to fill it, so he went out and found a used one and bought it, and when it broke down, he simply found the parts and fixed the damned thing himself. Nothing stopped this guy; nothing was beyond him. I believed he could do anything."

The sailing trip became the number-one topic of conversation among the Roehlers's friends in Malibu. A yacht was big stuff, an around-the-world cruise, glamorous. Everywhere they went, people asked them about it.

"It's almost become a community project," Roehler boasted.

Verna was anxious about the Mexican voyage from the start. Sailing was new to her, and Mexico, to her, meant dangerous waters, uncertain laws, even bandits and pirates. Fred tried to reassure her.

"Don't forget, we'll be close to port all the way down, and you can have that dog you and the kids have been nagging me about. If a stranger comes on board, the dog will let us know. We'll do lots of practice sailing until you feel really comfortable."

"By the time I've finished with her," Fred told the family, "Verna will be handling the *Perseverance* like our old station wagon."

But some were not so sure. Barbara Leonard, the Roehlers's neighbor who had often babysat for Jeanne, bumped into Verna in the supermarket and casually asked how things were going. Her reply was uncharacteristic of the always positive Verna, as Mrs. Leonard remembered. "She said things were not going well at all and that she was not happy. She complained that she and the children were having to give up all their goals and the things they liked to do, drop their entire lifestyle, in fact, in order to pursue Fred's ambition to sail around the world."

That summer, Fred Roehler had taken care of an important piece of unfinished business. July 12 was Cam Zeitner's wedding anniversary, so when Verna climbed the stairs of her small apartment over the garage of the Broad Beach duplex and told her, "Come with me, Mom, we've got an anniversary surprise for you," Cam followed excitedly.

On the beach Fred and the Reverend John Hagar, minister of the Malibu Methodist church, were waiting. This time there was no grand piano or admiring friends and relatives, no children, flowers, or ballyhoo. In a three-minute ceremony, Fred Roehler and Verna Jo Johnson, with Verna's mother as the sole witness, were married. If they were going sailing early in the new year, it was important for all the loose ends to be tied up. This time, said Fred, it was legal.

On the night of December 3, 1980, Verna arranged to go Christmas shopping and have dinner with Paddy Leitelt. It was a belated birthday celebration, for the two women had not seen each other since before Verna's thirty-sixth birthday, on September 13. The first week in December, however, brought one of Southern California's savage winter storms and the night was wet with lashing rain, whipped by fierce winds blowing down the canyons to the ocean. The highways were slick and treacherous with rocks tumbling down the steep canyon sides, making driving after dark a nightmare. Paddy was thinking about canceling, but at 6:00 p.m. Verna called her. She sounded upset, even desperate.

"You are coming, aren't you? I don't care where we go, we can even stay in Malibu, but please come and get me. Fred said I can go out."

Paddy parked at the top of Verna's hill and was surprised to find her friend waiting for her in the pouring rain. "She ran out to meet me and I saw she'd left her car lights on," Paddy recalled. "I said, 'You idiot—turn off your lights or you won't have a car when you get back.' She was agitated, forgetful, you know, like she'd been afraid I wasn't going to show up."

The two women drove in Paddy's car through the canyon, seventeen miles to the sprawling housing tracts and shopping malls of the San Fernando Valley. At a department store, Paddy started buying Christmas presents. Of the two, Verna was normally the one who enjoyed shopping, as Paddy was usually hard up. But that night, Verna didn't seem to have the heart for it. When she tried to put a purchase on her Visa card, it was rejected. "She was embarrassed and angry," Paddy recalled. " 'This is Fred's way of keeping me from using the card,' [Verna told me]. He doesn't pay the damned bill.' "

At a local Mexican restaurant, Verna got drunk quickly.

"We'd been there for a while," Paddy recalled, "when these two guys came over and tried to pick us up. One of them was a loan customer at the bank where I was working, so I knew him. The other was married to a well-known actress and was driving around in her Rolls-Royce. He kept telling us how his wife was always gone, and how he had to go out and have affairs because of it. They tried to get Verna and me to leave with them. I said, 'No, thanks.' Verna looked up over her drink and said, 'I'll have you know I'm a happily married woman.' But she said it with such sarcasm in her voice that I was really shocked. They kept trying, but Verna kept repeating, 'But I'm a happily married woman.' The way she said it gave me the creeps."

It was a painful memory of Paddy's last encounter with her best friend.

Fritz and Charlotte Roehler arrived at Sea Level Drive on December 30, 1980. Verna arranged to have lunch that day with three of her friends at a restaurant on the beach. One of them remembered Verna quietly griping about her mother-in-law. Charlotte doted on her son, she said, and he could do no wrong in her eyes. She made Verna feel inadequate, as though nothing she did was right. But she was willing to play along because the Roehlers weren't staying long.

Before she hurried off to buy lobster for the Roehlers's traditional surf 'n' turf dinner, they talked about the trip to Mexico.

"She was excited and looking forward to it," her friend recalled, "although she was apprehensive. She still wasn't very comfortable on the boat, so I asked her how she was coping. 'I'm at total peace with myself,' she told me. 'If the Lord wanted my life tomorrow, he could have it. I'm ready to go.' "

She had no clue how prescient this conversation would prove to be.

The New Year had gone peacefully for the Schoonhoven family in Colorado. But on the evening of January 3, John Schoonhoven got the awful news that once again, his grandchildren were motherless. There had been an accident at sea. Their boat, The *Perseverance*, had capsized, and though Fred had tried to save them, Verna and Douglas were dead.

He phoned his daughter Linda. "Come over right away. Something terrible has happened."

At the front door, her ashen-faced father greeted her with "It's about Fred . . ."

"What's that maniac done now?" Linda shouted.

"Don't ever let me hear you talk like that about him ever again," John Schoonhoven snapped.

A memorial service was held at the Malibu Methodist Church for Verna and Douglas. The family had asked that only those invited come and that everyone else pay their respects later at the house. The request was largely ignored. Everyone in the community, it seemed, wanted to say a formal good-bye. Kimberly, Heidi, and Kirsten cried. Fred Roehler was dry-eyed and stoic. Cam Zeitner tried to smile and welcome Verna's friends, but she was finding it hard to maintain a brave front.

The quiet condolences and the murmured expressions of grief masked the fact that the Malibu community inside and outside the church was instantly divided. Those close to Jeanne were outraged and convinced that Fred had killed a second time. Others—those who knew sparse details of Fred's first marriage but had become friends with the Roehlers after Fred had married Verna—were simply appalled at that kind of unwarranted and vicious speculation.

The memorial service was brief. Afterward, the Roehlers's beach house was packed with people, children running underfoot everywhere. Lady, the puppy, ran around barking excitedly. Neighbors brought crates of wine and beer. It was an old-style wake—a family rite. And while some thought the party atmosphere strange, others agreed it was just the way Verna would have wanted it.

Fred Roehler sat alone in his bedroom. As each guest arrived, they went in to see him and offer their condolences. He accepted them silently, hugged old friends, and shook hands with neighbors, but when John Leitelt arrived, Fred clung to him, weeping.

"Oh, John," he sobbed. "They hit their heads on the rock. There was nothing I could do."

13

The Investigation

Santa Barbara, January 6, 1981

Santa Barbara, a Mediterranean-style Southern Californian resort town that has been justly called the most beautiful city in America, has one of the highest per capita incomes in the world. And alongside the millionaires' yachts in the marina, the Polo Club, and the Coral Casino's very private beach club, are the street people—the alcoholics and the dispossessed—for whom the mild climate and the tree-lined grassy verges by the ocean provide more pleasant al fresco accommodations than the dusty streets of Los Angeles, ninety miles down the coast. With them comes crime, and the sheriff's department usually has its hands full.

On this day, phones were ringing off the hook and the already busy bureau was stretched to near breaking point when Santa Barbara coroner's deputy Larry Gillespie, still puzzled by the strange phone call he had received minutes earlier from Candy Hinman, a woman in Malibu, approached homicide detective Sergeant Bill Baker.

"I don't know what we've got here, Bill," he said. "I'm not even sure it's our jurisdiction, but this woman seems dead sure we should look into it."

"Oh yeah," said Baker. "I clipped something about that accident out of the paper the other day." He rummaged through his desk drawer and came up with a two-paragraph news story from the *Santa Barbara News-Press* about a rescue at sea four days before. It had happened at Santa Cruz Island, which fell under the jurisdiction of Santa Barbara County.

An hour later, Baker finally got his head above water long enough to grab a detective, Fred Ray, one of his senior investigators.

"Fred, take a look at this, will you?" He passed the clipping to the lanky cop. "And talk to Gillespie," he added over his shoulder as he retreated to his desk.

Fred Wayne Ray had been a Santa Barbara detective for ten years, in major crimes for three. Tall and tailored, with a small, well-trimmed mustache and carefully barbered brown hair, at age forty-two, he looked enough like a cop to be a caricature, right down to his rather loud taste in sports jackets. Lean as a pole, he was a compulsively hard worker. Known affectionately in the department as "Fresno Fred" because of his origins in the Central Valley of California, he was divorced and had full custody of four teenage children, three girls and a boy. Keeping them on a sheriff's pay was a struggle, so he moonlighted as a gas company meter reader, a roofer, and a house cleaner, and he managed four apartment buildings. In his spare time, he grew Cymbidium orchids.

Tightly wound, with the kind of high energy that got him by with only five hours of sleep a night, Fred Ray had developed a reputation as a tenacious investigator who, once having been given a scent of a crime, couldn't be pried away from it until he'd run down every single lead. He was persistent to the point of exhaustion, and like many cops married to the job, his own ten-year marriage had finally collapsed from the strain. He sang in the church choir on Sundays. He was religious and clean-cut, the only cop anyone knew who winced every time someone swore.

Pocketing the clipping, Ray went off to find his partner, Claude Tuller, a homicide novice. Five years younger than Ray, four inches shorter, and fifteen pounds heavier, he was as phlegmatic as Ray was packed with nervous energy. Only his heavy, two-pack-a-day smoking habit betrayed any anxiety whatsoever. He'd spent five years as an Air Force policeman, and before becoming a detective, had worked in the Santa Barbara County jail. Florid of face, the sandy-haired Tuller also came from Fresno, but he proudly wore a large class ring from the University of Redlands. Father of four sons, he was known in the department simply as "Dad." The perfect foil for the fast-moving Fred Ray, he was generally content to take a back seat, respectful of his colleague's wider experience. Anxious to learn, he would follow wherever Ray led.

"Not much to go on here," Ray told him. "But Gillespie got a tip that there may be more. Let's go talk to the Coast Guard."

For the rest of the afternoon Ray and Tuller talked to every Coast Guard officer who had been on the rescue on January 2. None of them had any reason to believe that the drowning of the young mother from Malibu and her child had been anything but a tragic accident.

But that phone call from Malibu had worried Larry Gillespie, and Gillespie wasn't an alarmist. If he thought something might be wrong, then Ray and Tuller wanted to know a whole lot more about this Fred Roehler before closing the file on the Santa Cruz drownings.

January 7, 1981

Five days after the drownings, detectives Ray and Tuller set out early for their 11:00 a.m. interview with the survivor Fred Roehler at his home in Malibu. It was only a seventy-five-mile drive from their home base, but for Tuller and Ray, Malibu was alien soil. They drove past the oceanfront homes belonging to people recognized the world over. Santa Barbara, their beach community base, was more established. There, houses had stood since Spanish colonial times. Money was old, earned in Pennsylvania, or in Detroit, in cars. Malibu marched to a different drummer, and Ray and Tuller didn't understand its ethos.

The Roehler house wasn't at all what they'd expected. It was the scruffiest place on the street. On the beach level, there was only a front door and a garage, with the living accommodations upstairs. An ocean-facing balcony ran across the front of the house, but the window on one side was broken and a sheet of plastic had been hung to keep out the wind. The blue-painted stucco was drab and faded, and the white trim was peeling. A pile of building junk lay in the side yard. It needed a makeover, and fast.

Roehler greeted them in faded Levi's, a T-shirt, and rubber flip-flops. He gave them a bone-crushing handshake and a wide smile, and then led them up a narrow, carpeted staircase to the first-floor living room. On the way up, happy family photos of Roehler, a smiling wife, and four cute children gazed down at them from the walls.

The living room was furnished with a motley collection of unmatched odds and ends, the sort of stuff that spelled weekend place. Roehler showed them to a breakfast area off to one side of the Pullman kitchen where they arranged themselves around a small wooden table in three straight-backed chairs. They could hear the rhythmic crash of the surf on the sand below them as they spoke. The perfect host, Roehler was composed, relaxed, and friendly as he sipped from a mug of tea. He offered them coffee, which they politely declined.

Ray carefully set his briefcase down at his feet alongside his chair, surreptitiously switching on the small Sony tape recorder inside. He opened a small spiral notebook as Roehler picked up a sheaf of handwritten notes from the table in front of him.

Outside, the sun was shining, and the sounds of children playing on the sand wafted up to them. Breakfast leftovers sat on the kitchen counter.

Ray cleared his throat ceremoniously and began. "Can I call you Fred?"

"Certainly. Please do."

"Okay. I'm Fred also."

They had received a phone call, Ray explained. It really didn't amount to much, he was sure, but since the accident had occurred in Santa Barbara waters, they were obliged to investigate. It certainly looked like nothing but an accident, and they were there only to clear up some small points.

Roehler said he understood. He had missed their passing reference to the phone call.

Then Ray introduced his sole note of caution: "The only thing I would suggest that maybe we do is—you know—remind you that if there's anything wrong with this at all, that . . . you know . . . that you have certain rights, too, so I don't know if it's necessary at this point—but certainly I would want to make you aware of every—er—every right that you have. Plus, I'm sure there's gonna be some civil problems as far as insurance or whatever . . . I don't know if there is any insurance. . . . "

He let the question hang.

"Uh-huh." Roehler was noncommittal.

" . . . but I'm sure there's gonna be a lot of legal things that you're gonna have to . . . you know, consult with. Don't you think, Claude?"

"More'n likely, yeah," Tuller agreed, giving his colleague a moment to take a breath after his long-winded and inarticulate preamble.

"So for your own protection and your own edification, too, I should remind you that you do have the right to remain silent and anything you say can and will be used against you in a court of law. You have the right to an attorney and to have him present with you before and during questioning if you wish one. Do you understand that?"

"I do."

Ray glanced nervously at the closed briefcase at his feet. " . . . And having those rights in mind, do you still want to discuss this with us?"

"Certainly."

It was not a full reading of Miranda rights. Ray had done it off the top of his head and somewhat reluctantly. They did not really consider the man they'd come to talk to a suspect, and the atmosphere was so congenial that Mirandizing him at all seemed almost an insult in light of what had happened to his wife and stepson.

"Okay," Detective Ray continued, leaning on the table and placing an arm around Fred Roehler's shoulders in a gesture of comfort. "I know it's going to be really difficult to talk about this. I remarked when I first heard about it on the news—I'm a diver, I go out in the ocean a lot—and I thought, 'What a tragedy.'"

Roehler nodded silently, his eyes downcast, quietly acknowledging their sympathy. "You know," he said, "we had a service for both of them on Monday and we had friends over afterward. A lot of my friends are really into sailing and all these things, and they remarked over and over, 'How many times have you dumped a boat, and everybody just got wet and got back in and everything was fine?' That's part of the things that I find, you know, perverse, as it is. My son was a good swimmer. He had just mastered standing up on a boogie board. He was a small boy, but very agile, and he was a good swimmer. But I think part of the thing that got him was the fact that he was wearing a life jacket, that he was trapped underneath the boat."

"Oh, he was trapped under the boat?" Fred Ray asked, picking up on the one kernel of solid information.

Roehler hesitated. "Well . . . and again, that's something I can only surmise because initially I was trapped under the boat. I had a camera on, and the camera strap got hooked in the oarlock. I drew a picture of that. I don't know if you're familiar with the boat, but it was a sixteen-foot rowing dory . . . and somehow, either on the metallic part or on the wood dowel part of the oarlocks, it got wrapped around the camera strap when the boat turned over, and then I was held up against the seat where I was . . . there was no air space and I basically thought I'd had it. I was just about out. You know, it's one of those things. I was trying to break that, and I couldn't break the camera strap and I couldn't break the parachute strap, and then for whatever reason, I relaxed a little and was able to get it undone and get out."

Roehler seemed in no doubt that the strap on the camera he'd been wearing around his neck had trapped him under the boat, causing him to struggle for his life.

During the entire interview, Roehler answered every single question. In fact, he often gave them much more information than they asked for. As raw material for an investigation, Ray and Tuller had never had better, as Roehler, occasionally consulting his handwritten notes, calmly told them about buying the yacht *Perseverance* and his family's plan for a six-month sailing cruise.

As he spoke, Ray was impressed by his recall. The notes, however, worried him. He'd seen guys like this before: meticulous, covering every detail. No matter how you sliced it, this was odd for a grieving husband.

They had gone out in the dory on the day of the accident, Roehler said, to test a new camera they'd bought for the Mexico trip.

"Did you happen to take any pictures on the island that day?" Ray asked nonchalantly.

"That's what we were doing, but I never got a chance to even take a picture. We had just gotten the dog about . . . maybe a month . . . I'd have to look at the records."

Ray let the non sequitur pass. He'd let Roehler tell the story in his own way.

The sail to the island was uneventful, Roehler told them. He described his mother taking the wheel, the anchoring of the boat, and the family stopping for lunch.

Tuller asked what time they had moored. (He was dying for a cigarette, but a "Please, No Smoking" sign had caught his eye when he'd entered the house.) Roehler told them it was close to noon, though he hadn't seen a clock at the time.

He continued to talk with very little prompting. He was like a tape player, wound up, running on one tone. So far there had been no awkward moments, no emotional outbursts. He seemed in control of himself; he had gone through a tragedy, but he was holding up admirably.

After lunch, Roehler said, his brother, sister-in-law, and the two girls, Heidi and Kimberly, had climbed into the inflatable dinghy to go ashore. Young Douglas had demanded that he be allowed to go in the dory despite his stepfather's suggestion that he go with Scott, Ginny, and the two girls.

"So, I was about to let him go in the boat and my wife came on deck and said, 'Well, I'd like to take the dog ashore, but I don't want Doug to row me.' And I said, 'Well, okay.' She wasn't used to the Nikon camera, and she said, 'Bring the camera along and we'll take some pictures.' She went and got the camera and the dog, and Doug did not have a life jacket on at the time, and I told him to go below and get a life jacket on."

Roehler shuffled his notes and continued. "I got in the boat and then Doug climbed down in it. He sat in the aft end and Verna passed me the dog down. Then she gave me the camera and I put it around my neck, and then she sat on the forward part of the boat, sort of a built-in air reserve seat type of thing, and she threw down two more of the green flotation cushions. She was sitting on one of those and she was leaning against the other one in the back. And then I gave her the dog and we pushed off."

"Was she wearing a life jacket?" Ray asked.

"No. She had—I don't know if she had a sweater on, but she had a brown ski-type jacket . . . it was a short-waisted thing . . . jeans . . . I can't remember what . . . and Verna said, 'Well, why don't we row over by the rock so we can get a picture of . . .'" As he talked, he sketched a small pen drawing of the relative position of his yacht and the dory, vis-à-vis the other boats in the anchorage, as they rowed toward the corner of Bird Rock.

"So, I said okay, and figuring that what we would do would be to take the pictures and then go back over and find the rest of the kids and go up on the island. When we got over there she said, you know, she kept giving me . . . 'a little ahead, a little to the left, a little to the right,' kind of thing, and finally, she thought we were in the right place, so I put the oars in the boat and then I slipped off the seat and put my butt right down on the floor of the boat. And then she gave me the dog around my left side, and I passed the dog over to Doug. And I was just getting ready to get the camera out when the dog jumped over the side. And I grabbed the dog by the back leg and Doug obviously didn't know or didn't see, or whatever . . . that I had the dog, and he went to go for the dog and I went and caught him by the collar as he was reaching over the side of the boat . . . and then, I just don't know whether she slipped or thought she was helping me or what . . . but my wife hit me in the back . . . and then the boat turned over."

There was a long pause.

Fred Ray was again acutely aware of the crash of surf on the sand below and the loud ticking of the old-fashioned wall clock. It seemed a long time before anyone spoke.

Tuller looked furtively at Roehler from under his eyebrows, his head ostensibly bent over his notes. It was all being told very matter-of-factly. He could have been describing a fender bender on the freeway. There were apparently no screams or cries for help, no violent thrashing in the water, no frenzied struggle for life.

Roehler drained his mug of tea and carefully laid it aside. What he saw when he'd finally freed himself from his underwater trap and come up from under the dory was his stepson, lying on his side.

"It would have been on his left side. He was vomiting and it was yellow . . . a yellow vomit . . . He could have been caught underneath there, even battling that while I was trying to get out, and maybe when I got out, I put the boat up enough for him to come out, you know. And I think about Verna the same way . . . when the boat rolled . . . it definitely got all three of us . . . because it's a fairly heavy boat."

For the first time, Roehler seemed to be choking back tears. "He wasn't breathing," he gasped. "She wasn't either. I just thought she was resting." His voice strained into a high-pitched strangled cry and for fully half a minute he tried to regain his composure.

The clock chimed noon. They had been talking for just an hour. Roehler seemed to have an almost complete and quite remarkable recall. If anything, he was inclined to get into too much detail, seemingly able—for the most part—to divorce himself from the painful emotions of his recent loss.

"So, he wasn't breathing when you first saw him?" Ray asked.

"No, because his mouth was just sort of fixed open . . . just sort of hanging open . . . and I probably would have thought that Verna was okay except that I knew she would have been saying something. She wasn't saying anything . . . I thought, 'My God, is she not breathing free?' . . . I just couldn't believe it."

"She had her head out of the water?" Tuller asked.

"Yeah . . . just at the water's edge . . . it was just clearing the water. It wasn't high up and it wasn't down in the water . . . and then I saw that he was really in trouble, and she was not helping him, you know, and the dog was swimming around. It had a leash on, and I kept talking to the dog because . . . telling it to just stay down. Finally, she settled on my back and put her paws on the back of my head, and that was okay because she really wasn't pushing me down.

"And then after we went to the Rock and I got rid of the dog, Doug just got colder and colder, and she was harder and harder to hold up and I really thought we'd had it until I saw another boat coming down from the west. And he was way out, and I thought, 'Oh God, he's not going to hear me either,' and for some reason they did, and they came over and I kept telling Doug and Verna, 'We've made it. We're gonna make it. We're really gonna make it. Come on.' And it took them a while to get to us. I don't know why."

His voice became quieter, and the detectives had to strain to hear.

"And then we were too close to the rocks and the guy threw us a rope and I thought, 'God, I can't do anything with that rope because I'm holding both of them.'"

His voice broke, but again he collected himself quickly. "And then finally I grabbed both with one hand and then grabbed the rope and the guy backed the boat up so he could pull us away from the rocks. And then we pulled over by the ladder and there was a man on board, and he reached down and grabbed Doug and pulled him on board, and then there must have been another man on board, 'cause two of them grabbed Verna and pulled her up.

"And then the guy said, 'You're okay. You can come up now.' I said, 'Oh, God . . .'"

At that point, tears rolled silently down Roehler's cheeks. He wiped them away with the back of his hand. "I told the guy . . . 'I can't move . . . my legs aren't moving.'"

After several unsuccessful attempts to get him out of the water, Roehler said, the man from the *Morning Star* came over in his dinghy and removed the camera from around his neck.

"And then a little wave or something basically sandwiched me between the boat and the dinghy, and then I just went out . . ."

He began to weep again. The detectives gave him time to recover.

" . . . And I woke up at St. John's." His voice was a whisper. "And I finally spelled my name for them, and I asked about Verna and Doug, and they said something about they were in the hospital and were okay. Then they brought a priest in and a doctor, and they told me about Verna and Doug."

He began to weep again, quietly.

He had sent his friend Dick Velthoen out to retrieve the dog off the Rock the next day. "I last saw her three or four feet above the water line. And I said, 'Dick, I really feel the dog's still on the island.' And he said, 'The Coast Guard says she's not.' But he found the dog. She had spent the whole night on the island."

The thought of the dog alone and cold for a long night in the middle of the ocean seemed to affect him more than anything else that had happened, and he wept profusely, his shoulders hunched and shaking with sobs.

Ray and Tuller stayed with him for another hour. He answered every question with quiet precision, describing distances, what Verna and Doug were wearing, and detailing again his own attempts to save them.

As the chiming clock on the living room wall struck 1:00 p.m., Fred Ray ended the interview, but needed permission to search the *Perseverance.* He had not brought a search warrant.

No problem, Roehler told them. Dick Velthoen had the key; all they had to do was call him. He could not have been more cooperative.

Ray decided to press his luck. "Fred, do you think somehow . . . there's a way we can figure out . . . to make sure there's no foul play or anything like that with this?" Turning innocently to Tuller, he said, "You're the expert here—do you know how to go about it?"

"Well, a couple of ways," Tuller ventured. "If you're willing to have a polygraph examination . . ."

There was barely a moment's hesitation. "Sure," Roehler said.

"Or how about a voice stress test?" Tuller offered.

"Would that be all right with you?" Ray asked.

"Yeah. I think I would probably have to talk to my attorney, and then find out just exactly what . . . really . . . I should be doing." The same would apply, Roehler conceded, on second thought, to the polygraph.

Bang goes that chance, Ray thought. Lawyers were as likely to let their clients take a polygraph as seagulls were to migrate to the desert.

Roehler had nothing further to say on the subject.

Ray closed his notebook. Tuller could feel the cigarette pack burning a hole in his pocket.

Roehler folded his notes, stood up, and drew in a chest full of air.

But Ray wasn't quite finished. He had just one more question. "Er . . . Fred . . . were they both insured?"

"Yeah. The whole family was insured."

Ray reopened his notebook. "Was that in her name, or your name?"

"Well, we had just set it up because we were gonna be taking this trip. We had just set up a trust and gone through the whole estate planning thing with Bill Fairfield."

Fairfield was his lawyer as well as his good friend.
"Okay," said Ray. "How much were these policies for?"
There was a slight hesitation. "I think there's $400,000 each on myself and Verna, and $60,000 on each of the four children."

14

Murder for Profit?

Malibu, January 7, 1981

Detectives Ray and Tuller finished their interview with Fred Roehler around 3:30 p.m. and drove onto Pacific Coast Highway. They stopped at the Trancas Coffee Shop opposite the beach and ordered sandwiches and coffee.

"Phew," Tuller said, lighting another filter-tip, his second since leaving Roehler's house, and inhaled deeply. "Four hundred thousand bucks . . . that's gonna buy a helluva lot of gas for his yacht."

"No kidding," Ray agreed. "And how many people do you know who insure their kids for sixty thousand bucks apiece? Let's go hit him again—today," Ray decided. "Once he talks to his lawyer, we may not get another chance."

Ray got on the phone. "Sorry to bug you again, Fred, but there are a couple of extra things we'd like to ask you about. We need to come over and talk to your parents anyway, that way we can finish it all up today."

As before, Roehler was pleasant. "Yes, and my mother-in-law is around, too. You should talk to her as well."

Fritz Roehler described the events of January 2 in an unemotional, detached narration, as if he had been a spectator rather than one of the main players. He told them of the family leaving Ventura Harbor early to make high tide, of taking a nap after lunch and waking up to find Kirsten asleep in the salon, and then almost immediately receiving a visitor on board who told them about the accident and asked for oxygen. After the helicopters had taken the bodies away and whisked Fred to the hospital, they discovered they couldn't raise the anchor.

"I said, 'Hell, we want to get out of here before dark, just cut the damn line,' but somebody from another boat radioed over that those anchors cost $800 to $900 and he told us he'd come aboard and help."

Fritz said his son and daughter-in-law were planning their cruise to Mexico. They were going to take off for about four months, but first, Fred, who had been off work for some time, had to settle some back-pay matters with his employers at Point Mugu. "He's been off with a bad back," Fritz explained. "Every so often it goes out on him."

"How long's he been off work?" Ray asked.

"I think about almost a year, but he was supposed to go back on the sixteenth of this month."

"Has he been getting any money?" Ray asked casually.

"No, but I understand his back pay is supposed to be paid before he goes back."

"How were they going to finance their trip to Mexico?"

"They're quite well off financially, to be honest with you."

Their son certainly seemed to have had a lot of tragedy in his life, Fred Ray noted. He had also lost his first wife, hadn't he?

Fritz nodded his assent.

"Oh, by the way, how did she die?"

"She had an aneurysm," Fritz replied. "A blood vessel broke in her brain, as near as we can figure. That's what the head neurologist at Westlake Hospital told us. She lived about six or seven days on machines that were hooked up."

And hadn't Verna also lost her husband in tragic circumstances?

"As near as I can understand, he was a structural steelworker and he fell some thirty stories from an open elevator shaft, or something like that. In fact, they are going to . . . the bodies are to be cremated and Verna's husband Bill's ashes are in a niche in one of those funeral homes, and according to his mother and father, they want all their ashes brought out and all three of them spread at sea."

"I guess Verna was pretty wealthy, too, wasn't she?" Ray inquired.

"Well, she has real estate. I mean, I don't know about wealthy, because I think her only source of income—well, she was a teacher's aide at school or something like that. She got Social Security for the children. I think that's what it consisted of."

Then it was Charlotte Roehler's turn. Once she got started, there was no stopping her.

"I really feel bad about this, you know, for two reasons. I have been dying to get out here and get on this boat. Last year I went shopping for boats with them and then my brother and his wife, who were headed to Hawaii, came out and got on the boat and had a ride, and I was just P.O.'d that they beat me to it, you know."

Charlotte described the early part of the journey. She told them that Douglas had wanted to go in the dinghy with Scott and Ginny, but Fred had suggested instead that he stay and go in the dory with his mother and father.

Then, with great emotion and excitement, Charlotte recounted the dreadful moments when they realized their son, his wife, and stepson were in terrible trouble. She had tried to keep everyone's spirits up.

"So, then the kids all start crying . . . I thought to myself, this can't be real, this can't be real . . . what do you do? Not only to try and help them, but to help the kids. And I had 'em all quieted down and they were all praying, and we were on the radio. I don't know how to work any of that, but my husband was trying to get the information, you know, on the radio . . . and then they said that they were suffering from . . . what they call it when you get cold . . . ?"

"Hypothermia," Ray said.

"Yeah, hypothermia."

The whole thing gave her a feeling of helplessness. "I feel that if I would have been on top I could have heard 'em holler or something. I give swimming lessons. I've had life-saving and I think about it, and I might have done something foolish and dove over the side . . . and you know . . . 'cause I'm not used to swimming in the ocean."

"Had there been any tensions or anything during the day—any quarreling?" Ray asked.

Charlotte straightened. "No. Believe me. So help me God. This is so unreal . . . when I see some of these other people . . . how they live . . . how they raise their children, and they're walking around and here is this beautiful little family . . . and I mean, there was love in this family . . . and, I mean, discipline . . ."

"Was Doug a good swimmer?" Ray asked. "How would you classify him, you being a teacher of swimming?"

"An advanced intermediate. He could handle himself. He had a life jacket on." Charlotte continued, "The way I have it figured, he had to come up under the boat and hit his head. He's quick and he was fast, he was gutsy. God!"

"Was Verna a very good swimmer?"

"She's a good swimmer. They've taken them all to the Y and everything and had advanced lessons for the kids and all. They've all had a lot of swimming lessons. Kirsten was taking lessons. She could swim. They all could."

Charlotte told the detectives how happy she'd been when her son had met and married Verna. "They each had two children and they all went to this little church and the minister is who got these two families together, 'cause they felt so sorry for them. They needed a father, and they needed a mother, and he was the instigator of getting them together and all . . . and it was a marriage of families, not just Fred and Verna, but the children and everything."

She told them about the tragedy of Fred's life, the death of his first wife Jeanne. And now his second wife was gone too. She was overwhelmed with the enormity of her son's despair.

"You get to the point, you don't believe in anything. Hey, it's supposed to be the golden years. You raise them all, you educate 'em. We'll be married forty years this summer," she continued, "and we're joined right here at the hip, and if he goes, I want to go with him."

Charlotte finally paused. "I'm sure you want to talk to the others."

The detectives rose and prepared to leave, but Charlotte had a last word. "I'd trade places with Verna. So help me God, I would."

Detectives Ray and Tuller found Verna Roehler's mother, Camelia Zeitner, in her simply furnished studio apartment over the garage of her daughter's Broad Beach Road duplex. She was in her mid-sixties, silver-haired, with a thin, soft face and pretty eyes. Cam looked worn, the signs of a difficult life etched on her pale face, but she held herself proudly and tried valiantly to keep her voice steady as she welcomed them. She may have lived modestly, but the view of the ocean out her windows was the same one that some of her neighbors had paid a fortune for.

Cam and her daughter had had a close relationship, and Kimberly and Doug were the joy of their grandmother's life, especially since her husband died.

Cam had been on the edge of poverty most of her life, and maintaining a genteel front had consumed much of her energy over the years. People in her position didn't ask too many questions; they took what was offered in kindness and gave thanks for it. She was devoutly religious. God arranged the inequities of life, she felt. One day it would all be explained to her, but for now, her faith would pull her through.

But still nagging at the back of her mind were her own doubts. Why were the police here? She didn't think she could bear it if there was any more to her daughter and grandson's death than an Act of God. She wanted to help her grieving son-in-law and his remaining family get back to normal as quickly as she could. If that meant having to put up with a lot of questions, so be it.

Her voice shook as she gave Ray and Tuller a list of those she considered Verna's best friends. Paddy Leitelt, she said, was Verna's closest friend. She had lived next door to her in the other half of her duplex before Cam had come to live there. She had known Verna the longest. It was a name that had been missing from the list of Verna's friends Fred Roehler had given them, so Ray made careful note of her address.

This was Ray's fourth interview of the day, and he was tired, so he got right to the point. "Do you know if Fred and Verna were having any marital problems?"

"Oh, definitely not." Cam was firm. "This is what makes it so hard to accept, this accident, because you know, you see the marital problems and you see people who aren't worth—that's not fair to say—worth living. I've never heard them raise their voices to each other, and that's hard to say of any couple. And I'm around them a lot because I live close."

"Any financial problems that you know of?" Ray asked.

"No. Definitely not. I don't know about their finances. They never skimp on anything. They never seem to be concerned if they spend an extra dime rather than try to find a bargain or something like that. I can't help but be a little bit envious of people who don't have to count their pennies."

Ray nodded sympathetically. "So, no problems that you're aware of, and you're pretty close?"

"I hope I am close. I don't think you could find me much closer. I mean, my daughter and I were extremely close. We shared a lot. She shared before she got married and since she's been married; I mean, if there was something she was keeping back, you'd almost feel it."

"Verna's first husband Bill died quite strangely?"

Ray's question seemed to startle her.

"Well, if you want to look up records, it's on his death certificate as a suicide. That's hard for Verna or me to ever have accepted. That was thoroughly investigated. Bill had some problems, but there, too, was another good marriage. I mean, nothing to do with their marriage. I never could understand it."

"What happened? Was it an accident?"

"We feel accidental. If you're asking me questions, I feel like I should be honest with you. I shouldn't have said it . . . because it was never talked about. Bill fell off a building where he had been working, and to all our knowledge, he went there to check up on something. Where did you hear your information?" Cam asked edgily.

"Oh, just talking to members of the family . . . Fritz."

"They probably don't know what the death certificate said."

"Fred's dad told us he fell down an elevator shaft."

Cam was nervous now. She'd let a family secret out of the bag unnecessarily.

"I probably shouldn't have even said that. I would rather you didn't even bring it out in somebody else's conversation."

Ray apologized. "We're nosy and we really have to find out. But you know it's our job. Say it wasn't an accident, say it was suicide . . . just say that. What would have caused it?"

"Well, Bill had"—here, Cam struggled for the right words—"what do you say? Psychiatric problems? Depression? He had been to a doctor for it."

"What was causing the depression?"

"We never knew that . . . it had nothing to do with their marriage."

"Did Verna know Fred then?"

Ray's line of questioning was worrying Cam. Why were the police here anyway, she wondered. Was it just routine after an accident? Why were they asking these sorts of questions?

"I wish you would find out, could find out what actually happened," she said, referring to the deaths of Verna and Doug, her voice trembling.

Did she have reservations still? Fred Ray asked her.

No, it wasn't that. She had no doubts at all about what Fred had told her, it was just . . .

"I'm personally hoping for our own sanity that they were both hit on the head with the boat as it capsized, because they were both good swimmers," Cam said. "Because the fact that, you know, Doug had his life jacket on, which should have saved him. Verna wasn't the most expert swimmer, but she could swim. The cold water sure would have gotten to her, though."

Ray returned to the subject of Verna's first husband, asking if Bill had been insured. How much money had he left Verna?

Cam said she didn't know. She hadn't sustained such a good relationship with her daughter by poking her nose in where she felt it didn't belong. "It was nothing pertaining to me, and I didn't ask," she explained. "If she wanted to tell me, she would have . . . I mean, there was nothing secretive about it. I knew she was taken care of, as far as I didn't have to help . . . but as far as was it $100,000 or $50,000, I couldn't give you an amount. I may have heard it a long time ago. If she was in dire circumstances, I might have known more about it."

It was dark outside, and the detectives wanted to make sure they had time to see Fred Roehler again. They were about to end the interview, but Cam wanted them to know that she had mixed feelings about them being there. Her first instinct, she said, had been to resent their presence at a time like this, but then she'd had second thoughts. "I mean, if there had been any suspicion of foul play, then you have to be thankful there's somebody who steps in and looks into it . . . something like this."

"Yeah, well," Ray's tone was placatory, "it doesn't have to be really an indication of foul play. Any tragic death or vehicle accident has to be investigated."

"But . . . I mean, you can't help but wonder, in my mind, the kind of questions you're asking . . . if you're suspicious."

Malibu Soccer team Lions, 1978. Fred Roehler in sweater. Ivor Davis in black and white shirt. Douglas Johnson is second from left, front row. Gideon Davis is seventh from left, front row. *Photo from author's collection.*

Fred Roehler, Sally Ogle Davis, and Ivor Davis at Folsom Prison visit, 1982. *Photo from author's collection.*

Fred Roehler and family at County Fair in San Luis Obispo, August 1980. *Trial Evidence.*

Fred Roehler and his stepson, Douglas Johnson, 1978 Malibu Beach wedding—to Doug's mother, Verna Johnson Roehler. *Trial Evidence.*

Verna Johnson Roehler at wheel of yacht Perseverance, 1981. *Trial Evidence.*

Fred on his yacht. *Trial Evidence.*

Fred and his first wife Jeanne. *Trial Evidence.*

Family photo of the late Jeanne Roehler with her children. *Photo courtesy of Schoonhoven Family.*

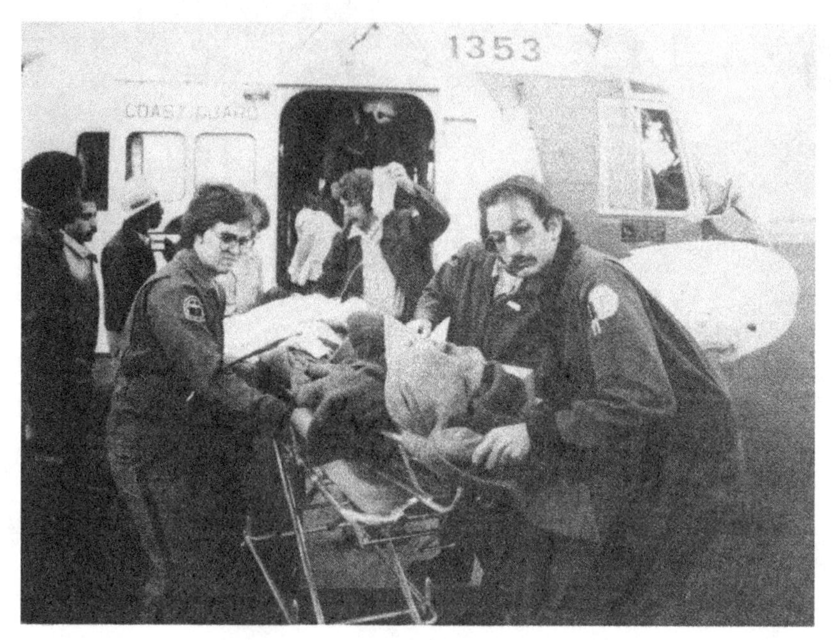

Fred Roehler is moved from rescue helicopter to hospital in January 1981. *Photo courtesy of the Santa Barbara News Press.*

Fred in handcuffs after arrest. *Photo courtesy of the Santa Barbara News Press.*

James Farley, Fred Roehler's chief defense lawyer. *Photo courtesy of the Santa Barbara News Press.*

William Fairfield, Fred Roehler's best friend and lawyer. *Photo courtesy of the Fairfield family.*

Fred Ray, Santa Barbara Sheriff's chief investigator. *Photo courtesy of the Santa Barbara News Press.*

Claude Tuller, Santa Barbara Sheriff Chief Investigator. *Photo courtesy of the Santa Barbara News Press.*

Judge John T. Rickard—Trial judge in Roehler murder. *Photo courtesy of the Santa Barbara News Press.*

Stanley Roden, Santa Barbara District Attorney. *Photo courtesy of Stanley Roden.*

15

The Death of Jeanne Roehler

Santa Barbara, January 7, 1981, 6:20 p.m.

Ray and Tuller had been interviewing for seven hours straight when they sat down again with Fred Roehler. They'd come to Malibu to investigate the deaths of Verna Roehler and Douglas Johnson, but there was another death they hadn't even touched on when they'd first talked with Roehler. Now they wanted to know more.

"How did Jeanne die?" Ray asked. "We've gotten two or three different stories."

Roehler's answer was scarcely direct.

"She had been a stewardess for United Airlines . . . I'm trying to think of where a narrative of the whole thing turned out to be . . ."

Ray's mind went into overdrive. *A narrative of the thing?* He'd simply asked how his first wife had died, and Roehler was responding with "a narrative of the thing." This guy needs a script to tell him who his kids are, Ray thought.

Roehler began the "narrative" in his flat, Midwestern accent. "In essence, she was on the phone with a girlfriend. She had gotten back from a trip. Heidi was our oldest and she was in the hospital, Los Robles, for tonsils, tonsils out . . . and I had Kirsten at home, and I had just come back from Heidi when Jeanne came home. And she was talking to a friend on the phone, and I went out and got into the hot tub, and about a half-hour later she came out and sat down and asked me what I was drinking. I said all I had was a beer, and she said she'd really prefer some wine rather than mine. So, I went back in the house and she said, 'Would you check Kirsten when you go inside?'"

The story had obviously been told many times before; he was talking fast, and Ray would have bet the recitation never changed.

"And I went into the kids' bedroom and changed her and then I got a bottle of wine and some ice, and when I went back outside, she was in the pool, facedown."

There had been no sound. Jeanne Roehler had apparently drowned in her own backyard, in total silence.

As if reading their minds, Roehler went on. "And we had two dogs, a German shepherd and a Dachshund, and they were both just lying there, looking in the water. The house is probably . . . from Kirsten's window to the pool would be about fifty to sixty feet. It was a warm night and the windows were open and there just was no sound at all. The dogs didn't bark. The big shepherd, which my parents have now, used to bark every time someone would go in the water."

"What happened?" Ray asked.

"Well, I pulled her out and I started mouth-to-mouth with her, and I called the neighbor who lives next door, for him to call Dr. Morgenstern, who lived across the street. And Dr. Morgenstern came over and started doing a cardiac bump and I was doing mouth-to-mouth, and the paramedics came and they got her . . . and everything's fine, and then they transported both of us to Westlake. She was in a coma and, like, six or seven days later, she died of pneumonia."

"But you don't know what . . . nobody knows what happened?"

"The autopsy didn't show anything, and we talked to United's medical people about it, and she had vertigo a couple of times, and I can't recall the exact name . . . it's an inner ear problem. But all those were just sketchy and sort of far-fetched. We just didn't know."

As soon as Ray and Tuller arrived back in Santa Barbara they contacted Larry Gillespie. They felt that the information they had gathered—$400,000 insurance on Verna Roehler and $60,000 on her son, the strong indication that Douglas Johnson had been virtually forced to go out in the boat, and the knowledge that Jeanne Roehler had also drowned—gave them enough to take to the DA.

Santa Barbara Deputy District Attorney Terry Cannon was planning to leave the DA's office for private practice and was looking for a crackerjack case to go out on. He listened intently as Ray filled him in on Fred Roehler. Cannon was a passionate man of action and he'd been in a few tight corners in his time. Like Fred Ray, Cannon was bothered by Roehler's finely detailed story.

"It doesn't feel right," he said. "There's no way in this kind of panicky, semi-hysterical situation, under this kind of stress, he could recall this kind of detail."

Ray agreed. "Yeah, but one thing doesn't fit. Why would a guy bump off his wife and kid on a family outing with his folks along for the ride? And that anchorage isn't exactly a deserted spot, particularly on vacation weekends."

"Maybe that's the beauty of the thing," Cannon said. "Happy family out for the day with the kids, Grandma and Grandpa, and a dog. Who'd think of that as a setting for murder? All that's missing is the apple pie. And his first wife just happened to drown, and he just happens to be a rich man today thanks to the fact his second wife is no longer with us." Cannon paused. "So, we have the motive, we have the opportunity, and we have a guy who makes his living in the water and could certainly pull something like this off. What we don't have is evidence. Let's take another look at those bodies."

It turned out to be more difficult than they thought. The Westwood Mortuary in Los Angeles told Larry Gillespie that Verna and Douglas's bodies had already been cremated. No bodies—no case.

"Are you certain?" Gillespie asked.

They would recheck.

Minutes later they were back on the line. "You're in luck—we're so swamped that we're running two days behind. The bodies are still here."

Gillespie breathed a sigh of relief. "Put a hold on them. This is a homicide investigation. I'm on my way."

On January 9, 1981, at 8:00 a.m., Terry Cannon, along with the beginnings of his investigative team—Detectives Ray and Tuller, Larry Gillespie, and three cops from the Sheriff's criminalistics bureau—gathered at Santa Barbara's Cottage Hospital to supervise the second autopsy of Verna Jo Roehler and Douglas Johnson. They only had one day to find what they were looking for, as the judge who'd issued the warrant insisted the bodies be returned to the mortuary within twenty-four hours.

Just before he left the morgue, Cannon took a last look at the bodies of Verna Jo Roehler and Douglas Johnson stretched out on the examining tables. They looked too alive, he thought, to have been dead for a week. It seemed as if at any moment they'd open their eyes, say "How ya doin'?," and jump off the table. Cannon had a son the same age as Douglas. He turned his head away. "If you find anything," he whispered to Ray, "I want this case."

Santa Barbara County does not have a resident professional coroner. Pathology duties are performed under contract to the county by an outside medical team led by a clinical pathologist, rather than specially trained forensic pathologists. So Dr. Dewitt Talmadge Hunter had only a limited background in criminal pathology. His experience was with natural death, and he had never been called upon to re-autopsy a body. But the Santa Barbara sheriff's department felt they had a crime on their hands, and the doctor knew that unless he found some evidence of physical injury, it would be virtually impossible to pursue that crime. With this in mind, he took scalpel in hand and began his dissections.

The initial work was slow and routine. A minute reexamination of Verna's body revealed little that was unusual. Only a broken fingernail on a finger of her right hand had not been recorded in the previous autopsy. Could it be a defensive wound, suggesting some kind of struggle, he wondered? There were a few superficial bruises on her head, but nothing significant.

However, when Hunter turned to Douglas's tiny frame, he thought he saw more. There were superficial bruises, he said, on the left and right thighs and the right heel, even an abrasion on the boy's right shoulder and the right side of his abdomen. No district attorney was going to get excited about that, though; it could hardly be considered unusual for an eight-year-old kid.

As Hunter worked, a cameraman from the sheriff's criminalistics division videotaped the proceedings, the first time an autopsy had ever been recorded on tape in Santa Barbara. It was a measure of the importance they attached to the proceedings.

Hunter examined the internal organs that had been neatly sealed in a plastic bag in Douglas's abdominal cavity by Dr. Craig Duncan in Ventura.

"These lungs don't look like drowning lungs to me," Hunter offered, "but we can't draw conclusions from that."

But when he got to the skull, he became uncharacteristically animated. "There are bruises here," he said. "Look."

Detective Ray leaned forward and looked through a magnifying glass; on closer examination, he could see a definite pinkish discoloration, three to four inches in length, and a second one, one-half to two inches wide on the right-hand side of the back of the boy's head. Slightly below it and more to the center, a more elongated bruise, approximately one to one and a half inches in length, extended toward the right ear.

"Those have to be the result of sufficient force applied to the outside of the head to cause the skin to split and tear here," said Hunter.

With the camera carefully documenting his every move, he took cross sections of the bruised portions for later study. Then, for a second time in six days, Douglas Johnson's brain was removed from his skull, cross-sectioned, and set aside for microscopic studies later.

By 4:15 p.m. the autopsy was over.

The investigators drove to Terry Cannon's office to give him a report.

"Nope, that's not good enough," said Cannon. "It's just too bitty; we can't make anything stick with a few superficial bruises. These could have happened when they were pulled out of the water. Hell, the Coast Guard could have done that. Tell Hunter to have another go. Tell him to find me something I can go to court with."

With the judge's deadline for the return of the bodies looming, Hunter went back and subjected them to an unprecedented third examination. The next morning, Verna and Douglas were finally returned to the mortuary in Los Angeles and cremated almost immediately.

Fred Ray had thought about keeping them in Santa Barbara. "That's where our evidence is coming from," he said. "Maybe we'd better keep them around."

"No way," said Larry Gillespie. "They've got to go back to Westwood. Hunter's got his slides and tissue samples, and that's the best we can do."

No one told Fred Roehler or any member of his family what had happened in the past twenty-four hours. As far as Roehler knew, the bodies had been cremated one week earlier.

From the moment they realized that Fred Roehler had profited to the tune of almost $500,000 from the death of his second wife, detectives Ray and Tuller realized they were simultaneously investigating the murders of two wives, not one.

They contacted the Los Angeles coroner for his report on Jeanne Roehler's death and learned that the routine autopsy had found no evidence of foul play. They tried in vain to persuade the Los Angeles Sheriff's Department to reopen the investigation considering subsequent events. There was no reason to assume, they were told, that after six years, anyone would change their minds. The sheriff's refusal was all the more frustrating to the two detectives because of what they were hearing daily from Jeanne's colleagues at United Airlines.

Long layovers at airports provide plenty of time for exchanging advice and confidences. Stewardesses knew more about each other's lives than their own family members. And there wasn't a flight attendant Jeanne had worked with who couldn't give an almost clinical rundown on the state of her marriage.

Jeanne Sias, the woman who'd made the long phone call to Jeanne Roehler the night she died—the last person to speak to her besides her husband—told the detectives that a definite date had been set for Jeanne and Fred to separate. Jeanne Roehler had told all her friends she was afraid that if Fred ever found out about her affair, he would kill both her and her lover, and leave the country. Jeanne Roehler, Sias told them, was so fearful that she took Fred's loaded gun from their house and gave it to a friend to hide.

Lori Swanson, another United flight attendant, told Ray and Tuller that she had flown several times with Jeanne during the last weeks of her life, and that she'd shown up for work with red bruises on her neck. When quizzed about them, she'd said Fred had tried to kill her.

"Oh come on, don't exaggerate," Lori had chided.

"No," Jeanne said, "the bastard tried to kill me last night."

The same day they interviewed Swanson, Claude Tuller got a telephone call from Joyce Feldman, another United stewardess who had flown the Chicago turnaround flight with Jeanne on the day she drowned. She said Jeanne, for the whole month before, had made no secret of her unhappiness, or the fact that she was seeing someone else. It was common knowledge, she said, that Jeanne was planning to divorce her husband.

By now Ray and Tuller were also getting calls from women in Malibu on an almost daily basis. Trying to sift the gossip from the truth was not easy, but they decided Barbara Leonard, a neighbor of the Roehlers, sounded genuine.

The tall, red-haired mother of three had babysat for Fred and Jeanne for more than a year right after Kirsten was born. The story sounded familiar: Jeanne was very unhappy and fearful of her husband. She told them Jeanne had taken a gun to Verna Johnson's house to get it out of the way. Jeanne had been happy while Fred was in Kauai and, far from encouraging him to come back for her birthday, she had been dreading his return. Just a week before she drowned, Jeanne had told Barbara Leonard that Fred had finally agreed to split up.

"He's going to move up north to a rental we have in Oxnard," Jeanne had told her.

But after Jeanne's death, Fred assured Barbara Leonard that he and Jeanne had worked out most of their problems and that he had been optimistic about their future together.

At the time of Jeanne's death, Barbara said she'd had grave doubts that it was an accident, but when she had told friends of her suspicions, they had convinced her that indeed, it had happened the way Fred said it had.

"Now, however," she concluded, "how anyone can believe that Verna and Doug's deaths were accidental, I just don't know."

16

Murder Most Foul

Santa Barbara, January 10, 1981

It was Saturday, normally their day off, but by ten in the morning detectives Fred Ray and Claude Tuller had driven the eighty-five miles from Santa Barbara to the small home of John and Paddy Leitelt in the broiling California desert. They were Verna's closest friends and her former next-door neighbors. They had seen her through her widowhood and remarriage, but they had left Malibu for good the Christmas Eve before Verna died. They hadn't seen her since Paddy and she had dined together a month before their departure.

There was obviously no love lost between the Leitelts and Fred. Ray and Tuller could see that immediately. Roehler had come between them and Verna. He'd edged them out of her life and her duplex so that living in Malibu became too expensive for them. Was their animosity toward him simple resentment at an outsider who'd caused the rift . . . or something else?

Paddy, a slender petite blonde, said they'd known Fred from the time he was married to his first wife, Jeanne. Paddy and Verna had been friends of Jeanne, and the three of them had spent a lot of time together. Roehler's first marriage had been on the skids; Paddy was in no doubt about that. Jeanne loved to gossip. She'd lay out all of her problems no matter how intimate. Everybody knew about them. Jeanne had no secrets except from Fred.

She and Verna had known all about Jeanne's long-standing affair, Paddy told the detective. "But Fred didn't know any of it. Jeanne said he'd told her he would kill her if he ever found her fooling around, or if she ever tried to leave him."

Fred and Jeanne's sex life was raked over the coals every time the girls got together.

"Jeanne could be quite wicked," Paddy remembered. "We'd be sitting around the pool, and he'd come out in his tiny little bikini bathing suit that didn't leave much to the imagination—you know, the kind they wear in Europe—and she'd say under her breath, 'Here comes the minute man.' She used to call him Mr. P.E."

Jeanne had told her friends for years that she wanted a divorce, but Fred wouldn't hear of it.

It was in October 1976, the month Jeanne died, that Paddy said things came to a head.

Fred called his wife from Hawaii and Jeanne told him she was going to leave him.

"Jeanne told me Fred started crying on the phone and begged her not to leave, at least until he got home."

Then a week before her death, Jeanne told her Fred had suddenly had a change of heart. He'd agreed to the divorce. Jeanne was delighted it would all be settled amicably. In any case, she had made up her mind to leave, with or without Fred's consent. Even so, Paddy said, after Fred's return from Hawaii, Jeanne had taken a gun her husband kept at the house over to Verna's duplex and asked her to keep it for her.

"She just didn't want it around," said Paddy. "She was very frightened of it."

It had taken Ray and Tuller some time to catch up with Candy Hinman, whose telephone call had begun their investigation. By now her story had received lots of corroboration.

Candy had known Jeanne, she told them, since their children were toddlers. They would visit together about twice a week for coffee, where Fred was often the subject of conversation. Jeanne made no bones about the fact that she wanted out of her marriage.

Candy told them about one occasion when Jeanne had shown up at her house sporting a black eye. She told them that the day before Jeanne died, she had run into her at a local bank and Jeanne told her that Fred had finally agreed to a divorce and was planning to move up to Oxnard. She said they would have to sell the Calpine house because they couldn't afford to live in Malibu on their individual salaries. Fred had warned her to keep quiet about their impending separation.

Despite her suspicions after the death, Candy introduced Fred to her friend Gloria Hunnicut, and they had begun dating.

For weeks after the drownings, through January and February of 1981, the detectives scoured Malibu, interviewing family and friends and anyone else who had seen the Roehlers up close. As someone who had spent some social and recreational time with Fred, I was also targeted by them. I knew the cops were obviously looking for negative stuff about Fred, but in my view, everything was totally positive.

"Fred is a victim of cultural misunderstanding," I told the cops. "He didn't actually fit into the 'let it all hang out' Malibu crowd. Sure, he was different. He came from a tightly run, Midwestern family, and so he disciplined his kids. Pity more parents didn't do that. He also alienated some of Verna's friends by pushing them out when he married her. And by doing this, they took an instant dislike to him. Then along comes this terrible tragedy and people say, 'Well, Fred was kind of weird—and this justifies all that negativity.'"

While Tuller and Ray were scouring Malibu, Santa Barbara Deputy District Attorney Terry Cannon was poring over the transcript of their interviews with Fred Roehler.

"The guy's a master at deflection," he told Fred Ray. "He packs so much irrelevant detail into his answers that you almost forget every time he's hit with a solid question, he's nowhere near answering it."

If a case was to be made against him, he would have to be pinned down. Roehler's story had to be cast in concrete.

"He's such a detail man. If we nail him, it's those details we're going to nail him with," Cannon told Ray. "Go back and run him through it one more time. And guys, this time get me something I can take to court—something I can run with."

Chapter 16

Four days after the second autopsies were completed on Verna and Doug, Fred Ray received a phone call from Dr. Hunter. He was in a state of high excitement, stuttering over the phone, so it took Ray a while to understand what he was trying to say.

"I think I may have what you're looking for," Hunter finally got out.

Ray raced across to the DA's office. "We've got him," he told Terry Cannon. "More premortem injuries. No way these could have been accidental. The medical people will knock the hell out of his story."

"Terrific," Cannon exclaimed, "but we're a long way from home. We need a motive. Let's take a look at that insurance."

Fred Roehler had been an insurance agent's dream, recalled Raymond Wylie, formerly of the Travelers Insurance Company. In the two years since taking out the mortgage on his Sea Level Drive house, Roehler must have kept and filed away every insurance flyer that ever came through his mailbox. In fact, he'd gone further, sending out blanket inquiry letters to insurance companies throughout Southern California, one of which, yellowed with age, had landed on Wylie's desk. He'd immediately called Roehler and set up an appointment with him for August 28, 1980, at his home.

Wylie was delighted to learn that Roehler had much bigger things in mind than the simple mortgage insurance the original flyer had solicited. He was having an estate plan drawn up to include life insurance for his wife, himself, and each of their four children.

A quick survey of the assets Roehler presented convinced Wylie, who'd been with Travelers for only five months, that he was in over his head, and he made an appointment with Roehler for the following week to include his supervisor, Tom Costanza.

Arriving at the appointed time at the Roehler home, Wylie said it looked as if a mini-insurance convention was going on. No one was at home, but two agents from a rival company were waiting outside in their car. Another agent had apparently just left, and the business cards of several others were stuck on the front door.

Later, on the phone, Roehler apologized for the mix-up and assured Wylie that there would be no other agents at their next meeting.

Fred Ray, having taken a statement from Wylie, decided to find out just exactly how extensive Fred Roehler's insurance shopping had been. He and Claude Tuller spent a day on the phone using the Los Angeles yellow pages, calling every listed insurance company in the city. There was scarcely one major company that didn't have someone who remembered Fred Roehler, the guy who lived "on the sand" in Malibu and was looking for an estate plan. He was a hot prospect; he and his wife owned extensive real estate, and they all wanted the account.

Everyone told the same story: Roehler wanted them to insure his family because they were planning to be gone on a sailing trip for several months.

Tom Costanza of Travelers told Ray and Tuller that Fred and Verna Roehler had signed their insurance documents at their home on September 25, 1980. "He told us the family planned to go away for Thanksgiving and he wanted everything to be signed, sealed, and delivered before they left," Costanza stated.

Thanksgiving came and went with no policies. By this time, Roehler was calling Ray Wylie a couple of times a week.

"He was very unhappy with us," Tom Costanza remembered, "and he had every right to be. He wanted to know what the hell the delay was in getting him the policies. Finally, he hit us with an ultimatum. Another company, he said, had offered to produce immediate coverage—we either put up or shut up."

The delay had been caused by Verna Roehler's high blood pressure, and Travelers offered to go ahead and ensure the rest of the family and finish Verna's policy later. But Roehler was adamant. "He told us it was all or nothing," Costanza remembered. "We either insured them all then and there, including Mrs. Roehler, or he would take his business elsewhere. It was one helluva account to lose, and we had invested a lot of time getting it."

Costanza pressured his people to get moving, and finally the company agreed to issue the policies immediately, covering Mrs. Roehler with a one-month binder until more detailed medical information could be obtained.

On Thursday, December 4, 1980, Ray Wylie personally delivered the policies to the Roehler home and collected the quarterly premiums. On December 16, Tom Costanza carried Verna Roehler's insurance contract to their home and collected the second-quarter premiums for all the policies. They were exactly as Fred Roehler had ordered: $400,000 each for father and mother, with $60,000 for each of the four children.

Then Costanza dropped the other shoe. There was a little something extra Roehler had neglected to mention to the detectives. The Roehlers had bought accidental death coverage on each other to the tune of an additional $300,000 each, with double indemnity on each of their four children. If either of the adult Roehlers died in an accident, the insurance payoff would not be the $400,000 the police had believed, but $700,000 on each other, and $120,000 on each child.

On December 29, Tom Costanza told the detectives, he discovered that he had neglected to charge them the additional premium for the accidental death coverage on Verna. He immediately contacted Roehler, who promised to mail him the payment immediately. Two days later, on December 31, 1980, the check ensuring that Verna was covered for accidental death arrived in Costanza's mail.

Santa Barbara, January 20, 1981

When Fred Ray and Claude Tuller faced Fred Roehler across his kitchen table for a third time, the atmosphere was very different from that of two weeks earlier. This time the two investigators believed Fred Roehler had killed his wife and her eight-year-old child, and that he'd done it for money: $820,000, to be exact—not the $460,000 they had previously believed. The death of his first wife, too, as far as they were concerned, stank like a frightened skunk.

The house on Sea Level Drive was still in turmoil. Roehler was in the middle of putting on a new roof. A cement mixer sat churning in the backyard. The remodeling was moving forward at speed, even though the mistress of the house had died just two weeks before.

This time no refreshments were taken. The interview was businesslike, interrupted only by the constant sound of hammering from a workman on the roof. Roehler seemed a little stiff, more wary than when they had last seen him.

"I see you're staying busy, Fred," said Ray. "It helps keep your mind off things. I guess if you were sitting around doing nothing, I bet it would be really difficult."

Roehler nodded silently. Ray read him his rights, having first switched on the tape recorder, this time in full view, and plunged immediately into his questioning.

Then, without looking at his notes or seemingly giving his next question any consideration at all, Ray asked, "Did you and Verna have any marital problems?"

"No," Roehler said, issuing a flat, unelaborated denial, delivered with neither emotion nor surprise, without irritation or anger.

"How would you describe your relationship? Your marriage, I mean."

There was a long uncomfortable pause and Ray was content to let it go on if Roehler wanted it to. Finally, Roehler looked up at them.

"I would say we had as good a relationship overall as anyone I know. We shared the same aspirations. We had gone through, really, a learning process for deciding what we really wanted to do with the children and buying the boat and all those things." He sighed deeply, a pained look: "We shared interest in each other, things that we liked to do, friends that we had, common friends. I don't really know what else."

Fred Ray had never been called upon to describe his relationship with his wife, but it occurred to him that Roehler didn't have the vocabulary for the job; he didn't know how to describe a relationship. How did he feel about her? Did he love her? Did she love him?

"Were you having any financial problems, or are you having any financial problems now?" Ray asked.

Roehler's reply was so quiet that they could barely hear his unelaborated "No."

At their request, he described the planned trip to Mexico, admitting that Verna had some fears about the shipping lanes and the fog. But they would have been gone, he said, for only four to six months, and she had begun to look forward to the adventure every bit as much as he had. It was going to be the trip of a lifetime.

Santa Barbara, February 14, 1981

On a chilly winter's morning, Detective Fred Ray shipped Fred Roehler's small orange dory to the swimming pool of San Marcos High School in Santa Barbara, taking along with him a woman detective from the sheriff's department, a ten-year-old boy, and a professor of mechanical and environmental engineering at the University of California at Santa Barbara.

With Ray playing Roehler, his female colleague, Verna, and the boy, Douglas Johnson, the trio reenacted the capsizing scene at Bird Rock on that bleak day just over a month earlier, exactly as Roehler had described it. Their tests were videotaped.

Back at the office, Ray called Terry Cannon: "We had a heck of a time trying to get that boat to turn over at all," he said. "It works like one of those bouncing rubber toys—you tip it one way and it bounces back. Now we're waiting for the engineering report."

When it appeared, the report was decisive. That dory, turning over even at the maximum rate possible, could not have created nearly enough force to cause any significant bruising to Douglas's head.

It had been a good week for Terry Cannon. The same day he was given the engineer's report, he received a letter from a pathologist in Texas famed for his work in forensic experimentation. He had studied Dr. Hunter's latest tissue samples and slides from Douglas's head. He was certain there were at least four separate injuries, and there was no doubt about it, he said: Those injuries had occurred prior to death.

Bill Fairfield had been in and out of town continuously since the deaths of his friend's wife and stepson, so it wasn't until three months later that Ray and Tuller were finally able to interview the man they believed might have handed Roehler a motive to murder.

Fairfield was nervous. His field of law was far removed from the criminal; estate planning, tax law, good, clean, corporate stuff—that was his specialty. Fairfield hadn't been around crime since an early stint right out of law school as a deputy DA. His father-in-law had been a cop; his brother-in-law was an FBI agent, and later, a Superior Court judge. The defense side of the table was not a place he'd ever expected to find himself, yet here he was, on behalf of the man he considered his best friend.

"Fred and I are extremely close," he told the detectives. "And I value my friendship with him a lot more than I do my attorney–client relationship. I've kind of been, you know, as a result of Jeanne's death and some of the other incidents that have happened to him prior to that period of time, some of the hard luck that he has had . . . I have a big shoulder to cry on."

He was most anxious to clear up any misconception there might be about Roehler's large life insurance purchase. It was he who had suggested that Fred buy the insurance as part of their estate plan.

The process had really begun in 1977 when Fred had brought a slightly nervous Verna into Fairfield's office just as she was preparing to move in with Fred. She was concerned about keeping control of her property and wanted to make a will so her own money and her duplex wouldn't be jeopardized by their living arrangement. He had helped them prepare wills in which Verna appointed Fred guardian of her two children, the guardianship to pass, if he died or was incapacitated, to her late husband's sister. She was also concerned about using Fred's name, since they did not yet intend to be legally married. So, Fred had given Fairfield a prepared statement to add to his file, which read:

> I am married to Verna Jo Johnson, also known as Verna Jo Roehler in the eyes of God and my peers, but not legally. It is our intention to marry legally in the future. However, at present our tax status, pension and other payments make it imprudent to be legally married at this time. It is our intent to live as husband and wife, and for that reason all references in this will to "my wife" are to her.
>
> There are four children included in the term "my children." They are Kim, Heidi, Doug, and Kirsten, two by my previous marriage and two by Verna Jo Johnson's former marriage.

Fairfield had witnessed the document.

With their joint purchase of the Sea Level Drive house in October of that year, Verna felt even more strongly the need to protect her own assets. She had just committed all of Bill's insurance to the new house, plus she had taken on joint responsibility for a refinancing loan on Fred's Calpine house. It made her feel insecure.

Any talk of estate planning was forestalled, however, when in October 1979, the athletic Fairfield had a massive heart attack and underwent a triple coronary bypass. On the evening before he was to go into hospital, his wife threw a party for him at which Bill got roaring drunk, but not so drunk that he didn't remember Fred Roehler saying to him, "Hey, when you get over this, fella, let's sit down and discuss my estate plan."

The next month as he lay recuperating in bed, Fred came to see him. "We need to get moving on this estate plan business," he told him, "so that we can get it all wrapped up before we leave."

They agreed to discuss it when Bill returned to the office. It was not in the office, however, but on Fred's new yacht, the *Perseverance*, that they next met. In brilliant May sunshine, they sat on the deck eating brown-bag lunches, and in between Fairfield's declarations of admiration for Fred's new toy, Roehler showed him a list he had prepared of his and Verna's assets, asking Fairfield to serve as trustee for the Johnson–Roehler family trust.

Fairfield agreed, with one proviso. He was concerned, he said, that there was no liquidity in their estates. It was all tied up in real estate. He didn't want to be forced to sell property at fire-sale prices in the event of an emergency, and he suggested that Verna and Fred buy life insurance to cover their liabilities.

Roehler's reply surprised him. "I don't like insurance," he said. "I'd rather have nothing to do with it."

But when Fairfield offered to call insurance agents for him, Fred immediately took charge. "No, thanks. I'll shop around myself."

On September 19, 1980, Fred brought Verna, now legally his wife, to meet Fairfield. For three hours they discussed the trust, until Fairfield was satisfied they understood its implications.

On the death of either of them, the trust would split in two, the survivors and the decedents' trust. He would prepare "pour-over wills," which meant that some of the decedents' assets would automatically transfer into the survivor's trust, so the survivor wasn't clobbered with heavy tax consequences. In the same way, it was important, he explained, that each of them own the policy of the other. If one of them died, the survivor would receive the insurance payout as his or her own property, and therefore, not subject to death taxes.

Consequently, on September 25, six days later, addendums were added to the Roehlers' Travelers Insurance applications, making Fred Roehler the beneficiary of Verna's policy and the sole owner of that policy during his lifetime. Verna was likewise the sole owner of Fred's policy.

In October 1980, Roehler told Fairfield that the life insurance coverage was complete, and he emphasized how important it was for the trust documents to be finished before Christmas, since they were planning to be out of town visiting Verna's sister in Northern California over Thanksgiving, and then they would be tied up with the Roehler family visit over Christmas.

On the last day of October, Fred and Verna dropped into Fairfield's office in Ventura to sign their wills, now redrawn as husband and wife, and to set the trust in motion. They were taking the children to a Halloween party and the four little Johnson-Roehlers were restlessly rampaging around the office dressed as witches and a pirate. Not surprisingly, no one paid too much attention to the matter at hand. In any case, there was not much to read. The actual property schedules involved in the trust were not included because Fairfield hadn't finished preparing them. So Verna signed without seeing exactly what properties were included, and in whose name.

When finished, the properties were dispersed exactly as Fred Roehler had requested. The Calpine house and the rented home in Oxnard were listed as Fred's separate property. The Broad Beach duplex was Verna's, and the Sea Level Drive house was community property, each spouse owning one-half. The yacht *Perseverance*, the purchase of which had been made possible by Verna's insurance money from the Broad Beach fire, was not included in the trust, and remained Fred's separate property outside the scope of the estate plan.

Since his marriage to Verna, Roehler had acquired a house on the beach in Malibu worth twice the value of his previous home, partially financed by Verna from her husband's insurance; a refinancing of his Calpine house, which he still owned, made possible by Verna's cosigning for the loan; and a $150,000 yacht, made possible by Verna's cash down payment. He had also acquired a $400,000 life insurance policy on himself and one on his wife for the same amount. Each policy would pay an additional $300,000 in the event of the accidental death of either of them, plus $60,000 life insurance policies on each of the four children, with double indemnity on each in the event of accidental death.

A few months earlier, Roehler had told his attorney that he didn't care for insurance. While Roehler had benefited over the years to the tune of several hundred thousand dollars from insurance, he had never committed himself to anything like the amount he was now undertaking. His Travelers policies brought his total insurance payments—fire insurance on all his homes and his yacht, and earthquake insurance on Sea Level Drive—to a colossal $8,000 a year, representing over 25 percent of his yearly salary from Mugu before deductions.

After backgrounding detectives Ray and Tuller, Fairfield said that just one week after Verna Roehler's death, he received a distraught phone call from Fred.

"He was absolutely beside himself. He told me he'd just opened the mail that had been lying there since before Christmas and he'd discovered another insurance policy he didn't even know he had. He wasn't even aware that it had been issued. He'd simply filled in an application for it and had heard no more about it. He was crying; he hadn't paid any premiums on it, but the effective date of the policy was January 1, the day before Verna and Doug drowned, and that threw him into a panic."

Fred Ray was taking notes so fast his fingers had gone numb: Roehler had another policy effective January 1—a policy he claims he didn't know he had.

"Fred said he felt terrible about the whole thing," Fairfield continued. "He said he didn't want the stuff. I almost got in the car and went down there, that's how upset he was. Fred asked me if he should pay the premium, and I said, 'No way.'"

Despite Fairfield's advice, however, Roehler did send in the premium payment on the policy he said he hadn't wanted and knew nothing about. It insured the mortgage on Verna's Broad Beach property, the sole piece of property that had belonged to her alone. As a result of that policy and Verna's death, her duplex now belonged to Fred, free and clear.

Driving back to Santa Barbara, Fred Ray shook his head. "Fairfield seems like a nice guy, but it looks like he may have been out of it with his heart surgery, and swallowed Roehler's tale hook, line, and sinker."

"Yeah," Tuller agreed, "but that's some trick—to get your lawyer to recommend $700,000 worth of insurance so you can say, 'Well, it wasn't my idea.'"

"Maybe Fairfield suggested the insurance in all innocence," Ray said, "but what he didn't know was that when Fred Roehler buys insurance, Fred Roehler collects."

Santa Barbara, March 25, 1981

After three months of investigation, Deputy DA Terry Cannon knew he had to go out to Bird Rock and walk through Roehler's version of what had happened. If he couldn't punch serious holes in Roehler's story, he'd never be able to convince a jury. So, on a cold gray March morning, with the waves pounding their launch and the wind cutting into them like a blast from the Arctic, Cannon and Fred Ray anchored at Little Scorpion and rowed in a small dory around the eastern corner of Bird Rock, to the point where Roehler said his boat had turned over.

What they learned that morning convinced Cannon that he could prosecute Fred for murder.

The prevailing current, Cannon found, flowed from west to east. If Roehler had simply draped the bodies over the upturned boat and hung on with them, in a matter of minutes they could have floated across the mouth of the anchorage and within hailing distance of *Perseverance* and other boats in the harbor.

But more, when Cannon tried to clamber up onto the rocks at the point where Roehler said he had tried to climb, he knew the story was fiction. The rock was completely covered with razor-sharp black mussels. After several futile attempts to climb up, Cannon's hands were gashed and bleeding profusely. Nothing in the hospital report said anything about cuts on Roehler's hands. In fact, his hands, neck, and head, where the small dog had supposedly scratched him, were unmarked.

"Whatever happened out here," Cannon told Ray. "It didn't happen the way Roehler said it did."

Chapter 16

On April 3, 1981, Fred Ray and Claude Tuller made the seventy-five-mile drive south to Malibu to arrest Fred Roehler.

In the house on the Malibu beach, the three little girls were up and going about their morning tasks, putting together their lunches for school and wolfing down the kind of incomplete, thrown-together breakfast kids make when there isn't a mother around to supervise.

It was 9:30 a.m. when the detectives knocked on the white-painted door of the blue, two-story oceanfront clapboard house. There was a long silence. They knocked again, louder this time. Tuller's heart was pounding as he felt for the reassurance of his gun.

Footsteps descended the stairs. The door opened a few feet.

Fred had hastily pulled on a pair of blue jeans, but his chest and feet were bare. He looked surprised, but not shocked as he recognized them. He knew they'd be coming. He just didn't know when.

"Frederick George Roehler," said Detective Fred Ray, "we have a warrant for your arrest for the murder of Verna Jo Roehler and Douglas Johnson."

Roehler asked if he could finish dressing, and they followed him around as he pulled on his shirt and tennis shoes. He was calm. That's what amazed them. He didn't protest. There was none of the usual, "Hey, you guys have made a mistake," or "What the hell is this?" or "You're out of your fucking mind!"

Ray had made hundreds of arrests. This one was eerie, quiet—unnatural. They could have been there to escort him to a business conference.

"Is it two counts?" he inquired calmly.

"That's right," Ray said coldly, "with special circumstances."

Under California law, "special circumstances" meant this was a death penalty case.

Still, there was no reaction. When Tuller cuffed him, he politely asked, "Is that really necessary?" He didn't protest again, but he asked them to pull the unmarked police car up to his front door so he could get in without the neighbors seeing.

In Colorado the next morning, John Schoonhoven was awakened at 5:30 a.m. by a call from California. It was a stewardess friend of Jeanne from United Airlines, and she was crying.

"Oh, John, did you hear? He killed them all."

For an instant, he felt his heart stop. What did she mean? Were all the children dead?

"Fred's been arrested for the murder of Verna and Doug. They say he killed Jeanne, too."

"I think Dad believed it for about twenty-four hours," his daughter Linda said later. "Then it was, 'Fred's innocent . . . victim of a terrible tragedy . . . persecuted by the police.'"

Their father's reaction left his daughters confused and bitter, but it was a position from which John Schoonhoven, at least publicly, was never to waver.

April 3, the day her eldest son was arrested on two counts of murder, was Charlotte Roehler's birthday. When her youngest son Scott returned from work that evening in Centerville, Indiana, his wife Ginny told him his brother was in jail.

That same evening, the young couple sat down with his parents for a celebratory birthday dinner. Scott had made up his mind: Nothing must be done to spoil Mother's birthday. The bad news could wait until tomorrow.

At seven the next morning, Scott took his father out to the back field behind the house and broke the news.

"We're taking the grandkids to the circus today," Fritz told him. "I'll tell her when we get back. I don't want to ruin her day."

The Roehlers entertained their grandchildren throughout the long Saturday with popcorn, cotton candy, and animal rides. Only after they'd dropped the children off with their parents and were driving back to Centerville did Fritz Roehler pull over to the side of the road.

The next morning, the Roehlers flew to California.

17

The Defense to the Rescue

Fred Roehler could not have found a more unlikely defender than James Matthew Farley. At forty-seven, he looked like the character actor he had once been. A bulky five-foot-eleven, his weight fluctuated between 250 and 280 pounds, and his broad Irish face was covered with a full gray beard and a head of thick, silvering hair. With his twinkling eyes hidden behind rimless glasses, he looked like an overweight friendly lion.

During the heat of trial, Farley had been known to escape to religious retreats to refresh his body and soul. Catholicism was the center of his life. The Agnus Dei was painted on the white front door of his Ventura house on Agnus Drive, and the last four digits of his home phone number spelled LAMB.

But there was nothing shy or retiring about Farley. Virtually self-educated, with an incisive wit and a deep laugh, he had a reputation as a lively courtroom performer. When he walked into a room, he immediately took center stage.

Farley was Bill Fairfield's choice. They'd known one another since the two were courtroom adversaries during Fairfield's days as a Ventura County prosecutor. They had offices just steps away from one another in the same Ventura building, and Fairfield had had Farley standing by since his own interview with the homicide detectives. Farley was a convenient—if not an obvious—choice, and from their first meeting, lawyer and client seemed well satisfied with each other.

From the moment he set eyes on him, Roehler was more than a client to Farley; he became a friend. Here was a man, Farley thought, facing perhaps the ultimate penalty, and all that seemed to concern him was how news of his arrest should be broken to his family. Roehler had requested that Dr. Paul Remis, the psychiatrist who had been treating him, be called to stay with his children following his arrest, to cushion the effects of their trauma.

"I looked at him from the standpoint of how a jury might see him," Farley said, "and he definitely made a good impression. I was struck by what a well-spoken and good-looking young guy he was. He didn't look like a murderer. Some of them do."

The day after Roehler's arrest, Farley and Fairfield met with members of Fred's family at Fairfield's office, and spent much of the time reassuring Verna's mother Cam, who was terribly disturbed by a recent conversation with the police. The officers had told her they had more than enough on her son-in-law to go for the death penalty, and that they were convinced there had been foul play in Jeanne's death, too. Now she was asking if Jeanne had also been insured. Why would the police say those things if they weren't true, she naively asked.

Farley moved quickly to repair the damage. The police were fishing, he told her, indulging in guessing games, hoping to confuse Cam in order to turn her against Fred, which would, of course, make their case considerably stronger.

Cam was relieved. She couldn't believe that Fred, who had been so kind and caring to her, could possibly be the man the police were describing. She knew her son-in-law. He wasn't acting. It was the first—and last—time that Verna's mother voiced even the slightest hesitation about Fred, at least in public. From that day on she was as firm in his defense as anyone could have wished.

Later, when friends asked her how she could be so positive of Fred's innocence, she would smile and say simply, "If he was guilty, the Lord would have given me a sign."

Roehler's arrest hit Malibu like a thunderbolt. Our town was instantly divided down the middle. Everyone in our small community wanted to discuss this shocking state of affairs, and that included my wife Sally and me. Wherever we went—to our children's school, the post office at Point

Dume, the local beauty salon—everyone who had ever come into contact with Fred had an opinion. The local dentist pronounced him guilty; the doctor, innocent. One high school coach voted yes, and another, no. One woman was thrown out of her hairdresser's, her hair still dripping wet, when she expressed the opinion that Fred Roehler was a killer.

Several of our friends who firmly believed Roehler was guilty refused to take our calls. Many who had been friends for years stopped speaking to one another. Upon my arrival at a friend's birthday party in the Malibu West neighborhood, the hostess pleaded: "Please, let's have a nice evening—for God's sake, don't bring up the Roehler case."

In Santa Barbara, District Attorney Stanley M. Roden had swept into office, replacing a corrupt, scandal-plagued administration. The old order had been virtually a rubber stamp for the sheriff's department. Roden was elected on a pledge not to prosecute unless he was convinced of the evidence against the accused. And he was a long way from being convinced on the Roehler case.

Not for the first time in his career, Roden's reluctance to go after Roehler was resented by his colleagues and the cops. The liberal DA was soft on crime, it was said at the watering spots where cops gathered after hours.

The evidence in the case was entirely circumstantial, Roden argued. The police had acted based on unsubstantiated rumor and gossip, mainly from a bunch of women. Judges hated that stuff.

But more important was Roden's gut feeling that Roehler simply didn't do it. "The guy's just unlucky," he kept telling Terry Cannon. "He's lost everything and it's beginning to look suspiciously like we're persecuting him. It makes us look like shit."

Cannon, however, continued to pursue the case with the enthusiastic help of the sheriff.

"The guy's good for it, Terry," Fred Ray told him after Cannon had returned from another heated exchange with his boss. "I just know it."

At a brief hearing on April 7, 1981, James Farley pleaded his client innocent to first-degree murder with special circumstances before a Santa Barbara municipal court judge. Roehler, in gray-green prison pajamas with his ankles chained together, looked depressed and ill. He did not acknowledge any of the familiar faces in the courtroom, just stared straight ahead as Farley requested that a gag order be imposed on the case. He fruitlessly argued for bail. Defendants charged in California in special circumstances cases are not eligible for bail. Here there were three separate such circumstances: the murder for profit of Verna Roehler; the murder for profit of Douglas Johnson; and the killing of more than one victim.

Farley also asked the judge to approve a defense request that Fred Roehler be given a lie detector test.

Two days later, Roehler was taken from his jail cell across a wide parking lot to the Santa Barbara sheriff's department to undergo the polygraph test. He had been fighting it since his first interview with the police, but Farley was very much in favor of the test. Even though it was controversial, inconclusive, and couldn't be admitted into evidence, Farley believed that a good result was a psychological advantage going into trial. Unbeknownst to him, his client had been preparing for the possibility ever since Fred Ray had first mentioned it to him.

Roehler was nervous as Jeff Boyd, the ex-cop hired by the defense, hooked him up. He kept coughing and clearing his throat, and as he talked about the events that had landed him in jail, his eyes filled with tears, and he dissolved into sobs. Boyd tried his best to put him at ease: All the questions, Roehler was assured, would be reviewed before the actual test began.

At 2:35 p.m., the formal testing began. When it was over, Boyd repeated four of the questions.

Had he ever lied about something important before 1981?

"No . . . Oh, wait a minute," Roehler said. He'd suddenly remembered that he had lied about his fitness to return to work after his back injury; maybe that was what the machine was picking up.

Did he ever get so mad at someone between 1971 and 1981 that he wished them dead?

Roehler thought for a moment. There was a problem with that one, too. There was his old neighbor Horace Bresee who he'd been trying to persuade to join him in shoring up their hill. Bresee had refused to go along with it and a dispute had erupted. "That may be what I'm thinking about here."

And the final question: Was he the person responsible for Verna and Doug's deaths?

The outcome of the test was a closely guarded secret, known only to Farley, Boyd, and defense investigator Russ Whitmeyer. It wasn't what they'd hoped for. According to their own polygraph test, Roehler was lying.

On April 21, I went with a group of friends to the court, hoping to get the judge to grant Fred bail, but in denying bail, the judge didn't allow any of us to speak.

Fred immediately wrote to us thus:

> Hello, Santa Barbara tourist,
>
> I am ready for getting the show on the road. Most any road out of Santa Barbara County will be fine, right after Slater (the judge) signs my motor check-out sheet. I promise not to take any of his towels, soap, or ashtrays. I have showered, been breakfasted, and am awaiting the limo. This is a special quiet time here at Camp Grenada, as the natives have full tummies and for the most part have returned to the womb until the 9 o'clock count. The radio is off, and the place is left with the sounds of an empty gym. The other good news is that very few of my roommates have figured out how to smoke and sleep so the air has a scent and clarity not usually experienced here.

It was typical Fred, with his dry wit and his ability to rise above a plight that would have sent most men into despair. But the reality was very different from the upbeat letters to supporters. Fred Roehler was finding the Santa Barbara jail unendurable.

A daily deluge of written correspondence, ranging from how to conduct his defense to conditions inside the jail, emanated from his cell to his lawyers. His health was suffering, he wrote, from the constant cigarette smoke surrounding him. He needed vitamins to counteract it. "If vitamins can't be had, let's look into a non-smoking section," he wrote, "and if that doesn't work, let's have no smoking in the facility."

His next order of business was a haircut: "I do not want an inmate style. I would give up a Wednesday visit to have a friend in the business in Malibu come up and trim me." The idea of a Malibu hair stylist making a house call at the jail was about as realistic as banning smoking.

Farley excused a lot of dictatorial commands, putting them down to his client's frustration. "This is his life we're messing with, after all," he said.

But of all the documents he fired off from jail, none was more chilling than the one he headed, "Why Not, at Santa Cruz on 1/2/81," in which he meticulously listed the reasons why it was simply illogical for him to have killed Verna and Doug. Each reason—there were thirty-eight in all—was separately numbered. For example:

> Loved and was a friend to both Douglas and Verna.
>
> Would not want to subject the other three children to the loss of Douglas and Verna.
>
> Would not have wanted to subject the other three children to my being jailed.
>
> Would certainly not have drowned them as it would look very suspicious, having lost Jeanne in the pool.
>
> Could have waited for the trip to Mexico and lost them both offshore with no one around.
>
> Could have waited till we were in Mexico and have them "done in by bandits."
>
> Would not have recovered bodies . . . the ocean is a big place, and deep. Very little effort to have them not wash up on shore.
>
> Would have beat them up on rocks to mask anything I would have done.
>
> Could have cut them up and had sharks in ten minutes.

18

Assembling the Troops

On the gloriously sunny morning of May 19, 1981, Fred Roehler's preliminary hearing began before municipal court judge John Slater.

Even though the defense rarely does more in a preliminary hearing than rattle the cage, preferring to keep their case under wraps until the trial, Farley told his team and his client there wasn't going to be a next step. He was prepared, he said, to mount a full-scale defense in the prelim.

"This case is nonsense," Farley said. "We're going to blow it out of the water right now." They would destroy all the flimsy autopsy findings, poke holes in the prosecution's dory experiments, and show the court just how treacherous those waters in the Santa Barbara Channel could be. It was a risky strategy, using up witnesses and resources that might have been reserved for the trial and showing their hand to the state. But Farley was so convinced of his client's innocence and the flimsy circumstantial nature of the state's case that he waded in with both feet. And those of us who thought we knew Fred Roehler agreed.

That night from his jail cell, Roehler wrote:

> I feel remiss only in letting myself see the open door a little too soon. This was for my family and in particular, my children. They are durable, but I do not wish to callous them. I have already written to all six children [he included brother Ron's three], to let them know it will take a little longer to get home.
>
> I drew the analogy that I had passed all the tests and examinations, but my teacher would not pass me to the next grade. I told them I was

> taking all my papers to the principal and showing him why I should be passed. I hope they understand. I hope I understand.

Within twenty-four hours after being ordered to stand trial, Fred Roehler launched into a frenzy of activity, firing off directives to his lieutenants. His troops were about to undergo a few changes. Bill Fairfield, his friend and personal lawyer, withdrew from active day-to-day involvement because he was to be a major defense witness.

On board came a husband-and-wife team of highly paid, highly skilled appeals lawyers, Edward and Wendy Lascher, Ventura-based, but with a statewide reputation. The Laschers would handle all major motions in the case and the finer points of legal research. They would also monitor the conduct of the trial for mistakes that might become the basis of an appeal should it be needed. Only a well-financed defense could have afforded to bring them on board so early. "At last," Jim Farley told them, "I have the money to do the thing properly."

The expensive and experienced team was assembled, but Fred Roehler was not about to surrender control to anyone. For him, this was literally a war to the death, and he wanted all the ammunition they could get.

Those crucial bruises pathologist Dr. Hunter had purportedly discovered on Douglas's head worried him. He wanted to make sure the jury would understand the issues.

"The medical testimony needs visual aids other than the photographs," Roehler wrote to his team. "The layperson will need a sandwich cutaway drawing." He illustrated the point with a sketch carefully labeled "Cross section of the skull of my eight-year-old stepson," showing five layers sliced through, with the hair and scalp on top, descending through the dermis and epidermis to the skull bone and the brain beneath.

Having just been bound over for trial in a capital case in which his life was up for grabs, Roehler wrote to Bill Fairfield asking what had happened to the attorney's fees he was supposed to get back from his wrongful dismissal suit against the navy. Wasn't it about time for those to show up? And while they were at it, he wanted Fairfield to sue Santa Barbara for wrongful arrest. He'd also been thinking that he might have a case against Lifespring, as well, the "cult" group he blamed for Jeanne's death. Surely they were liable for something.

Several months later, Fairfield did in fact sue Santa Barbara on behalf of Roehler for $10 million, but the lawyer managed to dissuade his pal from suing Lifespring.

As Fred awaited the most crucial test of his life, he stayed busy on the phone, calling his true believers several times a week—collect, from jail—including Sally and me. It was weird. He was giving *us* pep talks! He was always upbeat, assuring us that he was in good spirits and telling us we were all an essential part of his support team, ensuring that his lines to the outside world were maintained. Throughout the long trial, the team indeed held, thanks to the cheerleader and wannabe commander in chief behind bars.

His mind was in overdrive as he continued to deliver orders.

He wanted to get pictures, films, charts, and a variety of other documentation of Santa Cruz Island and Little Scorpion anchorage. In his head, he organized a mammoth operation involving boats and planes to map every inch of the spot. But this information-gathering operation, he warned, must be shrouded in secrecy.

"The islands, get a small plane . . . take a jeep down to the ridge. Requires cover story . . . entire operation should look like an ordinary day trip: Boats have fishing poles and beer . . . make it look good."

They should also take along a meteorologist, a professional surf observer, a lifeguard, a navy surf forecaster, and an engineer with ocean training.

"Jeez," one of the defense team said, laughing. "Why don't we just call out the fucking marines while we're at it?"

Deputy DA Terry Cannon was still trying to persuade his boss Stanley Roden of the legitimacy of his case. The DA had even made them redo the tests on Roehler's dory that they'd had done at the high school pool. Those tests were meaningless, he said. If they wanted to make any headway, they would have to take the boat out to Bird Rock and try to overturn it out there.

Cannon and Fred Ray spent hours banging their heads against the wall of Roden's spacious office.

"Stan, look at the logic," Cannon pleaded. "People kill. They find a method that works for them and they do it again the same way. And the next time they up the stakes. This guy has a history with insurance that smells from here to Malibu. He's been leading up to this all his life. This is his big payoff."

Roden was unimpressed. "Okay, but wouldn't you accept that it's one helluva leap from maybe collecting on a boat or a car to killing your wife and an eight-year-old kid? You wanna talk logic? What's the logic in murdering your wife and child with your parents looking over your shoulder?"

"But as Terry says, that's the way Roehler thinks," argued Ray, "in circles inside circles. This is a brilliant mind—sick, but brilliant."

"All right," Roden conceded, "but he's going to Mexico for how long? Six months or more? Can you think of a better place to lose somebody over the side and no questions asked?"

"Stanley," said Cannon, standing up to leave, "forget the pros and cons for a minute. Just tell me this—what are the odds that one guy can lose two wives, both by drowning, both when he's the only witness, and remember—he's an expert in water. A million to one? Maybe even more? Just think about it. That's all I'm asking."

On August 21, the Santa Barbara DA's office was hit with a bombshell. Terry Cannon, who knew every twist and turn of the Roehler case and who had pushed it so hard, suddenly resigned.

Stanley Roden was livid at what he regarded as an outright betrayal. Cannon had fought him every inch of the way to go after Roehler, and now, at the eleventh hour, with the department committed, much against his better judgment, his deputy was dumping it in his lap.

Terry Cannon insisted that he had delayed his departure for private practice for months to go after Roehler. Now he'd run out of excuses for himself and his family.

The talk around the DA's office, however, was that Cannon's decision had also been a pragmatic one. The Roehler case was an iffy proposition.

It was going to cost the county a bundle—and it just might not fly. Roehler could walk, and Cannon couldn't afford to go out into private practice on a defeat.

Roden was in a hole. Nobody besides Cannon knew the case.

In desperation, he sent for Pat McKinley, a deputy DA who had worked on the original arrest warrant for Roehler, and ordered the reluctant deputy to pick up the pieces.

Two weeks later, on a Friday afternoon, Roden marched into McKinley's office, collected the bulging Roehler files, and took them home with him over the long Labor Day weekend.

Early the following Tuesday, he arrived at the office and sent for McKinley. "I'm reassigning the Roehler case," he said.

McKinley breathed a sigh of relief. "Who's the lucky bastard?"

"I am. I've gone over it and I've changed my mind. I think Roehler killed them, both of his wives and the boy. Cannon was right; I was wrong. It's still not the strongest case I've ever seen, but we have a moral obligation to prosecute. However it turns out, he's going to have to answer." Characteristically, Roden felt no embarrassment at his abrupt about-face. He had not believed; now he did. In his mind, it was as simple as that.

The news that the DA was going to handle the prosecution was greeted with jubilation in the Ventura offices of Farley, Spencer, and Casey.

"What a mess!" Farley could barely contain himself. "Roden is stuck. He couldn't find anyone else to take it, now they're on their third prosecutor. Roden is rusty. He hasn't tried a case for years. It's looking better all the time."

On the surface, the tall, studious-looking Roden, with his thick-rimmed glasses and aloof manner, was not a warm man. He kept to himself, barely speaking to colleagues, preferring to communicate in brusque, impersonal memos.

By the time the Roehler case came along, however, Roden had been reelected for a second term, and while still not universally beloved by the sheriff and his men, at least he had earned their respect. The one thing everyone acknowledged about him was that his integrity was absolute.

He avoided even the slightest hint of impropriety, often to the irritation of his colleagues.

"If you lived next door to his third cousin in New York," one deputy said, "and you were pinched for dognapping, he'd squeal conflict and call in the AG [attorney general]. He worried about things no one else would have perceived as a problem."

"He sleeps with the damned Constitution under his pillow," a disgruntled cop griped.

Roden was competitive and hated to lose, but he wouldn't do it at any price. If he made the police dot all their i's and cross their t's, it was because, as one sympathetic colleague said, "He just wanted them to read the Bill of Rights occasionally."

Those who knew Stan Roden were fascinated by his struggle against Roehler as it developed. It was unlike him to pursue a man with such vehemence. It was all very well to say that to prosecute well you must hate the opposition, but it just wasn't like Roden.

An old friend and associate, one of neighboring Ventura County's leading defense attorneys, was hearing the local legal scuttlebutt that Roehler was innocent and Roden was making a terrible mistake.

"I kept asking him, 'Are you sure, Stan? Some people in Ventura that I respect think you're way off base.' And what finally struck me was his absolute conviction. He looked at Roehler as the worst kind of human being—someone who had every advantage this country had to offer and had twisted and abused it. Once he believed, he was determined—obsessed, almost—with the idea that this guy shouldn't get away with it."

19

Opening Statements

The trial of Fred Roehler began with pretrial motions on October 22, 1981, in the Santa Barbara Superior Court, Department 5, courtroom of Judge John T. Rickard.

Stanley Roden had been begging Rickard for more time to respond to a couple of defense motions. On October 22, he made his final appeal, pointing out the ridiculously short time he'd had to prepare. When Rickard returned from lunch, he magnanimously gave the DA until the following morning to answer the defense motions.

Roehler looked solemn. He was dressed in a blue suit, white shirt, and tie. His ankles had been chained together earlier but were now free, by the judge's decree. His beard had gone (it made him look shadowy and suspicious, the defense had decided), and his hair, long and curling over his ears in the morning, was shorter by the afternoon. His mother-in-law Cam had given him a haircut during the lunch hour. He seemed tense, but for someone who had been cooped up for almost seven months, he looked surprisingly healthy, if a little pale.

That day, the defense would argue possibly the most crucial motions the defense was to file throughout the trial. They were asking the court to exclude any evidence whatsoever relating to Fred Roehler's first marriage, or the nature and circumstances of Jeanne Roehler's death. They also asked that Roehler's prior insurance claims, be it on mortgage insurance, fire, or casualty, be excluded completely from his trial.

The DA was prepared to prove that Roehler had murdered his first wife and that his history with insurance companies would "make an underwriter blanch." Next, Roden passionately argued to keep the prior insurance claims in and allow the prosecution to examine not just the two drownings at Santa Cruz, but the pattern of a man's entire life.

The white-haired, erudite Ed Lascher, working himself up into a goodly state of indignation, hit hard at the fact that every single one of Roehler's insurance claims had been paid in full, making them all legitimate.

"I lack the imagination," said Lascher, "to understand how the fact that Mr. Roehler had a fire on an insured houseboat has a 'strong, unequivocal, clear, and logical connection' to that so-called murder out at Bird Rock. I lack the imagination," he continued, "to find a strong, unequivocal, clear, and logical connection between the washing out of his backyard during fire-prevention activities in Malibu and the fact that he committed a murder or had a motive to commit a murder.

"I understand," Lascher continued, "their theory to be that the motive for the killing was the fact that there is substantial insurance on Verna and Douglas, and nobody can deny that. Then what do they need to know that there was insurance on a houseboat ten years ago, for?"

Well satisfied with himself and certain that the law was on his side, Lascher sat down.

Roden shuffled his notes nervously. At this moment, tall, skinny, and stooped, he looked very much like a rather edgy stork shifting from leg to leg, dying to fly, but not sure if the effort would bring him crashing down.

He'd marshaled his strongest arguments for the inclusion of the evidence on Jeanne Roehler's death. Yes, he admitted, it was a leap of the imagination, to go from possible insurance fraud to murder, but from murder to murder was a shorter jump.

He told the court he had found no less than fourteen similarities between the death of Jeanne Roehler and those of Verna and Douglas four years later. The similarities were so strong and so unusual that they should be allowed to supersede Supreme Court rulings on the inadmissibility of prior behavior by a defendant.

When Judge Rickard cleared his throat, no one on either side of the house was in any doubt what his ruling would be. The defense motions were granted in their entirety. As far as Fred Roehler's trial was concerned, there would be no indication that he had ever had a first wife or that he had ever benefited in any way from earlier insurance payouts.

"It's all over for them," Jim Farley whispered to Lascher. "Stanley may as well fold up his tents and steal away."

By 10:15 a.m. on December 14, not a seat was left in Judge John Rickard's first-floor courtroom.

The jurors sat with fresh notebooks, rotating from side to side in their gray upholstered swivel seats. It had taken six weeks to pick them—the longest such process in Santa Barbara judicial history—due in no small measure to the presence at the defense table of a wispy blonde psychologist in her early thirties, named Cathy Bennett.

It had taken all of Farley's persuasive powers to get his client to hire her. She didn't come cheap, at $800 a day plus expenses, plus $25 an hour for her assistant. The Roehlers were flabbergasted at the extravagance, but Farley believed her services were essential.

"Fred, the jury is the key. Once they're selected, the case is essentially over. I must make them love me. She can help me do that."

Once the jury was seated, Roehler's gaze was firmly fixed on them. His legal team was expensive and experienced; nevertheless, it was he who had made the final decision on each one of them. His choices were often at odds with both Farley and jury expert Bennett, but he was adamant. He had filled pad after pad with notes on each one. He drew pictures of their eyeglasses and hairdos, noting everything from the fluorescent hand on one man's watch to the way one woman's eyebrows turned up quirkily at the ends. He was determined to know them inside out. He wanted jurors who understood the ocean—swimmers and divers and sailors. Only they would understand that he was telling the truth. They, too, had been cold and tired out there in the waves; they were bound to empathize with him.

There were six men, six women, and six alternates, for the most part solidly middle-class, ranging from a twenty-one-year-old meat cutter who loved to surf and said he didn't believe in "An eye for an eye," to a Santa Barbara fire department captain who had worked with Stanley Roden on behalf of the firefighters' union and had been an investigator for the arson detail. There was a gas company worker and a young man on probation for a misdemeanor break-in. There was also a middle-aged woman who worked in the department of the local hospital headed by the prosecution's chief witness, Dr. Hunter. She had five children from two husbands, both of whom had deserted her.

Farley had argued passionately against her; she certainly wasn't a peer, he said, and she probably hated men. But Roehler had insisted. She would understand how difficult it was to bring up and discipline children. She too had suffered. He didn't care that during questioning, she had told Farley, "Death for death—that's what I believe in."

Slowly, Stanley Roden unwound his six-foot-two frame from his seat at the prosecutor's table, planted his giant size-fourteen shoes behind a lectern, and began his opening statement.

The judge's ruling barring any reference to Roehler's first marriage, or his insurance history, had eviscerated Roden's case and cut him off at the knees. He knew better than anyone that he faced a virtually impossible task ahead.

He began with a simple question: "Why would anyone want to kill their wife and stepson?" And an equally simple answer: "Money—a lot of cash and a lot of property."

The last payment on the insurance policy taken out on Verna Johnson Roehler's life, he said, was made on December 29, just four days before she and her son died at Bird Rock. That insurance—$400,000, with $300,000 for accidental death—was term insurance, he told them, the cost of which would increase every year. The children's insurance on the other hand, in the amount of $60,000, with double indemnity on each child, was whole life, and the payments would not increase. The implication was clear: Roehler could not afford, nor did he intend, to pay these very expensive premiums on his wife's insurance for very long.

The defendant, Roden said, had bought almost three times as much insurance as he needed to meet his estate tax obligations in the event of his or his wife's death.

"But it doesn't matter how much insurance you need," Roden said. "You don't buy insurance unless you can afford it."

He would show that Roehler's financial base came from infusions of cash coming almost like Acts of God, at the eleventh hour, just when he needed them, without the continuing income to sustain his considerable obligations: his yacht, his houses, and not least, his hefty insurance premiums. Roehler, the evidence would show, hadn't worked in almost two years.

Turning to January 2, 1981, the day Verna and Doug died, Roden painted a picture of a calm, beautiful afternoon—a perfect day; a trip around Bird Rock in a dory, a boat designed not to turn over which had somehow mysteriously turned over, nonetheless; a man rescued after perhaps an hour to an hour and a half in the water, whose body remained warm and unmarked; and a woman and a boy, both excellent swimmers, who nevertheless had drowned in seconds.

Their bodies were autopsied; nothing untoward was found, because the coroner had considered it a routine drowning. But when those bodies were given a more thorough autopsy, premortem injuries were found—the kind that happen only before you're dead. And on the boy's head was found a distinctive pattern to those injuries—two, round, and two, straight lines.

"You won't need slides and fancy talk," Roden promised. "You will see them. It's as if you took an orange and hit it on something flat. It's going to make a roundish pattern. And if you took the same orange and hit it on the side of the table, you get a linear pattern."

They found similar roundish wounds on the back of Verna Roehler's head, Roden said, "and an interesting injury to the boy's shoulder, as if a pulling-down movement had caused it."

The prosecution would bring in an eminent biomechanical engineer, a woman named Dr. Carly Ward, to answer the key question: Even if the boat had turned over, could it have generated enough force to cause the injuries to either Douglas Johnson's or his mother's head?

The answer, said Roden: "No way!"

How, then, did they die? Not from a routine boating accident. Not from banging their heads accidentally on the dory or the cliff's rock. They died by an act of man—specifically the man who sat before them. There was no other alternative, Roden said. "What we have in this case, is cold-blooded murder."

The DA sat down. The jurors scribbled in their notepads as Fred Roehler turned toward them, his face blank. Then, slowly, deliberately, he shook his head.

Moments before he stood up, James Farley popped a nitroglycerine pill under his tongue. His face was flushed, his breath coming in uneven spurts. In the days leading up to the trial, he had had to battle his client for the privilege of making the opening statement for the defense. Fred Roehler had wanted to be the first to address the judge and jury.

"I'm putting additional pressure on Farley to let me make the opening statement," Roehler had written to his fervent supporters. "A number of jurors and most normal people would want to hear me . . . The judge wants to wrap this up and my verbal presentation—well-tailored, phrased and considered—could help. And I don't see how it could hurt . . . I will not unduly pressure Farley, but it is his task to deal with pressure."

Roehler had already begun to write his opening remarks, but somewhere along the way, he'd changed his mind. "We have all changed my mind," he wrote. "It will be Farley's job. I could come across as a smart ass, and we do not want to make [Judge] Rickard or the jury mad."

The opening argument was usually Farley's favorite part of any case, but this time he seemed subdued. "The evidence will show, ladies and gentlemen," he began, "that this was an accident and a tragedy in which a distraught father did everything humanly possible to save the lives of his wife and child." His defense, he told them, would revolve around the testimony of two main witnesses: the attorney Bill Fairfield, who had advised Roehler to enter into an estate plan for his family's protection, and to buy insurance to provide liquidity for that plan; and Dr. Martin J. Nemiroff, one of the world's leading experts in cold-water drowning, a man who effected rescues almost daily in the frigid waters off Kodiak, Alaska, where the summer temperature of the seas was similar to that in winter off Santa Cruz Island.

The defense, with the help of some distinguished pathologists, would prove, Farley said, that the so-called "head injuries" mentioned by the district attorney probably did not exist, and if they did, could well have been the result of the dramatic but futile rescue attempts. In fact, Dr. Nemiroff would testify that many such bruises occur in rescue operations, even to those doing the rescuing.

Summing up, Farley for the first time showed some of his famous passion. His voice grew louder, his large chest deflated like a pair of bellows as he slowly let out his pent-up frustration.

"The evidence will show," he roared, "this is not a cold-blooded killing—that it was a tragic accident, and that's all it was. And all the rest, the evidence will show, is speculation."

Sitting behind Fred's parents and family, we all silently applauded Farley's passion. Sally and I were firmly part of "Team Fred," and over a picnic lunch of sandwiches and lemonade on the picturesque lawns in front of the Santa Barbara courthouse, we all agreed that this charade of a trial would soon be resolved with Fred walking out a free man.

20

Death in the Afternoon

THE NEXT MORNING, RODEN BEGAN WITH THREE WITNESSES FROM Malibu, along with a former resident of the beach community and close friend of both Roehler wives, Paddy Leitelt.

The first, Dr. Jeff Harris, was the Roehler family (and my own family's) physician. With tousled blond hair and an unruly mustache, he practiced medicine from a trailer near the beach and liked to surf at lunchtime. He was a doctor of the 1980s, a practitioner of the New Age, holistic, hands-on, paying as much attention to his patients' psyches as their symptoms.

He said he had treated Verna for hypertension and had last seen her on November 14, 1980, when her blood pressure was 158/90. It often went higher—dangerously high. Her weight was 110 pounds. He had last seen Douglas in August for an ear infection.

Over Roden's objections, Jim Westwick, in cross-examination, asked Dr. Harris if he remembered prescribing asthma medicine for Heidi Roehler in preparation for a family cruise to Mexico. Harris recalled some vague conversation about an extended trip, but no specifics. Roden asked him if he had taken any notes of the conversation; Harris had not.

"Didn't they teach you to take notes in medical school, Doctor?" Roden snapped. Even this early in the case, he wanted to plant serious doubt in the jury's minds that this cruise had ever been seriously contemplated by Fred Roehler.

Two Malibu swimming instructors then followed each other to the stand. Robert LeMond had been teaching kids to swim in the area for fifteen years. He had dated some of Malibu's most beautiful women, Verna Johnson among them. He had taught Doug to swim when he was four and five years old, he said, and described him as a B-plus swimmer, a kid who genuinely loved the water.

Meta Vander Meyden taught swimming every summer in Malibu and had Doug in her classes from the age of five until the summer before his death. She had taken him from intermediate swimming and lifesaving right up to the advanced swimmers' class in the summer of 1980. Doug had taken the advanced swimmers' course and passed it twice, finishing the second time on September 2, 1980.

The final test for successful completion of the course was a tough one. The boy had to prove he could breaststroke for one hundred yards, sidestroke and crawl for one hundred, back-crawl for fifty yards, and use his legs alone for fifty yards. He had to show mastery of different kinds of turns and several different dives. In deep water, he had to disrobe, inflate his trousers, and then, using them as a flotation device, stay afloat for five minutes. She said he had done well in the course.

But under Westwick's quiet cross-examination, both instructors admitted that there was a world of difference between swimming in a pool heated to 76 degrees with concrete sides just feet away and being dumped out of a boat into the cold and uncertain ocean.

Paddy Leitelt was nervous. Verna's closest friend studiously avoided the gaze of Fred and his parents. Her resemblance to Verna Roehler was startling. She wore her hair the same way and she was about the same size. She could have been Verna's sister. Dressed soberly in a straight-from-the-office skirt and blouse, the pretty blonde shook as she sat down, her voice thin and quivery.

Her testimony was an exercise in frustration both for herself and for the district attorney. The court's earlier ruling meant she could tell only a fraction of what she knew: nothing about Jeanne, nothing about the state of her friend Verna's second marriage. She was dying to say more, but all she could do was establish her friendship with Verna and the fact that she and her husband and two children had lived for two years in Verna's duplex, within hailing distance of her friend. She said she had often seen

Verna and Doug swimming in the ocean, and she'd never seen the boy panic.

Roden showed her two snapshots. "Is this Verna? Is this her son?"

Paddy Leitelt could only nod her head, her eyes filling with tears as Roden passed the pictures to the jury. They had never seen photos of Verna or her son. Later, some of them said it was this moment when the enormity of what they were being asked to judge came home to them.

Having shown that Verna and Doug were more than able swimmers, Roden called Jack Burkhardt, Roehler's Point Mugu supervisor, to the stand. The DA now had to prove that Fred Roehler was a veritable dolphin in the water.

Burkhardt recalled a time when he and Roehler were diving off the Channel Islands, and he had run out of air at a depth of about forty feet. Everything had worked out fine, however, because Fred had been calm and under control. He had "buddy-breathed" with Burkhardt, sharing his own regulator with his friend until they'd reached the surface.

"More than most of us," Burkhardt said, "he had no problem handling the surge out there. I've never seen him panic."

Four days into the trial, the three crew members of the *Sound of Music* gave their version of what happened that afternoon in January.

Carlyle "Mike" Davis, the acting skipper of the sloop, was the picture of success in an expensive sports jacket, starched white shirt, and gold Rolex watch gleaming on his wrist. Gerald Formiller, the owner of the *Sound of Music*, was in his late fifties, his nautical navy blazer and white open-necked shirt revealing a deeply tanned neck. He looked dashing. Diane Wheatley, a tall, slim, silver-blonde, looking like the airline stewardess she had once been, wore a conservative dressed-for-success suit with a white blouse and severe black bow tie at the neck.

As far as Fred Roehler was concerned, from the moment the crew of the *Sound of Music* took the stand, they were his adversaries, even if they had saved his life.

"This whole damned tragedy was their fault," Roehler told his lawyers. "If the three of them hadn't screwed up the CPR, Verna and Doug would still be alive today. They were probably still alive when they were brought on board, but they were left lying on that deck while the *Sound of Music*'s dumb crew decided what to do with them."

Farley and Westwick knew it was important to show that the rescue efforts had been incompetent. If they could demonstrate that blood had been pumping, however slowly, through Douglas and Verna's arteries when they were hauled from the water, they could make a good case that the so-called premortem injuries had been inflicted by rough handling during the rescue.

Throughout the trio's testimony, Fred Roehler's face betrayed nothing, even when Formiller told Roden he thought it unusual that not once after he was brought aboard the *Sound of Music* had Fred Roehler inquired about his wife.

Roden had assembled scores of visual aids: navigational charts, maps, diagrams, aerial photographs, and slides. The court was beginning to look like a naval war room as the crew of the *Sound of Music* took the stand one by one.

"The sea conditions were calm," Mike Davis recalled. "It was just bizarre to see what we saw out there under those circumstances."

"Roehler's condition was much different from the other two," he said. "While their skin was gray and cold, his color was healthy and normal."

"Looking at him today, how would you compare his color?" asked Roden.

Davis swiveled his chair to look at Roehler sitting behind the defense table. "He looks a little paler now than he did then."

After two days of testimony, the *Sound of Music* crew had neither been particularly helpful to the prosecution nor especially damaging to the defense.

Roden wanted the jury to see that January day as a picture postcard, with a tranquil sea, sun shining and birds circling overhead. Unfortunately for him, other boat owners who had been in Little Scorpion anchorage that day and had followed the *Sound of Music* crew to the stand didn't quite see it that way. Ken Mueller, the skipper of one such boat, the *Sewickly*, said that much earlier in the day he had overturned a small sabot right by Bird Rock because it was blowing so hard. He added for good measure that his seven-year-old son had been terrified.

And on that unfortunate note for the prosecution, the court recessed for Christmas.

Charlotte Roehler told her family that she would not be celebrating the holiday that year—not family birthdays or anything else until she had her son back home with her. "We'll have Christmas then," she said. "Even if it's in the middle of the summer."

Stanley Roden's first objective when the trial resumed was to prove that Verna and Douglas had been assaulted before they drowned. He began by calling Dr. Craig Duncan, the acting medical examiner of Ventura County, and the pathologist who had performed the original autopsies. This was a considerable gamble on Roden's part, because Duncan was a hostile witness. As far as he was concerned, the deaths were perfectly consistent with a boating accident, and any other suggestion reflected poorly on his professional competency. Roden's whole case rested on his key witness Dr. Dewitt Hunter, the Santa Barbara pathologist, who, after doing a second autopsy, had purported to find bruises on Douglas's head. On paper, Duncan was the better-qualified medical detective, so Roden knew he would somehow have to belittle the Ventura coroner and convince the jury that his autopsies had been sloppy.

Duncan limped awkwardly to the stand. He was a young man, but a congenital hip deformity gave his body a contorted look. His thinning, dark hair was brushed forward across his forehead, and in a conservative blue suit, he seemed older than he was.

Roden immediately went on the attack, questioning his professional judgment, and in turn, Duncan became increasingly defensive and hostile. Demonstrating where he had made his incisions on a pair of Styrofoam mannequin heads provided by Roden, he insisted he had found nothing to indicate foul play.

Jim Westwick's cross-examination stressed Duncan's credentials. He'd been chief medical examiner in Rochester, New York, and had taught at Johns Hopkins University, with five thousand autopsies behind him, three thousand of them the result of violent death, including several hundred drownings.

Then, from a brown grocery sack, Westwick produced a medical-school model of a skull with removable sections showing the different layers of skin, tissue, and blood vessels. Westwick's model was obviously superior to Roden's rather amateurish mannequin; in fact, throughout the trial, the defense's visual aids would be considerably better than the prosecution's.

Westwick quickly got to the point. An autopsy was a violent occurrence, was it not? Bone was sawed through, tissues were sliced, blood vessels ruptured and gushed. For the next two hours, Duncan, agreeing, took the court through a short course in brain pathology. As he carefully demonstrated the dissection of Douglas's skull, Roehler slowly and deliberately averted his gaze. Charlotte and Fritz Roehler sat silently, their faces impassive. Cam Zeitner excused herself and fled to the outside corridor.

While cutting the membrane that covered the skull bone, Duncan explained that he had severed a number of blood vessels, which could account for the so-called "bruising." Those vessels would have bled profusely during any premortem injury, the blood covering the surface of the skull. Between the skull and the brain, he explained carefully, there were three layers of tissue. He had found no evidence of hemorrhaging in any of those layers during the autopsy, which meant there was no bruising prior to death.

While examining Douglas's skull, Westwick inquired, had Duncan found anything to suggest that a premortem blow had any relation to the cause of death?

Duncan was certain: He had found no injury whatsoever, just a typical drowning brain.

Westwick paused and slowly reached again into his grocery bag, pulling out a replica of a human skull and holding it in front of him like Hamlet with the head of Yorick.

Jurors gasped. It was a theatrical gesture and it worked.

Stanley Roden jumped to his feet and almost wrestled the skull from Westwick's hands. He made a great point of closely studying it, as if he expected to find something of great significance.

Using the skull, Duncan identified the three most important suture lines of the thirty or more that zigzagged across the skull like small tributaries from a main river: Any significant trauma to Douglas Johnson's skull, he said, would have produced separation along those lines, resulting in hemorrhaging. He had found none.

On Verna Johnson, he had also seen nothing—no suture separation, no injuries, no bleeding, no hemorrhaging.

Roden had had enough of this and called for a conference out of earshot of the jury. Westwick was turning his witness into an expert for the defense, Roden complained, and he was doing so on the prosecution's time. Twice Roden objected. Twice he was overruled. He had taken a risk by calling Duncan, and now he was paying the price.

Duncan was permitted to testify that after his own autopsy of January 3, he had seen microscopic sections of brain, scalp, skin, and the organs taken at Dr. Hunter's second autopsy, to see if somehow, he had overlooked anything. Dr. Hunter's slides, he said, had not changed his opinion in any way.

Over Roden's objections, Duncan speculated that Douglas's mild injuries could have been caused by hitting his head on the side of the boat as it overturned; being held against the rock; bumped against the rescue vessel by the surge and swell of the sea, or against the aluminum-and-wood ladder used by the rescue vessel; or, indeed, by any of the CPR efforts. Verna's injuries, on the other hand, were not injuries, he said; rather, they were possibly blood vessels congested by drowning that had leaked after death.

Duncan said he was almost certain that the wounds Dr. Hunter said he found on Douglas's head were caused by the first autopsy.

Duncan had been an excellent witness—for the defense.

Roden had a lot of ground to make up.

The next day turned into a marathon between Roden and Duncan. As the DA jabbed away, Duncan became angrier and more defensive. The more Roden bore in, the testier Duncan became. Their exchanges were petty and argumentative.

Roden showed Duncan a photo of Verna's left foot. "Do you see a bruise there?"

"No."

"Do you see any discoloration?"

"This photo was taken when?"

"I'm asking you—do you see a bruise?"

Duncan refused to be intimidated. "It is important to know when the photo was taken to interpret what I see on the foot in regard to postmortem interval."

Roden pressed further. "Do you see a bruise independent of when the photo was taken?"

"I don't see a bruise. No."

Roden pounced again. "Doctor, is it common practice to lose parts of the human body while you are doing an autopsy?"

"Oh, mistakes happen. It happens once in a while."

"Do you have any idea what happened to Douglas Johnson's larynx?"

"I sure do."

"What happened?"

"I think it ended up in Verna's bag of tissues."

"How did that happen, sir?" Roden could scarcely contain his glee. A man who could lose a larynx was capable of all sorts of carelessness.

"Well, I told you, the closeness in proximity of these bodies, and there are adjacent buckets in which the viscera are stored."

The jury was turning paler, visualizing the slaughterhouse aspects of the coroner's work.

And so, the grisly performance continued—Roden trying to portray Duncan as sloppy and careless, a civil servant under pressure, running an autopsy mill, disregarding injuries that Roden's more precise pathologist had had no trouble finding.

The jury was getting an education most of them would have happily done without. They now understood why in the *voir dire* they had been asked if they were squeamish. How is the brain sectioned? How does the blood leap from the vessels? In what order does the coroner cut up bodies? How much blood is there in a 110-pound female? Six liters? A 50-pound boy would have only two and a half to three liters of blood. Was Douglas's brain washed? Could blood have gotten onto his brain by being put into a bag with his other organs?

A spectator in the back of the court was snoring quietly. The jurors had stopped taking notes. The most galvanizing moment of the afternoon came when a tray of tissue-sample slides slid off Roden's desk and crashed onto the floor. For a moment, the prosecutor's evidence was in dire jeopardy. Order was quickly restored.

Before he finished his long session on the stand, Duncan managed to get in what to him was his most important point: Eight days after death, and following a first autopsy, by the time Dr. Hunter got to those bodies, the injuries were "hopelessly muddled." Had Duncan been present during Hunter's work, he could have at least clarified the messy picture.

Roden prepared to wind it up. In times of stress, his syntax tended to be anything but elegant. "Hypothetically," he began, "let's assume, with intentional and deliberate malice aforethought, with the intent of killing another human being, slamming the heads inside the boat twice, at least twice and maybe more times, and then drowning the person in the saltwater ocean—is that consistent with what you found, sir?"

Duncan's "No" was beside the point. It was a rhetorical question meant to plant in the jury's minds the image of Fred Roehler smashing the head of his tiny, helpless stepson somewhere on the boat, and then drowning the stunned child.

In re-cross, just before the day's end, Duncan confirmed that if Roden's scenario were correct—if a child of Douglas's age and weight had been slammed against the boat—there would have been much more severe injuries on the child's head. There were no lacerations, no tearing of the scalp, no fractures, no suture separations, no brain injuries, not even a break of the skin. The skin on Douglas's scalp, Duncan asserted, was completely intact.

Outside the courtroom, a Santa Barbara lawyer monitoring the evidence for the DA said, "If the jury is to find Fred Roehler guilty, they're going to have to ignore Dr. Duncan's testimony altogether."

The trial was in its twelfth day when Stanley Roden called Dr. Dewitt Hunter, the Santa Barbara pathologist who was the spine of his case. Listening to Hunter was like having a molar drilled. Thin and nervous, with sparse sandy hair and an ill-fitting jacket draped over his bony shoulders, Hunter's delivery was excruciatingly slow. His testimony was to hang heavily on the coursing of blood through bodies, yet his own looked as if it had a considerable insufficiency of the stuff. He stuttered, umm'd and ahh'd, his faltering answers delivered in obscure medicalese. He blinked compulsively and his hands shook. At times, during his three days on the stand, he looked like a candidate for intensive care. Roden couldn't have found a less impressive witness, yet somehow this unfortunate man had to be made to make sense.

Hunter's autopsy had taken some five to six hours, and it took even longer for him to reveal his findings in the courtroom. Often, he admitted, he could find little background research in the areas he was examining. Later, the defense's expert pathologists—many of international fame, stellar figures in the field and writers of standard textbooks—were to belittle Hunter's findings as the imaginings of a minor league player looking at things he didn't understand. Yet through it all, Hunter was unyielding.

Consuming glass after glass of water, clearing his throat frequently, he somehow managed to get through the ordeal of testimony as the jury struggled to stay with him.

It was quite possible, Hunter explained, and as Dr. Duncan had testified, that bruises which were invisible on the day following a death could become visible one or two days later when the blood had settled into the lower parts of the body. One cannot bruise a dead body, he insisted.

Reviewing an enlarged photograph of Verna's skull and collarbone, Hunter said he had found a premortem injury in her neck muscle and two premortem injuries on the back portion of her skull, but they were minimal. These injuries to her brain, Hunter maintained, were suffered "very, very shortly before death, perhaps a minute or a minute and a half before she drowned."

Roden finally had a clear unequivocal statement from Hunter that he could hang his hat on, and with relief, he suggested to the judge that it might be a good time to adjourn for the day.

Before being taken back to his jail cell, Roehler sent his father a note: "Hunter's putting the jury to sleep."

The next day was more of the same, with Hunter testifying that Verna's injuries could not have been caused by contact with Bird Rock;

the sharp barnacles on its surface would have torn her skin. In fact, he thought it very unlikely her injuries had been caused accidentally.

Turning to Douglas, Hunter said that an abrasion on his right shoulder beneath the neck was premortem. A wound on his thigh, as well as several bruises on his legs and one behind his right knee, was unequivocally premortem, the result of some kind of blunt force. Doug's injuries were also inflicted before death.

Then, with Roden guiding him every step of the way, Hunter prepared to reveal the crucial testimony that was at the heart of the prosecution case. "I observed profound premortem hemorrhages in four areas which could not have been apparent before the scalp was fully retracted."

Jumping up as if to a shouted command, Roden triumphantly pinned up large color photographs clearly showing four bruises on the base of Doug's shaved and scalped head. Cam Zeitner lowered her gaze to her knees and kept it there. Charlotte and Fritz Roehler paid close attention. Their son sat bolt upright, tense, his hands tightly clasping the wooden arms of his chair, glancing neither right nor left.

"There is no way," Hunter said, "other than premortem trauma, to explain bleeding in the tissues in this area."

As the court broke for lunch, Stanley Roden was exuberant.

The bruises were obvious in the enlarged photos. Even the jury could pick them out. Hunter's findings would be validated. The defense, on the other hand, was livid. "If you blow anything up that much," Westwick said indignantly, "you're going to find something—a pinprick of blood looks like a river under that kind of amplification. At that rate, if you pricked your finger, it would look like out-and-out carnage."

When court resumed, Roden produced still more pictures of Douglas's head, peeled like a grapefruit, and photographed from every conceivable angle. There was considerable swelling on Douglas's scalp, Hunter continued, and none on Verna's.

What did that mean? Douglas had probably lived longer after his injuries than his mother, the doctor explained. Those injuries were definitely premortem.

The testimony might have fascinated pathology students, but it was hard to say how much the jury was really absorbing.

A two-way microscope was set up as Hunter showed slides of actual brain tissue to indicate the difference between pre- and postmortem injuries. One after another, the jurors squinted, peering into the microscope, as Hunter told them what they were seeing.

He was firmly convinced, he told the jury, that the drownings of Verna and Douglas were not accidental. He could not rule out homicide.

21

Experts Go to War

For several days, Roden had bombarded the jury with enough blood, bone marrow, viscera, and buckets of body parts to decorate a slasher movie. Now he was beginning the phase of the trial one wag described as "everything you never wanted to know about physics."

If Hunter had been hard going, the next witnesses were even more excruciating. They came and went and were recalled and went again and reappeared with the regularity of the phases of the moon. It was interminable and almost intolerable. And what made it harder for the jury was that they spent days on end in their waiting room while Roden tried to persuade the judge to let his witnesses testify in open court. The more he tried to establish a foundation for their expertise, the harder the defense yelled halt. In most cases, the judge ruled for the defense.

Dr. Carly Ward, the biochemical engineer, was to occupy the stand for ten days. What she and her colleagues were to present was nearly impossible to translate into anything approaching language the jury could comprehend. At one stage, Roden asked the judge to allow her to supply a glossary for the jury. He was denied.

Carly Ward had done tests at Bird Rock as well as in a saltwater tank in a lab and had come up with complicated calculations to show how fast and with what force a dory could overturn. One woman juror was later to say of her testimony, "I didn't understand a word she was saying, but I was very impressed that a woman could be so clever."

But Fred Roehler did not dismiss her so lightly. After researching her background, he concluded she was a threat. She was, he said, the only prosecution witness they really had to worry about, the only one who could give the patina of scientific respectability to Roden's "Mickey Mouse case."

The fact that she was a woman seemed to make her even more objectionable. "If they get their way," he said, "we'll be knocking heads (no pun intended) with Ward, and the actual matter we should be showing will be swept under their expert's skirts."

Detective Fred Ray took the stand first to introduce a film of his dory testing at Bird Rock. The judge painstakingly admonished the jury that it was for the limited purpose of deciding how stable the dory was, as well as the maximum speed at which it would capsize. They were not—under any circumstances—to view it as a re-creation of what had actually happened in the ocean the previous January. It was classic legal game playing. Now you see it, now you don't, like instructing the jury to watch the reenactment of a man shooting his wife but only for the purpose of establishing the fact that a gun shoots bullets.

Jim Farley kept driving home again and again the difference between experiments where everyone in the boat knows exactly when it's going to turn over, and a genuine accident that comes upon people unaware. Science was marvelous, Farley seemed to say, but nature had a way of making its conclusions just so much empty speculation.

Dr. Ward's testimony stretched into the middle of February. The sum of her findings boiled down to one fact: She had calculated that the maximum speed at which the gunnel of an overturning dory and the head of a boy rising out of the water could come together is at 6.7 feet per second. One could almost hear the collective "So what?" from the jury box. When she finished, the DA, knowing full well that he had probably lost the jury weeks before, attempted to show the relevance of her findings.

Dr. Randall Smith, a San Diego neurosurgeon, testified about a research project he and Dr. Ward had completed to determine what amount of force it takes to injure the human brain. According to their published research, it would have taken almost eight times the 6.7-feet-per-second impact to the boy's head to produce serious injury.

The jury visibly relaxed. So that's what Dr. Ward's gobbledygook was all about! Roden had redeemed himself. That was why he had subjected them to the Ward marathon, even though it had taken him weeks and untold thousands of dollars to do it.

Now, pondered Roden, if the overturning dory could not have made those bruises on Doug's head, then what had? Roden called Santa Barbara criminologist Duane Mauzey. The jurors didn't know it, but Mauzey was simply an understudy for a leading player who was pulled from the defense's lineup at the very last moment.

Dr. Thomas Noguchi, "Coroner to the Stars," was an international figure, an acknowledged forensic genius, and the coroner of Los Angeles County. Headlines clung to Noguchi like smog to the hilltops of his adopted city. He'd conducted autopsies on some of the best-known personalities in America, from Marilyn Monroe to Robert Kennedy, from William Holden to Natalie Wood, along with a multitude of others who consequently had their anatomies and lives dissected for the benefit of the media.

Before the trial, Fred Ray had carted Roehler's dory to Los Angeles to try and enlist Noguchi's aid. Noguchi was intrigued. He made several visits to Santa Cruz Island with Duane Mauzey, donning underwater gear to inspect every inch of Bird Rock, the *Sound of Music*, the *Perseverance*, and the dory—especially the dory. On hands and knees, crawling into storage spaces, hanging from decks, clambering up and down nautical staircases, carrying a dummy's head and boxes of carbon paper, he delightedly bashed the dummy's head to see if he could duplicate the bruises on Doug's head.

But by the time the Roehler trial got under way, Dr. Noguchi was under such heavy fire in Los Angeles, his name the stuff of daily headlines following his firing by the Los Angeles County Board of Supervisors and his high-profile lawsuit to get his job back, that the DA simply couldn't afford to put him on the stand lest the defense make hay out of his tarnished reputation.

Hence Mauzey was called to deputize as a witness for the prosecution. The tools of his trade were quickly introduced: a life-size photo of the back of Doug's head; a ruler and a child-size dummy. Everyone's attention, however, was focused on Roehler's dory, which sat upturned in the well of the courtroom on two sawhorses, looking like a beached whale. The jurors eyed it as if it were a guillotine.

Mauzey had measured the four bruises Hunter said he'd found on Doug's head. He agreed with Roden that they were evenly spaced. Where could a pattern like that have come from? The only place he had been able to duplicate those marks, he said, was on the dory, and on a particular spot on the dory: amidships on the gunnel—the rail running along the top of the boat—and on a vertical support that held that gunnel in place.

Roden circled slowly and patiently, placing his feet carefully, one in front of the other. He paced in one direction, turned, and retraced his steps. There was an air of excitement. He had something, and he was enjoying the process of unfolding it—a magician preparing for his big finale.

Mauzey said he could reproduce the circular part of the bruise pattern and the linear parts of the pattern. Roden asked that the jurors in the back row be allowed to come forward so they wouldn't miss any of it. Mauzey pointed out the exact area he was talking about and demonstrated how he could strike the dummy's head on both the gunnel and the vertical support under it at virtually the same time. It had to be done twice, he said to produce the symmetrical pattern of two circular bruises over two linear marks. He had taken pictures of his test results on the dummy's head, he said, and they had been blown up to life-size.

At that moment, Roden produced the photograph and entered it into evidence, following it with a clear plastic overlay on which had been marked the exact replica of the bruises taken from Douglas Johnson's head.

There was absolute silence. Only their chairs squeaked as the jurors tensed forward. The clear plastic crackled in Mauzey's hands as he fumbled for a second before placing it over the blown-up photograph. The fit was absolutely perfect: round bruises on round marks, lines upon lines. Roden savored the moment, then slowly took his seat.

After a week of legal delays, Roden finally got his chance to make sure the jury had not overlooked Mauzey's testimony. On the starboard side of the boat, Mauzey testified, there was a small bump in the fiberglass on the vertical support just under the gunnel. On Mauzey's diagram of the four bruises on Doug's head, he pointed out that one of the linear bruises had a tiny tail at the end of it, making almost a fifth bruise. That tail, said Mauzey, had been made by that almost imperceptible bump in the fiberglass, further pinpointing the exact spot at which the boy's head had smashed into the boat.

Well satisfied with himself, Roden prepared to sit down. Then suddenly, he stopped in his tracks. Like the TV detective Columbo who always hit his suspects with the most dangerous questions just as he has a foot out of the door, he turned: "Incidentally, one last thing before you go . . ."

Just below the part of the boat where Mauzey had determined Doug's injuries could be reproduced, did he not find a small indentation?

"Yes," Mauzey agreed. "It's as though some force were applied from the inside of the dory pushing towards the outside . . . there's a slight curvature to the crack, which actually fits the curvature of a shoe."

Roden paused, hoping the jury would get the picture. Someone, he suggested, perhaps a large person, could have placed his foot against the side of the dory to steady himself while preparing to bash the head of an eight-year-old boy into insensibility.

For the first time in his long odyssey, Roden seemed content with his performance. He had presented nothing less than a blueprint for murder. Thanks to Mauzey and the invisible Noguchi, he felt he had shown not only that those bruises did exist on Doug and Verna's heads, but exactly how and where they had been made. He had held the jury's hand and spelled it out for them. He could do no better.

Farley and Westwick, however, were not nearly as concerned as Roden thought they ought to be. There were probably a million combinations that could reproduce that pattern, they were sure—assuming, of course, that such a pattern existed in the first place, which they were not prepared to concede for a moment.

"Mauzey's only the ventriloquist's dummy here," Farley said outside the court. "It's good old Dr. Noguchi pulling the strings, and this pattern business has his fingerprints all over it. I don't think the jury's gonna buy it. It's the same old nonsense Stanley has been pulling from the beginning, trying to make the pieces fit their bogus theories. It won't wash."

Roden's next witness, Dr. Charles Petty, called to buttress Dr. Hunter's testimony, turned out to be almost as helpful to the defense as he was to Roden. Petty was Dallas County's chief medical examiner, and a heavyweight in the field. He was tall, gray-haired, distinguished, and tweedy. The jury straightened up and paid attention from the moment he opened his mouth, turning to fresh pages in their spiral notebooks.

He began with a bombshell: Hunter's slides showed clearly, Petty said, that Verna Johnson Roehler was a very sick young woman. Not only did she suffer from hypertension, but she had quite pronounced heart disease. Her arteries had considerable narrowing, restricting the flow of blood. In the front row, Verna's mother looked stunned. She had had no idea that her thirty-six-year-old daughter, a woman who regularly ran three miles a day, could have been a candidate for bypass surgery.

Roden seemed equally shocked, and instead of moving quickly to minimize the damage, he asked Dr. Petty to elaborate. How significant was this heart disease?

The severe narrowing of her arteries, Petty explained, meant that "there is less capability of the heart to respond to stress and strain than would be normally expected. Does that answer your question, sir?" Petty asked.

It certainly did. It also explained why Verna could have died so quickly in a simple capsizing, despite her ability to swim.

Roden frantically tried to stem the damage his own witness was inflicting.

"Would it be easier to drown someone whose heart was in such a condition?" he asked.

"It might. Yes."

"And would it prevent the lady from defending herself?"

"Yes, it would."

Roden got little help from Petty about Verna's head injuries, however. Petty had detected what looked like hemorrhaging in her scalp, he said, but there were so few blood cells in the brain tissue that he could not be sure whether it was a genuine hemorrhage, or simply left over from a previous autopsy.

On Douglas, however, Roden was on safer ground. The boy's injuries were real, Petty said. It was unlikely they were caused by the dory turning over and striking him because both the boat and the boy would have been cushioned by the water, resulting in a much softer impact. Those injuries, Petty said, were caused by a force applied at several different locations, near one another, both in time and place.

Roden was relieved. He had neatly tied Petty to Mauzey's scenario. He then tried to wrap it up by having Petty confirm that both mother and child were dead before anyone tried to resuscitate them.

How much force would have been necessary, he inquired, to cause Verna Roehler's head injuries?

Farley leapt to his feet to object. All the DA's tests with the dory and the dummy applied only to Douglas, he pointed out. Where was the foundation for these questions on Verna?

The judge agreed. "It appears to the court there may be an insufficient foundation about Verna Jo," he said, and then called for a bench conference out of earshot of the jury.

"You don't have anything at all concerning Verna other than speculation," he told a confused Roden.

It was a crushing blow. Without Verna, where was his case? The money from Douglas's insurance was payable to the children's trust, not to Roehler, which Roden knew the defense would quickly point out. Only the big payoff from Verna's insurance would be pocketed directly by Roehler and thus serve as a motive for murder. After two months in court, it looked like the case was about to come crashing around his ears. The defense had never looked better.

Ed Lascher, Roehler's appeals expert, presented a thirty-page, closely reasoned argument to the judge on why Roden's case should be thrown out. He argued that no one had shown that Douglas and Verna had died of any cause other than drowning. Even the state's big medical gun, Dr. Petty, couldn't say for sure whether Douglas's injuries could have rendered him unconscious. The DA in his opening statement had promised to show that Verna Roehler had been in "very, very . . . good physical condition . . . at the time of her untimely death," but his own witness had contradicted him most emphatically. Lascher argued that Roden was, "conducting investigations to ascertain whether any crime had been committed months after the trial began." Lascher dismissed the DA's complicated tests as "Rube Goldberg experiments" that disregarded so many factors as to render them useless. The welter of medical gobbledygook failed to address the question of whether the injuries had actually caused either death.

Lascher was especially scornful of Roden's alleged motive. "A defendant," he declared, "is not to be put to death for buying too much insurance as a result of a too-rosy view of his finances, over-susceptibility to high pressure, or the negligence of his advisors."

The Roehler family was convinced that the DA was about to be left with egg on his face. "I've felt it all the way through," Charlotte Roehler wrote to her son. "The judge keeps looking over at me and smiling." He didn't believe all that garbage; she just knew he didn't.

After delivering the prosecution's reply to Lascher's motion, Roden sat in his office in a blue funk. "I think he's going to throw it out. We didn't do enough."

But on March 10, Judge Rickard ruled that the show would go on. He did, however, hand the defense a bone; he knocked out one of the three special circumstances, namely the murder for profit of Douglas Johnson, pointing out that Douglas's insurance proceeds were payable to the children's trust and not to Roehler himself. It made no difference whatsoever to the case. Two special circumstances remained: multiple murder, and the murder for profit of Verna Roehler. More than enough if the jury convicted him to send Fred to the gas chamber.

22

Fred Roehler, Star Witness for the Defense

IT HAD BEEN RAINING ALL MORNING AND MOST OF THE NIGHT, THE kind of California winter rain that saturates within minutes. The heavy foliage around the courthouse was dripping like a South American jungle as spectators, lawyers, friends, and enemies of Fred Roehler scurried out of the wet and scrambled for seats in the courtroom.

At 2:15 p.m. on March 11, 1982, Judge Rickard turned to the defense table. "Would you call your first witness, please?"

Jim Farley rose, moving heavily from his seat to a lectern some twenty feet from the witness box. "We will call Fred Roehler to the stand."

The courtroom was packed. Word had quickly spread that the defense's lead-off witness would be Roehler. The decision to have him testify had not been taken lightly. It wasn't until two hours before that the DA knew for sure he'd get the chance to go toe-to-toe with the man he'd been trying to pin the crime on for nearly a year. Some in his office thought Roehler would exercise his right not to testify, but Roden was confident.

"With his ego, there's no way he's going to keep his mouth shut. This is a tragic-accident defense. He was the only other one out there; he's got to tell his story."

The defense indeed had debated long and hard about calling Fred to the stand. I knew this because two days earlier, as a friend of Fred's, I'd been summoned to a defense-team brainstorming session led by Jim Farley. I was ready to fervently weigh in: "Sure, it could happen just the way Fred said it did," I told Farley before Fred took the stand. "In fact, just a few weeks ago the same kind of mishap happened to my own son Gideon, who is Doug's age.

"Gideon was turned on his head by a huge wave while surfing. And he went into total panic. He was in a terrible state by the time we pulled him out. But to a Machiavellian mind that scenario might sound too obvious, because here's Fred, a man who is more expert in water than 99 percent of the population. Fred is in his element in the ocean. He knows what to do. And because he's such an expert in water, I worry that this approach might rebound badly against him. It's a stretch: Fred was able to save the dog—but not his wife and not his young son!

"And Fred testifying in his own defense is rife with risks," I told Farley. "He's so matter-of-fact that the risk is the jury might think, 'This guy is so bloody cool and calculated that it's conceivable he did it.' And the worst thing you could have is for Fred to get on the stand and then deliver a 'Movie of the Week' performance."

Farley agreed, knowing full well that when a defendant takes the stand, he opens himself up to any and all questions relevant to the case. He can become the prosecution's sitting duck. In other ways, Fred might come across as the perfect witness to handle the pressure. He was intelligent, calculating, fast on his feet. Yet in other ways, he was anything but.

Farley was still jittery. "He's got that damned German stoicism and he's too precise, too picky and deliberate. He'd be the first to admit there's a touch of arrogance about him, and he looks God-awful after all that time in jail. He could come across as sinister."

"Why don't we get a makeup artist to give him some color," defense investigator Russ Whitmeyer suggested, only half in jest.

We all agreed that if Fred kept his emotions in check, he'd also be in big trouble.

Jim Farley was concerned about something else—the daily presence of Roehler's parents in the front row, and the impression they might be making on the jury. They seemed self-satisfied, smug, too flippant about their son's plight. "There isn't a helluva lot we can do about them, mind you," Farley told Westwick. "Would you like to try and move them?"

In the hours before Roehler testified, Farley became his coach. "Relax, Fred. I know it's not easy, but be as natural as you can. If you feel like crying, let it out. Don't be so darned brave. This is the jury's first chance to get to know you, and if they see you as too controlled or as some kind of robot, they won't believe you. They don't know you as we do."

There wasn't an empty seat as the star of the show walked slowly to the witness stand, up the two short steps, and swore to tell the truth, the whole truth, and nothing but the truth.

A supporter from Malibu turned to Ron Roehler, sitting in the second row, and whispered, "Here we go again."

"No," snapped Fred's brother, not shifting his gaze. "Here we start. We've waited a year for this."

Dressed in his blue suit, freshly cleaned for the occasion, a blue shirt, and dark blue tie, Roehler looked pasty, the deep bags under his eyes falling almost onto his cheekbones. His skin, despite his best efforts to soak up some sun in the jail's exercise yard, was the color of aged, mashed potatoes. Only his voice, higher-pitched than usual, betrayed his nervousness. Quietly he gave his age as thirty-nine and his address, as of January 1, 1981, as 31685 Sea Level Drive in Malibu.

"Who lived there with you on that date?" Farley asked softly.

"My family."

"Who is that?"

As he whispered the name Verna, his face became a contorted mask. A sob shook his large frame. He could not continue; it seemed impossible for him to utter his late wife's name. A court watcher later said, "I called him a murderer, but when he couldn't say his wife's name, I knew in my gut the jury couldn't convict him."

For the rest of the afternoon, Farley let Roehler tell his story, both men taking particular care to refer to Douglas Johnson as his son. Outwardly, Farley seemed relaxed, but he consumed what he said was "a jugful" of nitroglycerine pills to prepare for this moment. Even so, he could hear his heart pumping crazily.

Roehler sat stiffly in the box, like a man on a bed of nails, even though the tone of Farley's questioning was gentle and supportive. Roehler said it had been "a consensus" suggestion that they go sailing on January 2.

The trip, he said, was uneventful, except for his sister-in-law's seasickness. The seas were calm at Little Scorpion, though outside in the open sea it was choppier. It had been Verna's idea to take the dory out to take pictures with the new camera. It had also been Verna's idea that Douglas did not row her around in the anchorage alone, and it was she who suggested the photograph of Douglas holding the puppy with Bird Rock in the background and the *Perseverance* sitting in the anchorage in the far distance. She had been the one directing him to the exact spot where she wanted him to take the picture.

Then everything began to go disastrously wrong.

Farley pinned up an aerial photograph of the area, and rising from his seat, Roehler went up and marked with an X the point where the dory was positioned when it overturned. With a ruler, he showed how, while looking through his camera sight, he was able to have the yacht in the background and a piece of Bird Rock to the side of the picture in the foreground. He described how he was trapped under the boat after it capsized, caught up by something, and unable to get free.

"Do you know exactly what it was that was tangled up?" Farley asked.

"I do not."

The only thing Roehler vividly remembered was struggling and having the bobbing boat hit him as he fought to free himself. He opened his eyes briefly, but the salt water kept him from seeing anyone or anything. He said he spent anywhere from thirty seconds to a minute trapped like that, and he thought he was probably snagged on the oarlock. Eventually, he freed himself and surfaced on the side of the boat nearest the rock.

At first, he could see neither Verna nor Douglas, so he went back to the dory, ducked under it, made a wide sweep with his hand, found nothing, and came back up again. It was then he spotted them.

He had told the story so many times now that it was fluent, but it was recounted for the jury's benefit in a flat, emotionless voice, the pitch seldom varying, as he described his efforts to desperately get his family the help they needed.

With Douglas in his left hand and Verna in his right, he said, "I had them in different places. Sometimes on the clothing up behind the neck of their jackets. I think, sometimes, towards the end, I actually had their hair, because I couldn't hold onto the jacket, and I had big handfuls of hair, holding them by their hair."

The jurors were scribbling furiously as Roehler described swimming to the rock. There, he managed to do for, "the damned dog" what he couldn't do for his wife and son—push her up to safety on the rock. He hailed two boats as they left the anchorage, he said, but none heard him.

"I could see the people on the boats. I could make out the backs of their heads, but they wouldn't turn around."

Farley inquired whether, in the water with Verna and Douglas in his arms, he could see the *Perseverance*?

"Just a glimpse."

Then why had he swum toward the rock instead of toward the *Perseverance*? Farley asked.

The jury sat, pens suspended.

Roehler said that from his perspective, the rock was the closest thing he could get to, but when he got there, he was stuck, unable to get a foothold, swept up and down by the surge as if on an elevator. He couldn't even hold onto the rock without losing his hold on Verna and Douglas because the surface was slippery, covered with brown leafy algae and green sea anemones. By that time, he realized that trying to climb out was just wasting energy. He felt desperate.

His voice began to crack, his eyes filling with tears as he continued, almost in a whisper.

"I was very scared. I was sick from the vomit from Doug's mouth and salt water, and what was going on was really getting to me. It just got colder, and nothing was working."

"Did you think about swimming around the rock?"

"Briefly, but I decided I really couldn't. My legs were giving out and Verna was sinking."

It was fifteen minutes or maybe even longer, perhaps half an hour after that, he said, when he saw the *Sound of Music*. "I was really beginning to lose everything. I was trying to breathe into Verna and Doug and that was causing me to hyperventilate. I was sick because Douglas was throwing up and Verna had a little vomit. We were drinking salt water because the waves were breaking over us. I was cold. I was very, very frightened. I don't know . . ."

His voice trailed off into silence.

Most of the jurors had stopped writing. They sat still, their eyes fastened on Roehler's face.

Roehler said that even when the *Sound of Music* crew began their rescue, his ordeal was by no means over. It took ten to twenty minutes for them to reach him and throw their rescue line, and when it fell short, he just about despaired. "It was all tangled up. I thought, my God, what could possibly go wrong more than this?"

He, Verna, and Doug were towed by the rescue boat, pulled under the waves repeatedly, taking in still more salt water. And when at last, first Doug, and then Verna, was taken aboard, he was left floundering in the waves.

When the judge recessed for the day, Roehler seemed drained, absolutely without energy.

But Farley was delighted. "You're doing great," he told his client. "You're answering exactly what I'm asking you and you're letting them see the Fred I know and trust. Just one thing though, Fred, you're inclined to fix your gaze on one spot and leave it there. It looks like you're staring, not really thinking about what you're saying. Move your eyes around, look animated. Look at the jury. Look at me. If you catch yourself staring, change your gaze."

Farley's concern was well-founded. Roehler's eyes were bothering a lot of people.

"Those piercing pale blue eyes, I've seen them before," a spectator said in the hallway. "Those are empty eyes—killer's eyes."

Picking up where he'd left off the day before, Roehler told the court how difficult it had been to get himself up onto the rescue boat.

"I really felt there was a good chance that I was not going to get out of the water that day." Cold and frightened, his legs useless, he couldn't even raise his knees high enough, he said, to get them onto the ladder. He was hanging on to it by his arms when the ladder slipped, sending him underwater again. Then another man rowed over in a small boat to help. He remembered the man removing his camera.

"Then I was trapped between the motion of the two boats and I got hit in the back of the head. It was like a chop, and I don't remember anything else. Nothing."

"Do you recall being taken on the Coast Guard boat?" Farley asked.

"I do not."

"Do you recall being placed in the helicopter?"

"I do not."

Then, what was the next thing he did recall?

"I recall someone shining a light in my eyes and saying, 'His eyes are pearl,' and 'Try not to bang the IV' and something about . . . he's too long for the basket . . . watch his head. And it was a detached feeling."

"What do you mean, 'a detached feeling'?"

"I didn't feel my hands and I didn't feel my arms, and I didn't . . . I wasn't speaking. I thought there was a good chance I was dead."

Farley moved from behind the lectern and stood in front of his client. "There has been testimony, Mr. Roehler, that Doug and Verna had some bruises. Do you know what caused those bruises?"

"I do not."

"On January 2, did you hit either Verna or Doug with your hands, with your fists, or with any object at all?"

"I did not." Roehler's voice was strong, confident.

Farley took a deep breath, expanding his barrel chest to its fullest. "Did you murder Douglas Johnson?"

"I did not."

"Did you murder Verna Roehler?"

"I did not."

Farley stepped back to the defense table. "I have nothing further, Your Honor."

23

Roehler v. Roden

THERE WAS ONLY ONE THING IN THE ENTIRE TRIAL THAT FRED ROEHLER and the man intent on sending him to the gas chamber agreed on: The crucial time for both was about to begin. They were very different and yet not altogether dissimilar—both private men whose public posture was just the tip of the iceberg. Neither was emotional; both had been accused of coldness, both with quick minds, both with a capacity to tolerate the mountains of detail others shunned, both regarded by their friends as slightly different, even somehow better than other people, able to resist the blandishments of the herd. These were men who had made their mark in life by following the dictates of their own consciences. Both men had enemies, people who disliked them intensely. Both hated to lose.

For probably the first time in his entire life, what Fred Roehler said was about to be seriously challenged. Stanley Roden did not believe him. Roden did not think Roehler was a hero. Roden did not think him perfect. But Roehler had no doubt he could best the DA. In private, he and his family made fun of the prosecutor, Fritz referring to him as "Rodent," and his son calling him, simply, "Stanley."

Farley had carefully limited Roehler's testimony to the events of one day, January 2, 1981, avoiding anything that might lay the foundation for the DA to range further afield. It was a calculated risk. The jury would see a one-dimensional Fred, as a boatsman and lifesaver. It was like pulling the curtain and letting the jury witness one scene in Roehler's life and one scene only. Farley reckoned the more dimensions, the more room for trouble. He was playing it very, very safe.

Confident as the defense was, Roehler knew he was not going to skate lightly through the upcoming interrogation. For the benefit of his parents and loyal friends, he maintained his cool persona:

> Hello family,
>
> Well, at least it should not be boring, ha-ha. Please, please stay relaxed . . . Stanley's true colors will be flying when he has his turn. They had eleven months to make me lose my temper and failed. Stanley will not make it now, either. I say, please stay relaxed for a number of reasons. First, your own health. Second, my health, ha-ha. Third, we are better, nicer people than Stanley. Fourth, the truth will come out loud and clear. Anxious? Yes, I'm anxious coz I want to come home. That's my only concern. We have not set up a dog and pony show so there is nothing for me to forget—I can almost feel Stanley's paranoia at times . . .

Roehler was right about one thing: Roden wanted him to lose his temper. "He's an arrogant bastard," he told investigators. "If we can make him show it, expose that contempt he has for people, we'll have won fifty percent of the battle."

From the beginning, however, the pattern was set. When asked a simple question about sea conditions, Roehler let everyone know he wasn't going to concede even the most insignificant point. Roden showed him a photograph of the sea at Bird Rock. Would he agree that the conditions in the picture were like those on January 2, 1981?

No, he would not. "This was taken from a boat, Mr. Roden. I did not enjoy that perspective."

Roden produced Charlotte's snapshots, taken at the anchorage on January 2, which he had been careful to introduce into evidence earlier. Then did *this* picture accurately reflect the conditions on that date? Roden asked.

"Yes, of course."

"But wasn't the sea, as depicted there, perfectly calm?"

"Well, not exactly, because that picture showed mainly the inside of the anchorage," Roehler said, while outside, he had seen some indications that the sea might have been different.

Roden persisted. "Do you see any wind chop in that picture, sir?"

No, but he did see some wind ripples.

Could he define "wind ripples"?

"I'm sure on the Beaufort Scale of Sea States," Roehler snapped imperiously, "a wind ripple is probably defined."

He was doing exactly what Farley had instructed him not to do—airing his knowledge, trying to one-up the DA. It was simply his nature to show that he was smarter and quicker than some dumb, plodding civil servant, even if his life depended on not doing so.

Roden immediately countered. "And how would you, on the Beaufort Scale, define the sea conditions shown in this photograph . . . calm?"

"Calm."

"Flat?"

"Flat."

"One stage above glass?"

"No."

Roden let it rest and went on.

"Now, sir, how far would you estimate that you swam, with the dog on your head, with your wife in one arm and Douglas Johnson in the other arm, until you went past the blowhole to pull the dog to safety?"

"Probably on the order of 100 to 150 feet."

"Now was all of that done on your back? Was that 100 to 150 feet that you were swimming with the dog on your head, and your wife in one arm, and your son in the other arm . . . and was all that done while you were on your back swimming?"

"Not precisely. No."

"Was it done in any way with the assistance of your arms, for stroking purposes?"

"No arms."

"So, all the propulsion for moving you for 100, 150 feet with the dog on your head, and your wife and Douglas Johnson, was done with your feet?"

"That's correct."

He had no idea what time he left the *Perseverance*; after all, he didn't wear a watch.

Yet hadn't he told Detective Ray that it was between 1:00 and 1:30 p.m.?

Roehler was irritated. "I could give you any number you wish because I did not look at the clock. No one told me what time it was. I just don't know."

Roden thumbed through a bound transcript and quoted what Roehler had told Detective Ray. Roden looked up. "Now did you make that statement, sir?"

"If it is written there, I probably did."

"Why, sir, is your estimate of January 7, 1981, a few days after the occurrence, different from your estimate today?" Roden was ice.

Totally unperturbed, Roehler answered, "They were all within the realm of possibility, Mr. Roden."

Roden felt he had scored an important point. If Roehler left the *Perseverance* at the latest around 1:30 p.m. and it had taken him the five to ten minutes he'd originally said to row to the Rock, by the time he was picked up at 3:00 p.m. by the *Sound of Music*, he had been in the water, holding up his wife and the child, for over an hour. Roden was sure this was a feat the jury would have difficulty believing even of Hercules. Roehler's story had therefore been changed to make everything considerably vaguer.

Would Mr. Roehler run through that swim one more time, please?

Jim Farley was delighted. The story never varied. The jury would have to believe it.

Roden, for his part, believed exactly the opposite. With every telling, he thought Roehler's story became more and more incredible. Thus, both men fed into each other's game plan, and both believed they were scoring points.

Roden then turned his attention to the puppy, Lady.

At what point had the dog materialized in this whole story? Not when Roehler came up from under the dory, not when he swam around the boat to see Verna and Douglas, not when he saw his wife resting on the boat, not when he swam over to Douglas and breathed air into him. The dog had suddenly appeared from nowhere. Had she? Had the dog made any noise?

No, she neither barked nor whimpered.

Maybe the dog didn't make a noise, Roden was implying to the jury, because she wasn't there, and maybe she wasn't there because she had been deposited safely on dry land sometime before the drownings.

Wouldn't the dog have been in his way? Roden asked.

She certainly didn't help, Roehler said, but then he hadn't wanted the dog in the first place, just as he hadn't wanted guinea pigs and rabbits and all the other pets the children eventually persuaded him to agree to.

Some of the jurors were smiling. Farley too was smiling. Fred was coming over as an indulgent, loving father.

During a brief recess, Farley told his client, "He isn't laying a glove on you."

To the amusement of the court, Roden produced a woolly teddy bear to have Roehler demonstrate, on an awkward-looking Fred Ray, where exactly the dog had rested on his head and shoulders. Then he asked him to explain how he had managed to transfer the animal from his shoulder to the cleft in the rock while his hands were fully occupied.

He had moved Verna over to his left hand with Douglas, Roehler explained, and used the other hand to grab the dog by its rear end and push her onto the Rock.

Did he really think that small dog could have climbed up the sheer face of the Rock by herself? Roden's eyebrows were up in his hairline.

He hadn't surveyed the Rock. Roehler was snippy. He simply knew he had put her up there, and that she had later been found on the top.

Roden would continue doggedly for days, methodically building brick by brick what he saw as Roehler's edifice of lies. He told the police he had been badly hurt while being banged up against the Rock as he struggled to keep his wife and child alive, but in the hospital, there hadn't been a scratch on him. Now, he said the action of the water refracting off the Rock had kept him away from it and saved him from injury.

He had told Fred Ray and Claude Tuller that he had been trapped under the dory by his camera strap, which had wrapped itself around the oarlock. But Duane Mauzey of the Santa Barbara crime lab had tested the camera and found that with only fifteen pounds of pressure applied to it, the links holding the strap twisted and bent like so much linguine. Roehler's camera, links, strap, and all, was completely intact. So again, Roden pointed out that Roehler's story had had to change. Perhaps it was the lanyard of his jacket or the wood toggles on the jacket's hood that had held him? Roehler could not be sure—and anyway, he had only Roden's word that this was the same camera he'd had with him that day. He owned several cameras like this . . . how could he be sure which one Roden was showing him?

How was it possible, Roden asked, that struggling for his life against something holding him down underwater, he could be so unsure what he was struggling against?

"It is complete speculation, Mr. Roden. Your guess is as good as mine."

Roden decided to replay for the jury the scene seconds before the dory turned over with Roehler frantically reaching across the boat to grab Douglas in one hand and the falling dog in the other.

At that point, according to his story, Roehler had been sitting on the floor of the boat with his legs up over the seat.

Then could he please explain how in a split second he had been able to get his bottom up and his legs turned around to make that lunge? Roehler was six foot two inches tall, was he not? And all this had been accomplished in a split second? Try it sometime, Roden seemed to suggest; it's a physical impossibility.

For Roehler's third day on the stand, Roden arrived in court looking frisky. There was no other word for it. He had spent the evening before closeted with the defense exhibits. Now he pinned up a photograph that Farley had used earlier and on which Roehler had marked with an X the spot where he said the dory overturned, a point which he had described as slightly outboard of, and above, the eastern point of Bird Rock.

Roden turned slowly from the picture to face the court. Could Mr. Roehler explain why he told Detective Ray, just five days after the event, that the point where his dory capsized was slightly above and outboard of the blowhole, which was in fact some considerable distance from the point of the Rock? Hadn't he in fact drawn a sketch for Detective Ray marking precisely where he was?

Roehler quietly said he would yield to his earlier recollection.

Roden was insistent. "Well, is that where the boat tipped over, Mr. Roehler—slightly above where the blowhole was and outboard of it?

"I believe at the time I gave Detective Ray a sketch of the best estimate of where I thought it was. And that was the purpose."

But hadn't Roehler told the police that he had been positioning his dory for the purpose of taking a photograph with the *Perseverance* in the background? The reason for Roden's friskiness was about to be made clear.

"If you had tipped over where you told Detective Ray you had tipped over, that is, between thirty to forty feet outboard of and above the blowhole, sir, there's no way you could have seen the *Perseverance*, could you?"

"I don't know, Mr. Roden."

"Mr. Roehler, the other day you took a ruler and showed us how one would have a line of sight from the black X where you say your boat turned over to the yacht. Did you not?"

"I did."

Would he now, Roden asked, take the same ruler, and show the court how he could have seen the *Perseverance* from a point about forty feet outboard of and above the blowhole?

Roehler made no move to the photograph. "I gave Detective Ray my best estimate on January 7, Mr. Roden."

"And you found out subsequently, did you not, Mr. Roehler, that where you told him you were was impossible, because you couldn't see the *Perseverance* from that point?"

No answer was given. None was required.

Roden had had a good day—good enough for him to finish with a grandstand play that woke everyone up.

"Mr. Roehler," he began slowly, "on the day in question you were rowing with wooden oars, were you not?"

"That's correct."

"And didn't those oars float when they were in the water?"

Roehler assumed so.

Did he see the oars when he came up from beneath the boat?

He did not.

Did he see the oars when he swam around the boat and saw his wife and Douglas Johnson in the water?

"No."

Or at any time thereafter did he see the oars that should have floated?

He did not.

How then did the oars disappear? Were they perhaps disposed of because they had been used for some other purpose than rowing?

Slowly Roden walked to the center of the court. As he passed his desk, he scooped up a large wooden oar lying behind it and, clasping it in his right hand like a gladiator hoisting a spear, turned and shouted, "Mr. Roehler, didn't you use an oar just like this to hit your wife over the head twice?"

The answer was reasoned and quiet. "No, I did not, Mr. Roden."

The next morning, Roden refocused on Roehler's position at the base of the Rock. When he was struggling to get a foothold, Roden asked, did he notice any barnacles?

By now Roden had not only surveyed the rock, but he could have run guided tours around it. He very strongly felt that if the jurors could only see its razor-sharp surface, they would realize that Roehler was a liar. Again and again, he begged the judge to allow the jury to go out to Little Scorpion to see the rock for themselves.

No, said the judge. It was too dangerous. The court could not take responsibility for the jurors' safety.

Instead, Roden and Detective Ray went out to the rock themselves with the intention of bringing back a large portion of it for the jury to see.

The judge, while confessing he was "not in love with the idea," said that if Roden was unwise enough to try it, he wouldn't stop him.

After a great deal of effort, the loss of several chisels and a couple of saw blades, they gave up. The rock stayed firmly intact.

"I think I saw some, yes," Roehler said in response to Roden's question about the barnacles on the Rock.

"Did you see any other sea life that had shells on it, sir?"

"I did not do a survey of the rock," Roehler repeated through clenched teeth.

"Did you suffer any cuts on your hands?"

"I did not."

"While you were banged up against the rock, sir, did you suffer any tears on your clothing?"

"I really had no way of telling, Mr. Roden."

"Throughout this whole ordeal, did you suffer any injuries at all, Mr. Roehler?" Roden almost spat out the words.

Roehler replied weakly that the following morning when he took a shower, he'd discovered abrasions under both his arms and he had a bad headache.

The rest of Roden's examination stayed firmly on dry land. Why was it, he asked, that of all the property the Roehlers owned, the only piece he had taken out mortgage insurance on was the only piece owned solely by his wife: her duplex on Broad Beach Road?

Roehler explained that in the summer of 1980, he had filled in and mailed a routine insurance company solicitation card. Then in January, after his wife's death, he was surprised to discover that the company, without any further communication, had granted him a policy. He had absolutely no prior knowledge that this policy had been issued.

Roden fumbled through the papers on his desk and held aloft a letter, issued by the underwriting department of the Life Insurance Company of New Hampshire, dated November 7, 1980, and addressed to Fred Roehler. He read the second paragraph aloud.

"Thank you for your recent application for decreasing term life coverage. Before we can determine your eligibility for coverage, we need to obtain details of your medical history. We have requested a summary from Dr. Harris. As soon as we receive the required information, we will make an underwriting decision and will advise you promptly."

Roden replaced the letter on his desk as if it were a delicate piece of Waterford crystal.

"Did you get that letter, Mr. Roehler?"

"I don't specifically recall receiving that letter."

Then did he receive a second letter from the same company, Roden asked, this one dated December 10, congratulating him on taking home protection coverage? Again, Roden read aloud: "'Your decision is a wise one and will do much to safeguard a most important possession—your home.' This letter tells you the effective date of the policy is January 1, 1981, and your premium payment is $23.83."

It was totally unnecessary for Roden to point out that one day after the policy took effect, Verna Jo Roehler was dead, and her duplex passed on to her husband, free and clear.

"Did you get that letter, sir?"

"Yes, I did."

Roehler said he couldn't remember when he'd received the letter, but he knew he hadn't opened it until sometime after January 1, 1981.

"The only thing I can recall is that we got a lot of what we call junk mail—that goes in one spot. And we get mail that's fairly serious—that goes in another spot. We were planning a trip to Northern California for the holidays, and I didn't get time to go through the junk mail."

"You sent an application for insurance and got a letter back and put it in the junk mail? Is that what you're saying?" Roden dripped with disbelief.

"That's certainly possible, Mr. Roden."

"What you're telling us," said Roden, his voice rising in mock astonishment, "is that very definitely you didn't open this letter dated December 10, 1980, until January 7, 1981. You remember that, don't you, Mr. Roehler?"

"I can state that unequivocally, that's correct."

Even as Roehler was denying knowledge of the policy that came into effect the day before Verna Roehler died, an attorney acting for him was suing the insurance company in a bad faith suit over nonpayment of the $46,390 policy. The company eventually paid the policy in full.

Just as he had paid scant attention to the mortgage insurance, Roehler claimed he had never carefully studied the trust documents he and Verna had signed at the end of October 1980. This explained, he said, how he had missed the insurance company's mistake, making Verna and himself owners and beneficiaries of each other's policies. He had only given the documents a simple once-over, planning to ask his personal lawyer, Bill Fairfield, for details later. It was all very complicated, he seemed to suggest, not something a layman could understand.

Roden was ready for another grandstand play. He pulled out four pages of graph paper, closely handwritten, showed them to Roehler, and asked if it was his handwriting.

Yes, it was.

"Sir, with reference to page one of that document, it says, 'initial trust.' It says 'income.' It says 'trustee' and so on. Now, sir, these four pages are, in fact, a detailed outline of the trust agreement, are they not, sir? And you drafted this outline by going through the trust line by line, paragraph by paragraph, page by page, and making these detailed notes. Isn't that correct, sir?"

Roehler admitted it was.

"Then how do you explain your answer of a few minutes ago, sir, that you didn't do anything other than casually glance at the provisions of the trust?"

What he had gone through was merely the rough outline, Roehler explained, and it was the finished trust that he had only cursorily glanced at.

But weren't the two versions virtually identical?

If there had been any major changes, Roehler said, he assumed his lawyer would have told him of them.

Roden did another swift ricochet from business affairs to the Roehler family relationships. Stalking up and down in front of his witness, like a Doberman guarding a compound, he asked "Sir, it is true, is it not, that you thought your wife had terribly spoiled Douglas Johnson?"

"No, that's not true."

"It is true, is it not, that you did not get along very well with Douglas Johnson?"

"That's also not very true."

That "very" stuck out as if it had quotation marks around it.

Roden asked if Roehler knew Dennis O'Gorman.

Roehler said that they had once shared an office.

Hadn't Roehler told O'Gorman on more than one occasion that he couldn't stand little Douglas because he was a spoiled brat?

"Not even once," Roehler protested.

"Did you tell Dennis O'Gorman that Douglas Johnson was the only one who had a decent meal around the house and that anything he wanted, he got?"

"No, sir."

"During the same time frame, did you tell Mr. O'Gorman that Douglas Johnson was the favored boy? That Verna would spank the girls, but never Douglas?"

"I don't recall ever saying that. Further, it's not true."

"Did you tell him, sir, during the same time frame, that you had a strong dislike for Douglas Johnson, in fact resenting him?"

"I have never said anything like that about Doug."

Roehler's denials were almost irrelevant. Simply by posing the questions, Roden had achieved what he wanted. He had implanted in the jury's minds the image of a grown man resenting an eight-year-old boy.

For the rest of the day, Roden concentrated on money: Roehler's making of it, spending it, and acquiring it through insurance. When Jack Pritchett, the Malibu broker, valued the Roehler homes for the purpose of inheritance taxes after Verna's death, he arrived at $350,000 for the Sea Level Drive house and only $200,000 for the Broad Beach duplex. Could Roehler explain why just five months before, for the purpose of purchasing insurance, he had inflated the same properties at $800,000 and $400,000 respectively?

Were there any fires or perhaps floods between September 1980 and January 1981 that might justify the drop in valuation? Roden oozed sarcasm.

No, Roehler responded. In September it had been a question of potential value. They had done extensive work on the Sea Level Drive property, and they had built the foundation for a future 2,400-square-foot addition. Roehler said the figures were speculation as to what the house would be worth in a year when the work was finished.

Did the Travelers Insurance agent tell him to speculate what it might be worth a year from September?

"I don't recall Mr. Wylie asking me to speculate."

It was a bad moment, and evidence the two Jims had dreaded was coming up, but it wasn't too bad, Farley kept reminding himself. "Bill Fairfield will handle it for us when he's called."

And so, it continued, with Roehler taking blows even though his attorneys thought his explanations were reasonable and logical. But things were about to take a rapid turn for the worse.

The financial experts Roden called had testified to Roehler's dwindling resources. Was there any additional cash in his estate that they might have missed, Roden enquired.

Yes, Roehler said. He was glad Roden asked the question. He kept a little over $30,000 plus $3,000 in travelers' checks stashed in a deep freeze in his garage. This was news to Roehler's lawyers, both of whom were owed considerable amounts of money by their client, and who had on his behalf been pleading poverty to the County of Santa Barbara. In fact, that very day, they had argued before a different judge that Roehler should be declared indigent, and that the county should bankroll the rest of his trial, which the County, in fact, had agreed to do.

This was to rebound badly. It drew the inevitable "cold cash" headline in the *Santa Barbara News-Press* story by veteran court reporter Richard Aguirre, who covered the case from start to finish. What the jury must have thought of someone who secreted large sums of money away in bizarre places could only be guessed at.

Why hadn't he told Ray and Tuller about the cash when he was giving them a rundown on his finances?

"I didn't think it was any of their business."

Why didn't he use any of that cash to pay his outstanding property taxes?

Roehler said he had simply forgotten.

And why hadn't he paid the $2,000 owing on Verna's Visa card?

That was a subtle form of checks and balances on his wife's spending, he said.

Roden perked up. Was Verna's spending something of a bone of contention between them?

No, it was not.

Wasn't Mrs. Roehler's spending on herself and the children a constant source of dissension?

No, it was not.

With $2,000 owing on a Visa card and property taxes unpaid, why did Roehler take out $400,000 worth of insurance, plus $300,000 accidental coverage, on a woman who earned approximately $200 a month?

Roehler responded carefully. "We were balancing our estates. My wife's work and my work were about fifty-fifty. We did not get into the 'breadwinner' type of discussion, because I felt that my wife's value in the house was quite significant."

Stanley Roden showed up on St. Patrick's Day for his final head-to-head session with Fred with a clump of shamrocks in his lapel. It was the perfect complement to Jim Farley's kelly-green tie. But the defense attorney seemed to have considerably more bounce in his step. Roehler's lawyers believed that even with Roden hitting their client with everything he had, Fred was still way ahead on points.

"He's skipping around like a grasshopper with hiccups," Farley crowed, "and the jury's just not buying it. There's so many holes in his reasoning, it's like a piece of Swiss cheese."

The night before, however, Roehler had called a friend from jail and admitted it had been a mistake to mention the cold storage cache. "It made me sound like a hoarder and a flake. I should have kept my mouth shut." Nonetheless, the next morning he seemed to have his old confidence back. The dory had been brought into court again and the dummy and the woolly teddy bear were propped up on the stern. Roehler scribbled a quick note to his parents: "Poor Stanley is going to get a hernia with his experiments, and I am going to tell him I cannot recall the instant replay responses he wishes. I will try to sit in the damned thing [the dory], but that's about it. Why is it that I feel Stanley will not be finished with me today? Ha-ha. He was getting loud again, wasn't he?"

Roden indeed wanted Roehler to get into the dory to show the jury exactly where Roehler, Douglas, and the beagle puppy had been positioned at the instant the boat overturned.

Westwick and Farley objected, and Judge Rickard agreed with them.

The DA then suggested they all go out to the harbor and put Roehler and the dummy in the boat with the jury as witnesses. Again, the judge ruled against it, saying that any reenactment would be right there on the carpet with no one getting wet, and it would not include Roehler getting into the boat.

Roden hoped to demonstrate that Roehler would have had to have been a contortionist to have reached the boy and the dog from his position on the floor of the dory. He tried again.

"What is your shirtsleeve length, Mr. Roehler?"

Roehler couldn't remember. It was so long, he said, since he had bought a long-sleeved shirt.

Roden asked the judge for permission for the prosecution to go to Roehler's Malibu closet and find a shirt to determine the length of his arms.

No, ruled the judge.

Undaunted, Roden strode over to the dory sitting incongruously in the well of the court.

"For the record," he pointed out, "we have the dummy in evidence holding this poor excuse for a beagle here in his lap."

Roehler, on Roden's instruction, was now standing beside him holding a microphone attached to a long cord like a nightclub entertainer about to burst into song.

"Now, is that approximately the position of Douglas Johnson you described? Is that where he was, sir?"

"In the grossest terms, yes."

"In the grossest terms?" Roden looked pained. "Means . . . what, sir?"

Roehler exploded. "That damned thing does not look anything like my son, nor does it look like the dog. There is no lifejacket and no jacket on the boy. Nothing in my mind's eye that can identify with this mess," he angrily snapped.

Coldly, Roden asked him how he possibly could have reached the fifty-three inches (Roden had measured it) to make that grab for the boy and the dog.

"Could you help us, then, Mr. Roehler, place Douglas in the attitude you describe, half in and half out of the boat?"

Roehler was not about to do that either.

"This thing you've done here," he hissed, "doesn't remind me of my son. It doesn't look like him or anything else. It's not the picture I had in my mind. You could move that apparatus," he almost spat the word, "two feet forward and you would be very close."

He'd dodged the Roden trap, but for the first time in five days, Roehler really lost his cool. His eyes were flashing, his face flushed, his bitterness and anger spilling over. Standing just inches from the DA, he seemed volatile, almost threatening.

Roehler moved back to the stand and Roden shuffled his notes.

"Sir, prior to January 2, 1981, had you read a book called *Eyelids of Morning* by Alistair Graham and Peter Beard?"

"Irrelevant," snorted Farley.

Roden called for a sidebar. The book, he told the judge, had been found at Roehler's home when he was arrested. "There's a scene in the book, where a man gets into a situation in the water where he finds himself struggling for his life, and when he finally is rescued, he can't use his legs."

"Finally rescued . . . and what?" echoed Rickard. "Cannot use his legs, just like in this case."

Westwick wanted to know what that had to do with the offense of murder.

Roden explained that he didn't believe Roehler when he said he couldn't use his legs to climb onto the *Sound of Music*—that obviously he had picked up the idea from the book he'd been reading.

Objection sustained.

At 11:50 a.m., Roden announced, "I have no further questions, Your Honor."

That day we lunched with our friend Margaret Millar, Santa Barbara's famous crime novelist, who had a seat reserved for her in the courtroom. Millar, the wife of hard-boiled detective writer Ross Macdonald (real name, Kenneth Millar) was a savvy observer of life and crime, with a sharp tongue. She was not impressed with Fred Roehler, even though we strongly argued that in our minds, he was a victim himself, a modern-day Job.

"He did it," she imperiously declared.

24

The Defense Strikes Back

WITH ROEHLER'S SIX-AND-A-HALF DAYS ON THE STAND BEHIND THEM, Farley and Westwick now set out to bolster his story. They would call fewer than a dozen witnesses to do so. While Roden had presented a mountain of mostly technical evidence, the defense would try to use language the jury would understand. In any case, they were convinced they didn't have much to answer for.

"Roden's been speculating like crazy," Farley told Westwick. "Every two minutes he comes up with another theory. First Fred bashed their heads on the boat, then he killed them with an oar. Next, he'll have him strangling them. The man is desperate, and it shows. It's been five months of horseshit."

The defense's strategy was now simply to present their contention that Fred Roehler had not killed Verna and Douglas in the water, or anywhere else. They began by calling Martin J. Nemiroff, a thirty-six-year-old flight surgeon with the US Coast Guard in Kodiak, Alaska. Dr. Nemiroff spent much of his working day jumping out of helicopters, diving into freezing cold seas, dragging men out of submerged planes, helicopters, and boats, and then attempting to drag them like Eurydice across the Styx, back from the dead.

He had performed eighty cold-water rescues in the last year alone, and he defined cold water as anything below 70 degrees. In Kodiak, however, the water temperature in the summer months was approximately 50 to 55 degrees, almost exactly the winter temperature of the waters around Santa Cruz Island.

Cold-water drowning, he explained, was vastly different from submersion in warmer water. In cold water, a strange quirk of the body mechanism—a throwback almost to an earlier stage of evolution—went into operation. It was called the mammalian diving reflex. When cold water hit the face, he explained, it sent an emergency signal to the body, which immediately slowed respiration and heartbeat, redirecting the flow of blood away from the outer layers of the body toward the inner layers.

"What does it look like?" Farley asked.

"In its extreme form," Nemiroff explained, "in human beings, a person would be blue, not breathing, cold to touch, and might have unreactive pupils or eyes. There would be no signs of heartbeat or respiration. In other words, in its extreme form, the mammalian diving reflex makes a human look dead."

Because of that reflex, his research suggested, a person could be brought back to life after spending as long as one hour completely submerged in cold water. It explained why young children pulled from the bottom of frozen lakes, apparently completely lifeless, are sometimes later revived.

Nemiroff said he believed Verna and Douglas could have been resuscitated aboard the *Sound of Music*. Had paramedics kept their electric paddles on the two longer, they might well have detected a heartbeat. Nemiroff had found a pulse in cold-water drowning victims as slow as once every two minutes, and they had survived. He also wanted to make it clear that only in the movies do people who are drowning scream for help, their arms flailing all over the place. In cold water, they often slip silently under the waves. All that coming up three times with lots of panic and struggle was strictly a myth.

And did it surprise him that good swimmers might become incapacitated so quickly?

Nemiroff told the court about the "involuntary gasp" produced by an unexpected dumping into the water, such as in a boating accident. The shock often generates a sharp sucking in of breath, and with it, large quantities of water. It often leads to almost instant drowning.

In answer to a question from Farley, Nemiroff said that Douglas Johnson's life jacket might not have provided protection for him. On the contrary, it was an encumbrance that could have made it more difficult for him to swim. As for Verna, her heart condition could have drastically limited her survival time in the water.

Farley was nearing the crux of the point. Nemiroff agreed that in most drownings, or near drownings, the bodies are often injured because of the rescue effort. Bodies pulled roughly from the water during a rescue attempt are often bent in unusual positions, and because of this, they can often be subjected to minor injuries, he noted.

"I've seen various bruises. I've seen fractures occur. I've seen lacerations."

It was exactly what Farley needed, but then he went one step too far. "In your experience Doctor, is the rescuer himself sometimes injured in a rescue effort?"

"In my personal experience, I feel like I've been run over by a truck the following day. I have bruises on my shins. I have bruises on my elbows. I have bruises on my knees . . ."

It remained only for Stanley Roden to point out the obvious: Fred Roehler had emerged from his lengthy rescue attempt without so much as a scratch.

Roden went after Dr. Nemiroff with a vengeance, so much so that he later privately apologized to him. But he had little choice. Nemiroff was perhaps the best in the world when it came to cold-water drownings. If the jury believed him, he could take away an essential arm of Roden's case—namely, that Verna and Doug were dead when rescued, and the bruises Dr. Hunter found were premortem.

On Wednesday, March 24, Bill Fairfield nervously took the witness stand on behalf of his close friend, Fred Roehler. Fairfield looked pale and uncomfortable. To him alone fell the task of convincing the jury that Roehler's large insurance purchases were at his urging. For that and that alone, Fairfield believed his friend was now on trial for his life.

In the day and a half he was on the stand, Fairfield took responsibility for just about everything Fred Roehler had ever done, short of fathering his kids. It was he who suggested the insurance; it was he who told Roehler to inflate the values of his property for the purpose of buying more insurance. After Verna's death, it was he who told Fred to come up with the lowest possible property valuation for tax purposes. He was even willing to let himself be depicted as an incompetent attorney if it would help his friend.

He had also changed his mind about one important fact in the year since he'd spoken to the police. He told Fred Ray he had never discussed insuring the Roehler-Johnson children with his client, but under questioning by Jim Westwick, he remembered some "general discussion" on the subject. "I merely stated to him, 'What about insurance for the children?' And I believe all I said was, 'I don't know what to tell you. I know I have some insurance on my children, and if you are going, if you are truly going to have them become a part of the estate at some point in time, through a partnership or a corporation, you may want to consider buying it.'"

There was something about Fairfield that Roden simply didn't like. He had had to destroy Nemiroff, but he hadn't enjoyed it. Fairfield was different. Maybe it was because he, as a former prosecutor, was, in Roden's eyes, now shielding a murderer. Whatever the reason, Roden was never quite able to hide his distaste for the affable lawyer.

Roden said he assumed that as a good and prudent attorney, Fairfield had instructed his client that because of a change in California's tax laws, there would be a considerable reduction in state taxes should he or his wife die after January 1, 1981.

Fairfield said he had been out of his practice from the time of his heart attack in October 1979, and was somewhat out of touch with new developments in the tax laws. He had never advised Roehler of the change.

Roden then wanted to know why Fairfield had advised his client to inflate his property values for the purposes of buying insurance when he knew it would cost him more money. Fairfield said he hadn't told Roehler it would cost more, but had simply suggested it so his client wouldn't have to remember year after year to reassess his insurance needs, as property values rose.

But surely that wouldn't have been necessary for a man of Roehler's methodical nature, Roden suggested. Wouldn't Fairfield agree that the defendant was a very methodical person?

"Yes, sir."

"You said, 'Yes, sir' with a certain amount of emphasis. Do you mean he's a *very* methodical person?"

"Fred Roehler is a very thorough and a very methodical person."

"With a good memory?"

"With an excellent memory."

"And he thinks things through?"

Fairfield began to see where all this was leading. "I think Fred thinks things through fairly well."

The next day Roden attacked on other fronts.

Did the mortgage insurance policy on Verna's Broad Beach home—the one that came into effect the day before she died—have anything whatsoever to do with the estate plan Fairfield had prepared for the Roehlers?

No, it did not. Fairfield said he had not been aware of that policy, nor had he ever discussed it with the defendant or with the owner of the property, Verna Roehler.

Fairfield also confirmed that he had not discussed with Fred or Verna Roehler the accidental death benefits attached to the insurance.

"It wasn't part of your advice to him or her, was it, sir?"

"No, I didn't . . . we didn't get into a discussion with respect to accidental death."

During defense lawyer Jim Westwick's redirect, Fairfield, who had been close to the edge all day, finally broke down and cried when he talked about his feelings for Fred Roehler.

"Mr. Roden asked me if I am close to him. I am close to him; he's like a brother to me."

There was no need to say it. His whole demeanor from the moment he'd come into court had been that of a man whose love of Roehler was enough for him to put his credibility, even his professional integrity, on the line. And that was precisely what Roden's questions were designed to show.

Bill Fairfield had given Roehler his all. Never for an instant had he questioned his friend's innocence. If he had, he would have had to consider the terrifying possibility that he may have been the one to hand Fred Roehler a motive to murder his wife. He had also spent the last year shoring up Roehler's case, making sure the insurance claims were paid, taking care, as he always had, of Roehler's business. To now allow the question of Fred's guilt to enter his thoughts for even a moment might well have driven him mad.

The next few witnesses were designed to pile on the doubt. They ranged from a Santa Barbara marine meteorologist, who said the conditions at Bird Rock when the prosecution filmed their dory tests there were in no way comparable to those of January 2, to an electronics engineer, who produced photographs showing that it was possible for Roehler to have taken the pictures Verna wanted from the spot he claimed. Roden, however, quickly established that the engineer's photos were not taken from a yacht at sea level, which was where Roehler had described himself to be.

The defense got considerably more help from Tony Clinch, who recovered the beagle from the top of Bird Rock the day after the drownings and passed her on to Roehler's good friend, Dick Velthoen. January 3, he said, was virtually a carbon copy of the previous day, and both had a "very nasty sea." He had let his fourteen-year-old son out onto the rock to retrieve the dog and had to wait twenty minutes for the ocean to calm down before he could get near enough to get the boy back into his boat with the dog. In addition, he said he had seen a spot where he thought a dog could have scrambled up the sheer north face of the rock, just as Roehler had said she had.

Cam Zeitner also made a brief appearance. She was quite sure that the decision to take a trip on *Perseverance*, made on the evening of January 1, as the whole family sat around the dinner table in Malibu, was made by both her daughter and her son-in-law. In fact, she said, if one of them was pushing for it more than the other, it was Verna and not Fred.

The medical evidence for the defense was considerably more succinct than Roden's. After a Santa Barbara pathologist who stood in on part of Dr. Hunter's autopsy, Dr. John Blanchard, testified that he had reviewed the slides and was convinced there was no evidence of foul play in the deaths, the stage was set for the defense's big hitters. They had left the medical stars for last.

Richard Lindenberg and Werner Spitz were two of the world's most distinguished pathologists, and it turned out that their job was to destroy the prosecution's contention that there were actual bruises on Verna and Doug's heads, and that they were deliberately inflicted by Roehler. Any bruises were simply the result of clumsy rescuers or the two autopsies.

Both witnesses had been members of the Rockefeller Commission on CIA Activities within the United States, the body investigating the assassination of John F. Kennedy. Lindenberg, born in Berlin, was a neuropathologist from the University of Maryland, a world expert on trauma to the brain, consultant to the Luftwaffe from 1939 to 1945, and thereafter, to the US Air Force. Spitz, chief medical examiner of Detroit, had written the standard textbook on forensic science. He was a member of the American Academies of Forensic Science and regularly flew around the world as a highly respected consultant. They didn't come any more distinguished or Teutonic. Together they put on what the prosecution called the Franz and Hans Show, a Germanic two-step that had Stanley Roden grinding his molars into talcum powder.

One by one, Jim Farley showed Dr. Lindenberg pictures and slides of the bruises Dr. Hunter had found on Douglas Johnson's head, and one by one Lindenberg dismissed them with the disdain of an expert in Ming porcelain assessing a Target reproduction.

"These are not trauma . . . This is not intra vitam [during life] . . . The alteration here is not traumatic, there is no alteration here . . . This is not a hemorrhage . . . These are not premortem . . . These are artifacts from a previous autopsy."

Lindenberg was succinct. He'd brought his own teaching slides to illustrate real premortem injury. Each one came with its own story. Lindenberg was something of a raconteur. He told the jury about the twenty-five-year-old woman who drowned in her bath, and the Baltimore Orioles fan who got battered with a beer bottle by a rival team supporter.

"He hit her over the head and said, 'You fool,' and the fool fell to the ground and was dead." Lindenberg chortled. Now that was trauma. What he was seeing here was not.

Lindenberg's twinkling *gemütlich* folksiness was driving Roden crazy. He was an old hand at this. Hunter had put everybody to sleep; Lindenberg could make the gruesome testimony as acceptable as a Jimmy Kimmel monologue.

The injuries on Verna's and Douglas's heads, he was certain, were postmortem and were probably produced because Dr. Duncan, in the first autopsy, had cut too small an opening in the skull and had bruised the brain while trying to extract it for examination. Lindenberg had found bone meal in all the brain tissues, proving conclusively that they had been caused by the first autopsy. When Lindenberg began setting up his microscope to show the jury the bone meal in Hunter's "bruised and hemorrhaging tissues," Roden made a vain attempt to curb the doctor's exuberance.

"Is he going to be allowed to make jokes and 'folks it up' with the jury, or is he going to be restricted in the kind of comment he can make? We are going to have a television talk show here," he told the judge.

Before turning him over to the district attorney, Farley ran Lindenberg through the prosecutor's theory about the pattern of Doug's bruises.

Lindenberg said he had thought of everything that could conceivably have caused those funny parallel marks. "Suddenly it dawned on me. That there is a possibility—again, something that the experienced pathologist remembers—and that is that it happened at the time of the autopsy, and it has to do with the head resting on the headrest."

To Farley, it was a gift. "Doctor," he said, "yesterday I showed you the dory and the dummy. There has been testimony in this case—they developed a pattern by pushing the dummy's head against the dory gunnel and then down onto the gunnel support arm, and in that manner, they were able to produce the pattern of those four bruises."

That simply wouldn't fly, Lindenberg said, because two of those four bruises had to be thrown out right from the start.

"Why is that, Doctor?" Farley was having difficulty keeping his smile under control.

"Those bruises," declared Lindenberg, "are postmortem. I have no doubt about it, not at all—100 percent."

Roden was seething.

Charlotte Roehler thought Lindenberg was the star of the trial. "I decided to wear my very best suit today," she wrote to her son on the second day of the doctor's testimony, "since it is cool and there's a very important witness here today. I introduced myself to him last evening when the court session was over; he is a very dear man. I really enjoyed the few minutes I talked with him. I want to tell him later about your grandfather Otto Louis and Hilda Marie Alma—real German names—and Neuheart being another good German name. Sort of humor in all this, isn't it."

As he got up to cross-examine Lindenberg, Roden was not one whit intimidated. The more he needled him, the more the doctor's *gemütlichkeit* vanished. This was not a man accustomed to having his opinion questioned, especially by some small-town prosecutor. As Roden's questions became more and more aggressive, Lindenberg visibly stiffened.

"Sir, is it so difficult to understand what I say? It is so simple."

Roden never really managed to put a dent in Lindenberg's devastating opinions. The bruises were not inflicted during Doug's "death struggle," he insisted. It was 100 percent postmortem. And furthermore, to use a dummy to re-create the "bruises" was ridiculous.

"The dummy doesn't say, 'Don't do this, Father.' It doesn't fight or kick," said Lindenberg. "If Douglas had been struggling for survival, he would have thrown himself around." Even with his fractured English, Lindenberg got his point across. In the prosecution's scenario, it would have taken two identical blows to produce the two round bruises.

Werner Spitz was even more devastating to Roden's case than his colleague. He didn't have Lindenberg's flamboyance, but stressed repeatedly that any bruises were simply caused by the autopsy. As for Verna,

Spitz insisted that she was "a walking time bomb, in or out of the ocean, because her hypertension was severe and far advanced.

"I have come to realize," Spitz continued, "that if you are overzealous you see patterns. It reminds me like when we were kids, we used to look up at the sky and see faces in the clouds. This is a hazardous thing to do."

Farley couldn't have asked for anything better. Spitz was practically spelling it out: Dr. Hunter had looked too closely and found what was never there.

Roden's exchange with Spitz was more polite than with Lindenberg, but just as crushing to the prosecutor's case. The DA found himself painted into a corner, looking like someone who had no idea what he was talking about. As always with Roden, the more under siege he felt, the more convoluted his questions became.

Spitz begged for mercy. "Sir, would you do me a favor," he pleaded, "and ask me the questions a bit shorter? I forget the question by the time you finish reading it or telling it."

And from time to time, Spitz let his exasperation show. "You obviously have never opened a head," he snapped at Roden, "so you don't know what I'm talking about."

Roden's investigator, Dempsey Billey, took the stand on April 19. He stated that the day before, he, Roden, Fred Ray, and Mike Davis, one of the *Sound of Music* rescuers, had sailed back to Bird Rock. In wet suits, Billey and Ray had jumped in the water at the exact point where Roehler had struggled at the base of the rock, and both were able to push a forty-pound canvas bag wrapped in a life vest (representing Douglas) up onto Bird Rock. They'd also managed the same chore with a woman of Verna's size. But Rickard refused to let them show the videotape of these latest tests, noting that conditions at the Rock were in no way like those on January 2.

He also denied Roden's suggestion that the jury be taken out to the anchorage. The court could not be responsible for the jury's safety while splashing around in boats.

25

Closing Arguments

"WHAT, LADIES AND GENTLEMEN OF THE JURY," STANLEY RODEN BEGAN his closing argument, "does your common sense tell you about this case?"

Roden had spent enormous amounts of the county's money and more time than any district attorney had ever taken in Santa Barbara's history to present his case. Now he seemed to be saying, "Forget all the technical stuff we've bored you with, forget the myriad tests, forget the charts and weather maps and skull models; let's bring all this down to human terms.

"Look at the logic of it and see for yourself that Fred Roehler is a liar and a murderer."

Roehler sat grasping one knee with both hands as if he was holding himself in check. As he approached his fortieth birthday, the year he'd spent in prison was showing in the deep lines of his face, the gray in his hair, and his sunken eyes.

This was no tragic accident, Roden insisted. It was murder, cold and calculated. Only two things were alive when it was all over—a dog and a man—a man left with $800,000 tax-free dollars. That $800,000 worth of insurance was going to cost the man, who was clearly in financial trouble, $3,700 a year. He wasn't going to be able to keep that going for long.

"Now, what does your common sense tell you about that?" Roden paused, as if waiting for the jurors to lift their heads from their notebooks. "And not only does he get $800,000, but he also gets 25 percent of his wife's estate outright and all the income from the rest of it."

Eight hundred thousand dollars. The figure seemed to grow with each repetition.

"That represents a lot of freedom," Roden continued. "Freedom to travel, the freedom not to work."

The DA quickly ran through Roehler's financial picture, pointing out the weak spots, and then reminding the jury that this impecunious person was about to head out on a six-month cruise.

"What does your common sense tell you about that?"

"At some point, you're going to have to sit back and reflect on this by yourself, when the kids are asleep, and you're going to ask yourself, 'Did I do the right thing?' If the answer is 'Yes,' that's beyond a reasonable doubt."

Stanley Roden's closing argument was based on common sense. The two Jims—Farley and Westwick—believed they had sowed enough reasonable doubt in jurors' minds to get an acquittal. And Farley, in particular, allowed his firm faith in his client's innocence to influence his summation.

"You've seen this man sitting in court since October," said Farley, "and you've seen him on the stand for eight days under extremely searching examination. Does he fit the image the prosecutor wants you to accept of a scheming, cold-blooded brute? You've been watching, and you're asked to believe all this was because he didn't want to work anymore. Is that the impression you got from this man as he testified? Is this a high-stepping good liver?"

Farley's questions were almost childlike. He was playing with dynamite; the whole thing could well have exploded in his face. To all the questions, the jury could have answered yes just as easily as no.

If this was a crime, Farley noted, then Roehler had put his own life in danger to commit it.

Westwick was more pragmatic, and he hammered consistently at the holes and contradictions in the prosecution's case.

"Why are we here?" he asked. "Not because of Hunter's autopsy, not because of any distinctive pattern of bruises on Douglas Johnson's head, found after the trial began. The reason my client is on trial for murder is because of the insurance on his wife's life." And even if the advice the

Roehlers had received on insurance was 100 percent wrong, they had followed it in good faith.

Farley rose again to conclude for the defense like a grizzly trying to tiptoe into a campsite filled with sleeping vacationers. "What happened at Bird Rock was an accident and not a crime, but a terrible tragedy." He finished so softly that the jurors had to strain to hear.

The prosecution had the last word, once again hammering the reasonable doubt element.

"At some point," said Roden again, "you are going to have to sit back and reflect, when the kids are asleep, and you're going to ask yourself, 'Did I do the right thing?' If the answer is 'yes,' that's beyond a reasonable doubt."

On Monday, May 3, 1982, at 11:30 a.m., the Fred Roehler case went to the jury after some seventy witnesses, 392 exhibits, 7,495 pages of testimony in sixty-nine volumes, and a total cost to prosecution and defense of almost $2 million. The seven-woman, five-man jury (after three months one of the male jurors had been excused to take a new job and was replaced by a woman alternate) would be sequestered at a nearby hotel, an unusual step in Santa Barbara, but understandable considering the intense local interest in the case.

It was the one-hundredth court day and the judge, following his leisurely pace, took the entire morning to give his instructions. The people's case, Judge Rickard told the jury, rested substantially, if not entirely, on circumstantial evidence. Therefore, the law insisted that if two possible explanations existed for a fact, one tending to point toward innocence and one toward guilt, they were obliged to choose the one pointing toward innocence.

Roden thought those instructions virtually guaranteed at least a hung jury.

"Boy, he did just about everything but tell them outright to put him back on the street," Fred Ray grumbled.

26

The Verdict

The waiting seemed endless. At lunchtime, Sally and I sat with the Roehler family, nervously picnicking on the lawn in the glorious sunshine. Fritz Roehler kept up his nonstop quips, and Charlotte said that she was letting herself relax for the first time. She knew her ordeal would be over soon. And frankly, having sat through the mountain of testimony, Sally and I had to agree with them. The insurance stuff—the motive for the killings—was wishy-washy. Fred's lawyer and pal, Bill Fairfield, had sworn under oath that it was he who'd suggested Fred take out heavy insurance.

Ron Roehler sat by the courtroom door looking exhausted, his right leg elevated. He'd been his older brother's chief messenger boy for over a year, getting up in the middle of the night two or three times a week to make the 300-mile round-trip from his San Bernardino home to Santa Barbara, trying to reconcile the needs of his family—now doubled in size, with the addition of Kimberly Johnson and Fred's two young daughters—with his brother's long list of tasks.

I knew he was worn out. Several times, particularly on the weekends during the trial, Ron and his family and Fred's daughter had all stayed at our Ventura County house rather than making the long journey back to San Bernardino or having to pay for expensive hotels in Santa Barbara. Ron was also making payments on the Roehler houses, keeping the yacht maintained, and paying the mounting bills while continuing to run his own business. The strain had almost killed him. He'd been hospitalized with phlebitis during the trial; his own life was now in jeopardy, and he'd become so bitter over the terrible injustice he thought was being perpetrated on his brother that he had sought psychiatric counseling.

Ron's wife Elizabeth and their children were having to make sacrifices, too. Piano lessons and sports had to go because Elizabeth just didn't have the time for the children's activities. She had put aside her own plans to finish college. "I sometimes wonder," she said sadly, "if Ron and I will ever get back to being just our family again." She worried, too, that her in-laws were counting their chickens. "Charlotte insists she's going to walk out of here with Fred, but I think they should be prepared for anything."

Meanwhile, Fred Roehler was reviewing the past year for the benefit of his parents and children, now that it was all about to come right again, penning lengthy handwritten letters to friends and family:

> I equate the reaching of a verdict to finishing the work required for the Eagle Scout award, graduation from Purdue and Berkeley, all wrapped in a single moment. The moment will be as good as the other three for the same reasons. We have earned it. No gifts, no handouts, no inside track, just plain work. This moment is ours. We need not ask why we had to ever reach this point, but reach it we have. Do not detract from the moment with tension and worry. Quiet meditation, a sip or two of something, a walk through the courtyard, whatever is the best relaxer for you, enjoy it. Simply and respectfully, I do thank the Lord for each day we experience and the special promise of the new days yet to come. Have a good day.
>
> Much love,
>
> Dad/Fred

On the second day of deliberations, the jury asked to review the exhibits and to see the footage of the dory tests at Bird Rock. Judge Rickard refused the latter. He wanted to ensure that they did not use the film incorrectly to decide what had happened at the rock on January 2, 1981.

In the hallways and on the lawns, those for and against Roehler kept to their respective groups. As the days dragged on, the atmosphere between them grew more hostile. There were rumors of a hung jury. Hundred-dollar bets were being placed on the outcome.

By Thursday, Jim Farley looked like a man about to face a firing squad. He was in church every morning offering daily masses for his client, watching his own blood pressure escalate dangerously, torturing himself with the thought that perhaps his arguments hadn't been persuasive enough, that he'd somehow alienated the jury. But the longer it went, he told himself, the better it was for Fred. If they were going to convict him, they would have done it by now.

Stanley Roden agreed. He was becoming more and more withdrawn from his team, and increasingly despondent. At a private reception on Thursday night in Santa Barbara, he confided to a friend, "It looks bad. I think they're hung, and I can't see the County going for a rerun."

Toward the end of the week, John Schoonhoven, a pilot and the father of Fred's first wife Jeanne, flew in from Africa. He told friends that however it turned out, there would be little joy for him. His family had been torn asunder by the trial.

There was no sign of Bill Fairfield. The defense team had told him to stay away. It was only two years since his triple bypass; they thought the strain of waiting could kill him.

Sunday, May 9, was Mother's Day. Jim Farley was certain the jury would want to be home by then. "Those women have seen very little of their families for eight months," he said. "They're not going to miss Mother's Day at home. One way or another, it'll be over by the weekend."

At just after 2:00 p.m. on Friday afternoon, the jury asked to have Fred Roehler's testimony read to them. Forty-five minutes later, the word spread. They were coming back.

It was hot and stuffy in the Santa Barbara holding tank two floors above the courtroom. Roehler had carefully peeled off his shirt and sat sweating, bare-chested in the small room. He'd decided not to nap, something he'd admitted to doing frequently during trial recesses. Jury picker Cathy Bennett had told him he always looked awful after he was awakened from an afternoon doze and brought into court.

A bailiff appeared. "They want you downstairs."

"Is it the verdict?" Roehler asked.

"No."

Roehler quickly dressed, tightening his tie.

"I knew he was lying," he said later. "I can tell by now when people are lying to me."

Coming down the corridor to the courtroom he glanced out the window at the trees and the tourists basking in the sunshine on the lawn. It was going to be nice, he said, to be back home in Malibu that weekend.

Charlotte and Fritz Roehler took their front-row seats alongside Cam Zeitner.

"Isn't it wonderful. I'm going to have my son home for Mother's Day," Charlotte said loudly.

At the defense table, Jim Farley sat, tearing at his fingernails, his back turned to his client.

At 4:10 p.m., the judge ordered the courtroom door locked; there wasn't room for another soul. Bailiffs lined the back wall of the room and down the sides. The atmosphere was suffocating. Roehler stared straight ahead as if hypnotized.

The jurors filed in quickly, looking neither to right nor left, their faces unreadable.

Judy Austin, the clerk of the court, had become fond of Roehler. "When are they going to get this over with and let you get home to your family?" she often said to him. Her husband had died a few months earlier, and Fred had asked his family to send flowers to the funeral.

Now as she took the single sheet containing the verdict passed to her by the judge, her hand shook, and her voice broke:

"Guilty . . . of the murder of Verna Jo Roehler."

"Guilty . . . of the murder of Douglas Johnson."

"Guilty . . . of the two special circumstances: murder for profit, and the killing of more than one person."

"Oh no," Charlotte Roehler moaned audibly.

The deputies moved away from the walls, circling Roehler in the well of the court as if expecting an abduction. Roehler was expressionless, his knuckles white, hands tightly clenched on the arms of his chair. His family and supporters looked as if they'd been bludgeoned.

"It's not true" a friend mouthed across the room to Ron and Elizabeth Roehler.

"Hometown decision," snarled another.

Both Sally and I, who had covered every day of the marathon trial, were in total shock. Speechless.

"It's not over yet," Charlotte Roehler snapped as someone offered condolences. "This is just the beginning."

In the hallway, a TV camera crew locked its harsh lights on her. "Gossip kills," she hissed as her husband swiftly led her out of the building and down the street, hiding their faces behind her purse.

Roehler also hid his face from the cameras with a legal pad as they took him back to jail.

Outside, a Roehler supporter almost got into a fistfight with a jubilant Malibu resident.

"We were for Verna," said the beach dweller. "We were looking out for her."

Back in his cell, Fred Roehler quickly sent off a letter to his children:

> There is so much to say today. Your hurt from losing mother and Douglas will be refelt as you realize that a jury of twelve people have said I hurt both Mother and Douglas . . . The jury made a mistake. You will talk to many people who believe that, not just me. The mistake will be changed, but it will take more time . . . You will have many questions and I want to hear them all . . .

To his parents, he wrote:

> Do not let hate invade your heart. Now is the time for pulling together as a family and sharing both the grief that cannot be denied, but more importantly, sharing the knowledge that we know the truth and that truth will prevail . . .

He meticulously instructed his family on how to discuss the verdict with the children:

> Children to be told, stressing that the 12 people really did not understand us nor our family. These people got bits and pieces of us. They never traveled with us or sat at our dinner table. They never walked down the beach on a Sunday and sat while we read and discussed Bible stories. They did not share a family dreaming and loving.

Stanley Roden, looking gaunt, walked slowly across the street to his office. Word had spread. His entire staff slipped out into the corridor applauding as he silently passed by them to reach his own room. He closed the door quietly behind him.

A deputy shook his head in amazement, "That's what I do when I lose."

Half an hour later, Roden joined his prosecution team at a nearby Mexican restaurant for a celebratory drink. The atmosphere was euphoric. They had pulled off the impossible.

During the laughter and the backslapping, Roden slowly lifted his glass. "To Verna and Douglas," he proclaimed softly.

On Sunday, June 6, 1982, just a few days after he had been convicted, Fred Roehler phoned me again from jail to talk about preparations for the penalty phase of his trial. The same jury who had found him guilty would now have the power to send him to the gas chamber.

I asked him how he managed to stay sane.

"I have done no crime," he said. "Nothing was shown in court. I refuse to accept the stigma of newspaper reporters and twelve people in the box. Now it's a question of how gracefully—do you think that's a good word?—to get this stopped with the least amount of damage."

He felt sympathy for the jury who had convicted him, he said. The penalty phase would put tremendous pressure on them. "Can you imagine the strain? Those poor souls."

Frankly, I was utterly flabbergasted by his sanguine words. Sympathy for the jury!

In our own minds, the long trial had done nothing to change our opinion. We still felt that Fred Roehler was innocent. As journalists and friends, we naively believed we knew the truth.

Fred's attorneys asked me to be a character witness, so I joined sixty-three others who, one after the other, came forward to testify that Fred Roehler was a giant among men—a perfect husband, community member, and human being. There was something almost evangelical about our performance. These were testaments of faith.

"I hope it doesn't sound too good to be true," said his brother Ron. "Fred's coming across like a saint. But then, that's how he's always been."

During the penalty phase we felt for the first time that the strain on Fred was beginning to show. He simply wasn't rational. He was battling his attorneys to put him on the stand yet again, and he insisted that they show the film of his idyllic Malibu beachfront wedding to Verna. He wanted to somehow stick it to the jury and show them how wrong they were. He wanted to tell them his entire life story so they could see what kind of person he really was. Surely then they would have to acknowledge that they'd made a terrible mistake. And surely then, Judge Rickard would intervene, to "stop this farce."

His faith in the judge was being kept alive by his mother. Charlotte firmly believed that somehow, suddenly, after months of evidence and despite the verdict, the judge would wrest it out of the jury's hands and free her son.

And her son seemed not to disagree.

Farley and Westwick refused point-blank to let Fred testify again, but they couldn't persuade him not to run the eighteen-minute film of his Malibu beach wedding. It was screened without sound, with a courtroom narration by Reverend John Hagar, the minister who had performed the ceremony.

It came across like a fashion commentary. It was almost obscene. The jury hated it. Their antagonism was so strong one could feel it from the back of the room. They already knew that the idyllic "show wedding" had been staged mostly as a public spectacle. Fred couldn't seem to understand that. To him, that ceremony represented the epitome of perfect family togetherness, and surely the jury must also see it that way.

All stops were pulled out, including appearances by Heidi, eleven, and Kirsten, seven, as well as Kimberly Johnson, all shiny-eyed with pink bows in their hair, looking like illustrations from a kids' magazine, pleading with the jurors to spare their father's life. The attempt came to grief when after only two questions, twelve-year-old Kimberly collapsed in a fit of sobbing and was hastily excused. There wasn't a dry eye in the courtroom except in the jury box, where all twelve members looked ready to kill.

But they didn't. At the end of the ten-day penalty hearing, the jury that had found Fred guilty of the cold-blooded murder of his wife and her son sentenced him to life without the possibility of parole.

A minority, we later learned, had argued vehemently for the gas chamber, led by the woman deserted by her husband whom Fred had insisted on keeping on the panel. She was the last holdout. Others felt a life sentence would give Fred time to repent; some believed that for an intelligent man like him, life in a maximum-security prison for the remainder of his natural life would be worse than death.

Westwick had another theory: "They just couldn't kill the kids' daddy," he said.

At the sentencing, the judge, who had seemed so favorable to him, told Roehler he had changed his mind. He now believed after listening to all the evidence that he was guilty as charged.

Our Personal Odyssey: The Story Behind the Story

On January 5, 1981, just four days after we had heard and read about the deaths of Verna and Douglas, and as friends and neighbors of the family, we wrote the following letter to Fred Roehler:

Dear Fred,

At a time like this nothing we can say or do can soften that terrible blow of losing Verna and Doug. We can't tell you what a joy it was to see you and Doug on your first outings to play soccer and help us through that first season. New experiences with fathers and sons are always so unique. What touched us most was your devotion and utter dedication to Doug during those months and the obvious joy and delight you both got from each other and from those experiences.

Our paths, of course, crossed, although we were later on different teams. But we enjoyed watching you and Verna get such satisfaction from Doug's soccer as he grew older, and you both took such obvious delight and pride in his accomplishments. Even at that tender age, we always found Doug to be a great little sportsman, as well as a young gentleman in every sense of the word.

We will always cherish the memory of when we last saw you together. It was at the Apple Farm Restaurant in San Luis Obispo late last summer. You were there with Doug, Verna, and the girls, having spent what you told us was obviously a marvelous, warm family outing at the County Fair. And that is how we all saw you.

Our most sincere condolences to you and to Kim, Kirsten, and Heidi.

Sally and Ivor Davis

We sat through the eight-month marathon of the trial, our minds made up. We had argued bitterly with a friend, the formidable Santa Barbara crime writer Margaret "Maggie" Millar, wife of Ken Millar (hard-boiled detective writer Ross Macdonald), who frequently enjoyed a seat in the spectator section which the judge—a friend—reserved for her. After Fred's lengthy testimony, and even after we'd painted a picture of our friend as a loving father and husband, she was firm: "You've been conned. He did it."

Still, to us, the prosecution's case seemed a fantasy of pseudo-science and inept medical evidence, leaving much room for "beyond a reasonable doubt." We found plenty to back up our opinion. Doctors Linderberg and Spitz for the defense were the finest pathologists in the country. They found the DA's bruise-pattern evidence amateurish and ridiculous. They compared the theory to looking for faces in clouds. Was this the kind of cockeyed evidence upon which a man might be convicted of murder?

Santa Barbara County, we thought, had dug itself a deep financial hole and had to follow through to the bitter end, however it stretched to get there.

Before the trial, we had told Fred we wanted to write a book about his ordeal. He was in favor of the idea, though we made it patently clear that it would be our telling of his remarkable story, with our goal to pursue the truth. No problem, he said.

But the day the prosecution wound up its case and before the defense put on theirs, Fred phoned us from jail and told us to forget the book, since it was obvious he would be acquitted, and he didn't want his family to have to relive the whole thing. We had been there from day one and also felt he would walk.

Then, over the next week, as we carefully watched Fred testify, we came to feel that he was a lousy witness. We were not so biased that we couldn't see that. He was not a man to show his emotions, and we could see how he might come across to those who didn't know him as cold and unfeeling. Still, as far as we were concerned, stoicism was a virtue in times of deep distress.

The DA, we knew, couldn't wait to go for Roehler's jugular. Cross-examination by Roden had revealed petty inconsistencies in Fred's story, but it had been months since his arrest, and the whole tragedy at sea had occurred in an atmosphere of terror and panic. Was it any wonder that with more time to think about it, a few details of his story might have changed?

We were also impressed by the fierce loyalty of those who knew Fred Roehler best. Cam Zeitner, the devout mother-in-law, and John Schoonhoven, both with daughters now dead, were standing by him to the end. If that didn't speak volumes for the man, what would?

Even the judge seemed as favorable to the defense as he could possibly be. It was certainly the fairest trial we'd ever seen, except for the horrible inequity, as far as we were concerned, of Fred being on trial at all.

As journalists, Sally and I had covered several historic American trials of the twentieth century. We thought we knew how to listen to the evidence and read between the lines.

When the verdicts were read, we were in shock. What had we missed? Had we sat through the same evidence as the jury?

We weren't the only ones dumbstruck by the verdicts. Every attorney who had sat in on the key testimony said the same thing: The evidence was much too inconclusive for a conviction. The DA had labeled Fred a callous playboy who just wanted to sail around the world on his yacht, never having to work again. It was a cliché—certainly not the Fred Roehler we thought we knew, the man we admired.

Hours after the jury had found him guilty, Fred was on the phone. "Go ahead with your book," he said. "I've got nothing to lose."

We spoke to some of the jurors. They had virtually discarded the experts on both sides, along with their endless and expensive tests. What it boiled down to, they said, was that they simply hadn't believed that a man with Fred Roehler's vast experience in the water as a deep-sea diver in and around those islands could have fouled up so badly. And they hadn't liked what they saw of him on the stand; they didn't trust him. He didn't react as they would have; he didn't seem natural to them; there was something inhuman about him, like someone from another planet. He was cold and unfeeling—quite capable, they felt, of doing this terrible thing. He was a spoiled child and a liar who wanted it all, and wanted it now—and was prepared to kill to get it.

We began our deep dive. We had access to everything, most of which the jury didn't. It was as if they had looked through a window with 80 percent of the view obscured while we had 20/20 vision.

There were boxes full of documents and records relating to the trial; all of Fred's personal records, financial and otherwise, dating back to college; photographs; interview tapes and transcripts. We had an itinerary that would take us from one end of the country to the other.

The two crucial factors that had been excluded from the trial were Fred Roehler's history of insurance dealings and the intricate details about the death of his first wife, Jeanne.

We began with Jeanne. There had always been a sense of discomfort about that death. Stanley Roden had spent nine days trying to present aggravating evidence that Fred Roehler had also killed Jeanne. But again, he'd had much of his case cut from under him by the judge. The DA couldn't present evidence of imminent divorce; he couldn't have Jeanne's sisters testify, or her stewardess friends, or the marriage counselor they had consulted. Nevertheless, he tried to prove, four years after the fact, that Jeanne had also been murdered. He managed only to prove that she had virtually no alcohol whatsoever in her system on the night she died.

It was all too late. The trail had gone cold. After nine days of testimony, the judge ruled Roden had proved nothing, and there followed the extraordinary spectacle of the jurors, at the judge's instructions, actually ripping out all that Jeanne testimony from their notebooks and being told to erase it from their memories.

Once again, it was as if Jeanne Roehler had never existed. But we wondered: Did Jeanne's drowning remain a malignant scar in the recesses of their minds? And when it came to the final decision, did it influence their final verdict? Probably it did.

Fred had considered that his sole victory. "At least one good thing emerged from this whole fiasco," he said. "I've been found innocent on Jeanne."

Unhindered by any kind of limitations, we dug back into Fred's and Jeanne's histories. We interviewed Jeanne's sisters, her parents, her colleagues, friends at United Airlines, and her lover. A consistent picture emerged of a very unhappy young woman determined to get out of her marriage but at the same time terrified of the consequences of doing so. In court records, there were documents in their own handwriting that proved beyond a doubt that the marriage of Jeanne and Fred was ended in all but name only, and that just days before her death, Fred had led Jeanne to believe he would agree to an amicable divorce. In fact, several of Jeanne's flight attendant colleagues told us that Jeanne repeatedly said Fred had agreed to a divorce.

On more than a dozen occasions, we made the 800-mile round-trip to the grim Folsom State Prison in Northern California to visit Fred, spending five and six hours at a time interviewing him. Several times we took our young children—the same age as Fred and Verna's kids—and for hours we sat uncomfortably on hard benches in the outdoor visiting prison yard as scores of other inmates spent tense times with their families. As we interviewed Fred, we noticed growing inconsistencies in the telling of his story.

He had insisted repeatedly to his own attorneys and the police that he and Jeanne had never even discussed divorce. To us, when pressed, he finally admitted that Jeanne had asked him several times to let her out of the marriage. But then he digressed into long discussions about the self-help group Lifespring and how Jeanne's experience there had given her the strength to fight to save their marriage. We knew from our research that this simply wasn't true. We had come upon the account of their relationship they had written for their marriage counselor, and after that, there was no way, however hard we stretched, we could accept Fred's account at face value. We also knew that Jeanne had told friends and airline colleagues that she was passionately in love with another man, and that even though she had little prospect of making a life with him, she had determined that continuing to live with Fred was intolerable.

Maybe we were naive, but even though our conversations with Fred sometimes became tricky and acutely uncomfortable, we still remained true believers—even when Fred made some disturbingly contradictory remarks referring to Jeanne's inquest. Why, we asked him, did the Roehlers keep insisting that a coroner's inquest had determined she died of an aneurysm when the record showed she died of pneumonia following drowning?

An aneurysm, Fred said, completely unfazed, was one of several possibilities Jeanne's doctors had suggested as she lay in a coma. The family had simply fastened on to that answer as something people could more easily understand. Aneurysm was the convenient explanation that circulated in Malibu and at Fred's Point Mugu workplace, even though she had drowned.

And why had he told colleagues at work that if Jeanne insisted on a divorce, he would simply turn his back and walk out of the lives of his wife and children forever? His answer was feeble: "We talked about a lot of options, okay? About how different people survive a divorce, how they live after a divorce, and so forth. And I think at that point I was trying to show that there was so much pain and stuff involved that it would be analogous to going off by myself."

We had slowly begun to acknowledge a hitherto forbidden thought: Perhaps Fred had killed Jeanne to avoid a divorce and the chaotic disruption of his lifestyle. Could he have gotten away with it, and then, in some horrible twist, been punished for murders he did not commit—those of Doug and Verna?

At the same time, we were examining each of Fred's insurance claims in minute detail. They were all suspicious. Individually they did not raise a red flag, but collectively, when we knew more details, they were impossible to discount. There were some even the district attorney never knew about.

It disturbed us that certain common threads ran through his stories. His houseboat burned in Berkeley when he was on a picture-taking trip. Verna and Doug had died on a picture-taking trip. In both cases, Fred was rescued and so was the camera. When Jeanne died only the dogs were witnesses; when Verna and Doug died, a beagle puppy witnessed their end. There were people around, but in both cases, they were asleep: Fred's next-door neighbors, as Jeanne was drowning; the sleeping Roehlers on the *Perseverance* in the case of Doug and Verna.

The more time we spent with him, the harder it became to ignore the growing list of contradictions in Fred's story. He had sworn under oath in court that he had not had any problems with Doug. And certainly, I'd been impressed while watching father and son getting along so well during our coaching sessions and weekend soccer games. But when we challenged him on one visit with snippets of a tape recording made on board the *Perseverance*, which we had heard—the recording suggested that his attitude toward Doug was demeaning, not always that of a loving, understanding father—he became nervous and defensive, admitting, "Well, it was no secret Doug and I clashed." In fact, he had done his best to keep this a secret.

Although he had told Detective Ray that it was three months or so after Jeanne's death before he and Verna had dated without the children, he admitted to us it was very much earlier, and we knew from other sources that less than three weeks had passed after Jeanne's when they began stepping out.

He continued to insist to us that on January 2 he had asked Douglas to go in the dinghy with Scott and Ginny because the dory was still tied up. We knew from both his mother and his brother that Doug had begged to go in the dinghy. Fred had insisted that he wait to go with him in the dory.

The story of just whose idea it had been not to register that "show" marriage between Fred and Verna kept changing. First, it had been Bill Fairfield's idea; later, it was Fred's own suggestion, and still later, it became Verna's idea.

Insuring the children was another changing story: First it was Fairfield's idea, then, when Fairfield told the police he'd had nothing to do with it, it became a suggestion from his brother Ron.

Fred continued to insist that the trust was to have been the beneficiary of Verna's insurance. There were notes in his own handwriting, however, prepared before a visit with the insurance representative Raymond

Wylie, that clearly stated the policies were to be cross-owned, and that the trust was to be only the secondary beneficiary.

The list grew. Small, seemingly insignificant lies grew and multiplied. When we pointed out the inconsistencies, he would change tack and pull another answer out of the air.

At the same time, we were seeing in our visits to Folsom a man who had begun to resemble the same alien personality the jury had seen.

It surprised us that while in Folsom Prison, Fred displayed little curiosity about anybody outside. We told him about our visits to see his children and his old friends. He never ventured a single independent inquiry about how they were, or what they were doing. The frantic father of the trial, desperately concerned about how his children were adjusting to the tragedy that had befallen them, suddenly seemed to have no need to hear about their welfare or about those who were caring for them. This was in dramatic contrast to his personal letters, which were filled with selfless concern and consideration for others.

Receiving those letters ourselves and being shown countless others he'd written to friends and family made us very uneasy. They were so different to each person, in tone and language, that they seemed almost to be written by different people. To the religious, his letters were devout, full of faith in an ultimate purpose for what he was going through, crammed with references to a merciful God and the hereafter. To the cynical, his letters were dry, caustic, and skeptical. To the human potential crowd, they were full of self-awareness. This was more than just an attempt to be understood. The person writing these letters was a chameleon, able to change his coloring according to his surroundings, a mirror reflecting back what the person on the receiving end wanted to see. Foolishly perhaps, we sent Fred a copy of the classic 1979 book *The Culture of Narcissism* by cultural historian Christopher Lasch. But when we asked if he had received it, he abruptly said he had not, then quickly changed the subject. Later we realized that maybe some of the findings in that book might have hit too close to home.

Now that we were spending long periods of time with Fred at Folsom, we also found it disturbing that his feelings were displayed in strange, contradictory ways. He would shed heartfelt tears when discussing his own childhood and the idea of childhood in the abstract, but we saw few tears for his wife Verna or Douglas, or for his daughters who, years later, were to become the cornerstone of his "keep the faith" mentality.

Finally, after listening to descriptions of Santa Cruz Island, Little Scorpion anchorage, and Bird Rock, we sailed twice, with expert yachtsmen, out to the place where Verna and Doug died. We had expected a vast expanse of ocean, but the biggest surprise was how compact the anchorage was. From the corner of Bird Rock to the spot where the *Perseverance* was moored was only about a five-minute row. I, only a modest swimmer, had no difficulty undertaking the distance. For someone as strong and experienced in the water as Fred, the temptation to strike out for the yacht even in cold water and with two bodies in tow should have been irresistible. To reject that option and instead swim against the current, 100 to 150 yards, to the base of the sheer face of Bird Rock—a place from which it would have looked impossible to climb out—to spending forty-five minutes to an hour thrashing about in those freezing January waves, forced up and down by the surge of the sea against the jagged rocks, simply didn't make sense. Of course, according to his version—with Doug and Verna in each hand and a dog on his head—maybe that feat would have proved his superhuman qualities!

But it was when I swam more closely to the place on the rock where Fred had told us he'd stayed with Verna and Doug that we began to feel really disturbed. It was at the sheerest point on the cliff. Nearby was the blowhole through which the tide gushed with a deafening roar. The massive face of that spectacular rock, some twenty-five feet high at that point, would have blocked even the loudest noises from being heard in the anchorage. Even if Verna and Doug had been conscious, they would have had difficulty hearing each other, let alone expecting anyone else to hear their cries for help.

It was also frighteningly obvious that this spot on the rock, tucked into an indentation in the cliff, was probably the most shadowy place on the entire rock face, an indentation where even if they had been dressed in neon colors, the keenest eye would have had difficulty picking man, woman, or child out of the gloom.

The thought could not be ignored: Only someone who wanted to neither be seen nor heard might have chosen to stay there.

The only time during all our conversations in Folsom that Fred became agitated was when we told him we'd sailed twice to Santa Cruz Island, had swum in the waters around Bird Rock, had climbed up onto the rock itself, and been dive-bombed by seabirds.

We asked rather innocently whether he had been on the rock at any time on the day Verna and Doug died.

He was emphatic. Not only had he not been on the rock that day, but never in all the years he had swum or dived in those waters had he ever climbed onto the rock. It was obvious he was acutely uncomfortable, and it was clear he didn't want to discuss our visit to the island or Bird Rock.

Later, he complained that any conclusions we had come to from our visit were all wrong because we had sailed from Santa Barbara Harbor to the island instead of from Ventura Harbor, as he had done on January 2, 1981. In fact, we had sailed from both harbors. Why that would have altered or undermined anything we'd experienced when we got there was something he didn't bother to explain.

In our research, we listened to Fred's lie detector tests. It was eerie. Answering questions, he frequently broke down sobbing, but within a half-second, his voice returned completely to normal, without any trace of a quiver of emotion.

We had been given a much closer view of every aspect of Fred Roehler's life than anyone had ever had before, and we were coming up with a much different personality from the one we thought we knew.

We were losing our innocence; however, we knew that to really understand Fred, we would have to go back to his beginnings in his hometown of Centerville, Indiana, and do some digging into that ideal, storybook childhood and the wonderful family he spoke of so lovingly.

In March 1985, Sally and I flew to Indiana, carrying with us a six-foot-long stained-glass window Fred had made for his mother in the Folsom handicraft workshop. We were armed with a long list of Roehler's friends and neighbors he had supplied us with, and a pocket history of each of them.

We had expected glowing testimonials of the Roehlers and their handsome eldest son, but when we arrived, we found that only a handful of people would agree to talk to us. It was only when some relented that we discovered why. They feared we were private detectives hired by the Roehlers to get their son out of prison. That was just the kind of thing the Roehlers would do, we were told. The fact was that all of these close friends had no difficulty whatsoever in believing that Charlotte and Fritz Roehler's eldest son had committed murder.

"If there was money in it," one said flatly, "he did it."

We interviewed more than fifty people in that town. Many of them distrusted and feared the Roehlers, and those who didn't either despised or pitied them. We had probed more deeply and found things that could never have been presented in a courtroom. We spoke to several women Fred had dated. We spoke to friends he grew up with and neighbors who had known him all of his life.

One evening, we went for a drink at the home of a Centerville family who had known Fred since childhood. During a casual conversation, one of them mentioned a boat-burning incident from which Fritz Roehler had collected a large insurance settlement. We could feel hairs stand up on the backs of our necks. It sounded familiar and was the beginning of a trail that sent us around town, where we repeatedly heard similar stories.

It was no secret that the Roehler family seemed to have an inordinate amount of trouble with fire. Things burned, and when they burned, insurance money was paid, no questions asked. Everybody in town knew about these things; everyone marveled that somehow the Roehlers got away with it. If Fred benefited handsomely from unexplained fires, then surely he had learned well at his father's knee. Fritz Roehler, we were told repeatedly in Centerville, "would do anything for a buck."

The Roehler homestead, as described by those who knew the family, was a fortress presided over by Charlotte, a woman her neighbors regarded as completely out of touch with reality. To her, they said, children were an advertisement for a perfect family, in a fantasy world in which the Roehlers occupied an exalted position, and for whom no one else existed except those connected to her by ties of blood.

Of all her children, it was her eldest, Fred, who had apparently gone along with the myth, somehow elevating himself psychologically above his classmates. He was richer, cleverer, more handsome, and more successful, even when they had evidence to the contrary.

The Roehlers were unnaturally close. As described by one neighbor in Centerville, "They were like a pack of coyotes going out to forage in the outside world, then hiding back in their lair, picking off each other's fleas."

The night before we left Centerville, depressed by this fusillade of negativity about a man we admired, we received an urgent telephone summons from Charlotte: Would we stop by and see her before we flew home? First, she insisted on us sampling a glass of her homemade elderberry wine, which Sally and I sipped with a great deal of trepidation. She proposed a toast to our book and asked, "Is there going to be anything in it that will embarrass me?"

We tried to be diplomatic. There were surely things in all our lives that would embarrass our mothers, we said. And every family had some skeletons in their closet.

She drew herself up to her full height with thunder in her eyes and snapped, "The Roehler family does not." It was just two days before that Fritz had told us Charlotte's mother had died in a psychiatric hospital where she had been confined for over thirty years.

Back in California, we drove to Folsom and told Fred, somewhat hesitantly, about the strange and unexpected reception we had received in his hometown. He received the news blankly. Nobody in town really knew his parents, he said. "They left all their family and real friends in Pennsylvania." (This, even though they had lived in Indiana for over thirty years.)

Fred denied any knowledge of his father's questionable insurance dealings, but then admitted that on one occasion he "might" have warned his brother, Ron, saying, "The old man better be careful with his scams. One of these days he's going to get caught."

Soon afterward, however, it was as if none of that had been said. His father was once again a hardworking, God-fearing man; his mother, the ideal caring, attentive parent every child craved; his childhood, a paradise of goodness and light. Like his mother, Fred was rewriting the script, creating a version that pleased him better than what was real.

A few days after our visit, we received a letter from Fred. He wanted to review the transcripts of all the interviews from Centerville, with names attached.

We refused. We'd promised all those who had reluctantly agreed to be interviewed that the interviews would be confidential, and that we would not violate those confidences. We agreed to outline what was said and give him a complete list of the people spoken to, but we wouldn't tell him who said what.

He insisted he had to have those details in order to sift fact from fiction. Apparently, he could only do that if he knew precisely who said what.

We realized finally that his method of deflecting criticism was the same as his father's: attack first, rip the individual to shreds, and then anything they said was considered biased. Without the specific identities attached to the opinions, Fred's methods didn't work. He was virtually paralyzed.

This one-way communication, Fred decreed, would have to cease. Either we exchanged those names from Centerville with him or he would cut off all communications. Two weeks later he did.

We never heard from Fred Roehler again.

It took us a long time, much too long, to wake up to the fact that Fred Roehler was a man who could murder others—a stone-cold killer. We were emotionally involved from the start. It was our arrogance in thinking we understood human nature that led us to cling to our illusions for so long. We were wrong.

Sally and I changed our minds about him slowly and ever so reluctantly. We both had to accept the fact that he and his family had a lifelong pattern of insurance frauds, but it had seemed too great a leap from there to murder. Finally, we made that leap. Fred was not the man we thought we knew. He was a man without a conscience, a man who considered that only one person in the world counted: Fred Roehler. Anyone who stood between him and his distorted goals could simply be swatted away. His undoubted intelligence and ability to charm had had us completely fooled.

The terrifying thing was that he had so nearly gotten away with it. The bodies of Verna and Douglas were supposed to have been cremated two or three days before the Santa Barbara sheriff's department had asked to reexamine them. It was only because the crematorium was extremely busy that the cremations had been delayed. Without those corpses, there would have been no case.

And in our mind, there was more. We were convinced that Dr. Hunter's bruises and hemorrhage testimony, which had brought Fred to trial, were completely illusory. They really did not exist. An inexperienced pathologist in this field, pushed hard by the DA and the police, had studied already-autopsied bodies and come up with phantom injuries and bruises. Fred Roehler didn't need to beat Doug's skull on the gunnel of his dory or hammer Verna's head with an oar or anything else. At age thirty-eight, he was big and powerful, with formidable underwater lung capacity, a professionally trained navy diver. We speculated that he had almost certainly separated Verna from her son, perhaps by leaving Doug and their beagle puppy on Bird Rock, killing Verna, and then returning to finish the job. To kill a small, terrified woman and her eight-year-old boy, separately, would have been almost too easy for Fred. There had been no injuries on first wife Jeanne's body when she was dragged out of her own swimming pool, and there were none, we felt sure, on Verna and Douglas when they were lifted from the Pacific.

It was an almost Hitchcockian irony that at times perhaps even Roehler may have appreciated as he sat through the long trial. Without those bruises, he never would have been arrested. Yet the real irony lay in the fact that it wasn't the imaginary bruises that drove the jury to convict; it was Roehler himself. Sitting on the stand, day after day, impenetrable, rigid, arrogant, his pale blue eyes in a fixed stare, Fred brought about his own conviction.

At the time, many friends, Sally and I included, regarded his demeanor as fortitude. The men and women of the jury, on whom he had not had the opportunity to work his charm and his manipulative skills, had no difficulty seeing him as he was: an empty shell of a man doing a fair impersonation of a human being. The physical attributes were all in place, but behind them was a void that ultimately no amount of posturing could mask.

Postscript

On April 25, 1985, the California Court of Appeals denied Fred Roehler's appeal by a two-to-one vote.

On August 19, 1985, a petition for review to the California Supreme Court was denied.

On December 9, 1985, the US Supreme Court denied Roehler's petition to review his case.

In the ensuing years, while Fred was serving his life sentence without the possibility of parole, the Roehler Family Estate, under the financial guidance of lawyer William Fairfield, grew enormously. As astonishing as this might appear, Fairfield, under threats of a bad faith lawsuit, had persuaded the insurance company to pay the family the life insurance policy in full. The $820,000 was paid *before* the verdict was reached. In today's money, that amount would be worth over $3 million.

Since Fred's arrest and conviction, the Roehler Family Estate has grown thanks to wise investments carried out under the aegis of Fairfield. All the funds from the sale of Fred's Malibu house were used for a tax exchange to purchase an 870-acre cattle ranch in Idaho. Since then, all the ranch acreage was sold to developers who built exclusive, high-priced homes and ranches on the property, known as New Meadows, located on the Little Salmon River in Adams County, Idaho.

In January 2009, Fred Roehler's estate sued Fairfield for mismanagement of funds. The case was dismissed.

In the decades after his sentencing, the girls—Heidi, Kirsten, and Kimberly, who Fred describes as his "lifeline"—have remained united in their long campaign to try and persuade several California governors to set their father free. Following the COVID-19 pandemic, which began in 2020, Kirsten has led the charge to get her father paroled because of ill health and his "model prisoner" status. So far, all efforts have been in vain.

In 2021, Roehler told *Lost Hills* podcaster, Dana Goodyear, "I do think I will get out."

Back in the late 1970s, Fred Roehler told a colleague at Point Mugu, almost prophetically, "You just persevere, put up with all the bullshit they dish out to you, and eventually you'll get the brass ring."

As it turned out, his brass ring would be brass bars.

Author's Note

In the telling of this story, I have described events, locales, and conversations from personal notes taken, interviews, and my own memories. The contents of this book depend solely on the detailed daily coverage that Sally and I provided during the trial, which began in 1981, as well as follow-up research completed during the subsequent five years. This included one-on-one interviews with Fred Roehler in prison; interviews with other key figures and members of the Roehler and Schoonhoven families; and interviews with friends, neighbors, and Roehler's workmates. To maintain anonymity, at their request, in a very few instances I have changed the names of certain individuals.

The material in this book was also drawn from voluminous court testimony, tape recordings, transcripts, witness statements, and multiple other court and public records, as well as documents we obtained during preparations for the trial and its lengthy aftermath. All quotes, unless noted otherwise, were gathered firsthand through interviews Sally and I conducted, supplemented by our own follow-up investigation.

ACKNOWLEDGMENTS

This book has been over four decades in the making. Along the way, there have been innumerable twists and turns and delays, with a handful of inspiring and supporting players who helped keep this story alive.

My late wife Sally, whose vividly brilliant powers of description along with her superb prose, was unwavering from the moment we embarked on what for us turned out to be an incomparable lesson in humility.

A great many people made important contributions to this book, and it would be impossible to name and acknowledge everyone. Still, I would like to offer profuse and heartfelt thanks to the small army named here. And to those I have overlooked, my deepest apologies.

Stalwart friends like Clark and Diane Hubbard toiled by hand to help resurrect our anachronistic typewritten original manuscript and bring us into the twenty-first century and a world obsessed with all things Internet and AI.

Screenwriter/producer Frank Abatemarco's keen eye for a terrific story reignited the work after it had lain dormant, inspiring me to complete my literary mission. Authors and editors and colleagues all weighed in with support and guidance, including Marshall Terrill, Irma Wolfson, and Lew Harris, my former *Los Angeles Magazine* editor, who never gave up on the story from day one.

Cara Highsmith helped me over the finish line. Marla Daly, director of the Santa Cruz Island Foundation, constantly nudged me to show her a finished book. Thanks also to my agents Liseanne Miller and Charlie Serabian at Global Lion, and Rowman & Littlefield editor Becca Beurer.

Donna Fairfield, the widow of Roehler's best friend and personal lawyer Bill Fairfield, and Linda Velthoen, widow of Fred's sailing pal

Dick Velthoen, and their son, lawyer Mike—all of them, in their own way, suffered mightily throughout this long and winding ordeal. Their prodding and support was invaluable and encouraging.

I thank my daughter Rebecca Davis Suskind and my son Gideon Davis, whose psyches are still firmly intact, even though we insisted they travel hundreds of miles to spend tedious hours in the bleak, chilling climes of the Folsom Prison concrete visitors' yard.

My partner Louise Sherman stuck with me through thick and thin, particularly during my most irascible periods.

In researching and writing this book, scores of friends and colleagues and neighbors from Malibu to Ventura, from Centerville, Indiana, to Santa Barbara, did not hold back: Paddy and John Leitelt, Barbara Leonard, the late Florence Van Putten, documentary filmmakers George and Beth Gage, Mike Killeen, Rob LeMond, Dr. Jeff Harris, Gloria Hunnicut, and all those women from Fred's past who helped us to create an accurate picture of Roehler as a young man. *Santa Barbara News-Press* reporter Richard R. Aguirre, like us, watched the trial from his front-row seat in the courtroom and shared jury feedback. There are others too numerous to list, but they know who they are.

Dogged Santa Barbara County Sheriff's Office detectives, Fred Ray and Claude Tuller, shared their memories and emotions once the case was resolved. Investigator Russ Whitmeyer was a key part of the defense team, as was appeals lawyer Wendy Lascher and her late husband Ed, who toiled in vain to reverse the conviction. Roehler's defense lawyers, James Matthew Farley, in Ventura, and Jim Westwick, in Santa Barbara, were both always ready to share background information with us even in the heat of the trial, when we were all staunch members of the Roehler True Believers Club. I believe that Farley's passionate pleas for his client's innocence, along with his fragile cardiac system, may have shortened his own life.

We started off intensely disliking District Attorney Stanley Roden, Santa Barbara's version of Victor Hugo's relentless Inspector Javert from *Les Misérables*, because in our minds he was pursuing a friend, who, we believed, had been wrongly accused. Time heals. Long after we changed our minds, we realized that Roden had carried the mighty burden of seeking some form of retribution for Verna and Douglas Johnson.

Whenever I faltered in finishing this book, I would look at my own son Gideon, who is now middle-aged and the proud father of two sons. It was impossible to erase the image of what might have been for his school and soccer mate, the handsome, cheeky, and innocent young Douglas Johnson, who most certainly would have carved his own unique path in life had it not been so chillingly cut short.

Index

Note: Photo insert images between pages 130 and 131 are indicated by *p1*, *p2*, *p3*, etc.

About the Authors

London-born **Ivor Davis** is a former foreign correspondent, a columnist for the New York Times Syndicate, who was a witness to history: He traveled with The Beatles, was in the kitchen when Robert Kennedy was assassinated—and spent a lifetime writing about the rich, the famous—and the famous for the time being. He is the author of *Manson Exposed: A Reporter's 50 Year Journey into Madness and Murder*; *Ladies and Gentlemen . . . The Penguins!*; *The Beatles and Me on Tour*; *Five to Die: The Book That Helped Convict Charles Manson*; *Five to Die;* and *The Beatles and Me on Tour: 60th Anniversary Edition.*

Sally Ogle Davis was an anchor for BBC TV, and wrote for major magazines—from the *New York Sunday Times* to *Los Angeles Magazine.*